# JUDICIAL SETTLEMENT OF INTERNATIONAL DISPUTES

# By the Same Author

1. Judicial Review in the English-Speaking World, (1st ed., 1956; 4th ed., 1969).
2. *Föderalismus und Bundesverfassungsrecht*, (1962).
3. Constitutionalism in Germany and the Federal Constitutional Court, (1962).
4. Comparative Federalism. States' Rights and National Power, (1st ed., 1962; 2nd ed., 1965).
5. "Peaceful Coexistence" and Soviet-Western International Law (1964).
6. Federal Constitution-Making for a Multi-National World, (1966).
7. International Law and World Revolution, (1967).
8. *Conflit idéologique et Ordre public mondial*, (1970).
9. Parliamentary Privilege and the Publication of Parliamentary Debates, (1974).
10. The Illegal Diversion of Aircraft and International Law, (1975).
11. The International Law of *Détente*. Arms Control, European Security, and East-West Cooperation, (1978).
12. The World Court and the Contemporary International Law-Making Process, (1979).
13. Quebec and the Constitution. 1960-1978, (1979).
14. Conflict and Compromise. International Law and World Order in a Revolutionary Age, (1981).
15. Constitution-Making. Principles, Process, Practice, (1981).
16. Canada and the Constitution. 1979-1982. Patriation and the Charter of Rights, (1982).
17. (a) United Nations Law-Making. Cultural and Ideological Relativism and International Law Making for an Era of Transition, (1984).
    (b) French Language Edition: *Les Nations-Unies et la Formation du Droit*, (1986).
18. Supreme Courts and Judicial Law-Making. Constitutional Tribunals and Constitutional Review, (1986).
19. Aerial Piracy and International Terrorism (1987).
20. The International Court of Justice and the Western Tradition of International Law (The Paul Martin Lectures) (1987).
21. Nuclear Weapons and Contemporary International Law, (1989) (with President Nagendra Singh).

# JUDICIAL SETTLEMENT OF INTERNATIONAL DISPUTES

Jurisdiction, Justiciability and Judicial Law-Making
on the Contemporary International Court

*by*

## EDWARD McWHINNEY, Q.C.

*Professor of International Law and Relations,*
*Simon Fraser University, Vancouver*
*- Membre de l'Institut de Droit International*
*- Membre-associé de l'Académie Internationale de Droit Comparé*
*- Member of the Permanent Court of Arbitration*

MARTINUS NIJHOFF PUBLISHERS
DORDRECHT / BOSTON / LONDON

**Library of Congress Cataloging-in-Publication Data**

McWhinney, Edward.
    Judicial settlement of international disputes : jurisdiction,
justiciability, and judicial law-making on the contemporary
international court / by Edward McWhinney.
      p.    cm.
    Includes index.
    ISBN 0-7923-0991-X (acid free paper)
    1. International Court of Justice.  2. Jurisdiction (International
law)   I. Title.
JX1971.6.M4  1991
341.5'52--dc20                                          90-47843

ISBN 0-7923-0991-X

---

Published by Martinus Nijhoff Publishers,
P.O. Box 163, 3300 AD Dordrecht, The Netherlands.

Sold and distributed in the U.S.A. and Canada
by Kluwer Academic Publishers,
101 Philip Drive, Norwell, MA 02061, U.S.A.

In all other countries, sold and distributed
by Kluwer Academic Publishers,
P.O. Box 322, 3300 AH Dordrecht, The Netherlands.

*Printed on acid-free paper*

To Manfred Lachs

# Table of Contents

# Acknowledgements

The present study derives from lectures given by the author to the Sixtieth Session of The Hague Academy of International Law, in the Summer of 1990, under the title "Judicial Settlement of Disputes: Jurisdiction and Justiciability",and published in the *Recueil des Cours de l'Académie de la Haye*, 1990.

The intense public interest and discussion of the *rôle* of the contemporary International Court of Justice, heightened by recent attacks by the U.S. Administration on the Court and its judges in the wake of the Court's *Nicaragua* rulings, 1984–1986, have prompted the present publication in separate, monograph form, in a somewhat expanded version of the original.

It is a particular pleasure for the author to be able to renew and reinforce, in this way, long-standing ties to The Hague Academy – to its Curatorium, its distinguished sessional Faculty, and its students drawn, then as now, from all parts of the World and all legal systems, – first established, as student, in an earlier time period, 1951, that is sometimes, in retrospect, qualified as the "golden era",when great jurists of the stamp of Gidel, Scelle, Andrassy, Feinberg, Hsu Mo, and Wehberg were teaching at the Academy. These personal ties were renewed, as teacher, at the Fiftieth Anniversary session of the Academy, in 1973, when the author gave a course of lectures on the theme of "The Illegal Diversion of Aircraft and International Law",which were published in the *Recueil des Cours* for 1973 and later re-published, in somewhat expanded form, in separate, monograph form, under that same title, in 1975.

The author wishes to acknowledge the partial support accorded, in the research and preparation of the succeeding study, by the Social Sciences and Humanities Research Council of Canada. Barbara Wright of the Simon Fraser University in Vancouver typed all of the manuscript and otherwise assisted in its organisation and preparation for publication.

Edward McWhinney
The Hague, Netherlands
Vancouver, Canada

# Historical Contradictions in Contemporary State Attitudes to the International Court

The United Nations General Assembly, by Resolution adopted on 9 January 1990, officially designated the 1990s as the United Nations Decade of International Law. The Resolution recalled, in terms, in its Preamble, the earlier, by-now famous Resolution of 1970 on Friendly Relations and Cooperation among States, (Resolution 2625 (XXV)), and also the Resolution of 1982 embodying the Manila Declaration on the Peaceful Settlement of International Disputes (Resolution 37/10). The Resolution also specifically cited the *First* Hague Conference of 1899, which adopted the Convention for the Pacific Settlement of International Disputes and also created the Permanent Court of Arbitration, in going on to establish, as main purposes of the U.N. Decade of International Law, the "promot[ing] means and methods for the peaceful settlement of disputes between States, including resort to and full respect for the International Court of Justice".

The contemporary "great debate" over the principle of judicial settlement of international disputes involves radically competing conceptions of Court jurisdiction and justiciability at the present day. It is highlighted by the U.S. Administration's political and legal reactions to the International Court of Justice's rulings in the *Nicaragua* cases of 1984 and 1986. The contemporary debate is, however, no more than a latter-day *reprise* of a legal controversy first unloosed, with rather different State actors, in the aftermath of the International Court's earlier, much-attacked, single-vote majority decision in *South West Africa. Second Phase*, in 1966.

International Law *doctrines* on legal institutions and processes and even substantive legal ideas necessarily reflect, in measure, Municipal, national law thinking and attitudes. On the issue of judicial settlement, contemporary International Law could hardly remain unaffected by Municipal, national legal debates over the principle of judicial review of constitutionality. In particular, the long-range evolution, in Western legal

thinking in general and in U.S. legal thinking in particular, of basic conceptions of the *rôle* of the national judge in community decision-making
involves frank and open acceptance, by the courts and by their individual
judges, of the opportunities, and obligations of national courts for creative,
legislative, policy-making interpretations of statutes, executive-administrative decrees and other legal acts coming before the courts, and for a critical
re-examination of those courts' own past *jurisprudence* when it seems to fly
in the face of contemporary societal needs and community expectations of
what is right and reasonable.

A significant element in the formation, in the plural World Community
of today, of a new, inter-systemic, International Law consensus on the *rôle*
of the International Court and of the international judge, is the widespread
transfer or "reception", between different national legal-cultures, of distinctive legal attitudes and legal thought-ways worked out, experientially, in
any one particular society, at any one particular time, in response to that
society's own community needs or expectations. The distinctive American
constitutional law institution of judicial review has, by now, its own even
more contemporary Continental European analogues, with all the implications, from the successful judicial practice over the years, that the judges'
constitutional responsibilities go beyond any merely mechanical restatement of old legal *doctrines*, and involve, instead, active participation in
changing the law. This, – the American Legal Realist lesson –, has been
amply "received" and understood, by now, by several generations of
foreign graduate students who studied Law in the United States in the post-
World War II era. Those foreign students carried back to their home
countries, on graduation from major U.S. legal centres, basic U.S. constitutional law ideas on the *rôle* of the Courts in community policy-making, and
introduced them into main-stream legal thinking all around the World. One
of the curious historical ironies in the U.S. Administration's angry, reactive
measures directed against the International Court after the Court's
*Nicaragua* rulings of 1984-6, is that the Court majorities that decided
against the U.S. on the issues under contest in the *Nicaragua* cases applied
what amounted to a "U.S. constitutional law" approach that the great
liberal-activist judges on the U.S. Supreme Court in the Roosevelt era
would certainly themselves have understood and approved.

A still further, if more specific, historical contradiction in the *Nicaragua*
cases is to be found in the fact that the objection unsuccessfully raised by
the U.S. Administration, in the preliminary hearings in *Nicaragua*, that the
Nicaraguan Government's complaint against the U.S. was no more than a
part of a larger political problem which, *ex hypothesi*, a court should not
decide, replicated the Iranian Government's unsuccessful legal objection, in

*U.S. Diplomatic and Consular Staff in Tehran*, that the U.S. complaint against Iran could not properly be examined by the Court when "divorced from its proper context, namely the whole political dossier of the relations between Iran and the United States over the last twenty five years". [I.C.J. Reports 1980, p. 3, p. 19].

We are rightly reminded today that the present-day International Court has some direct ties of intellectual-legal consanguinity to late 19th century Continental European (including Imperial Russian) legal thinking on the merits of independent, Third Party resolution of international conflicts and of a Court-based system of settlement as a necessary part of that. The sometime enthusiasm in U.S. legal circles for international judicial settle-ment was a latter-day, supervening development, especially strong in the late 1940s and the 1950s when U.S. political-military power in international relations was at its *apogée*.

In examining the current paradox that the International Court majority, since *South West Africa. Second Phase* in 1966, has so largely accepted an American-style, judicial policy-making *rôle*, in terms of which the old, postulated *a priori* dichotomy between "Law" and "Politics" is rejected in favour of a more nuanced, essentially pragmatic approach to issues of justiciability, two points should be borne in mind.

*First*, the International Court judges' claims to constitutional-legal legitimacy in the exercise of such a new, community policy-making *rôle* are, – having regard both to the constitutional system of election of judges to the International Court and also to the actual patterns of voting practice in those elections, – at least as great as those of any of the great national, Special Constitutional Courts (whether *de facto* or *de jure*), of our times. For the International Court is now, in a very real sense, a representative tribunal, whose membership, in its ethno-cultural, legal-systemic, political-ideological, and even geographical make-up, fully reflects the new, plural, inclusive World Community of today.

*Second*, though the International Court, as a plural-systemic tribunal, is able to draw freely on all the World's legal systems for purposes of fleshing out the bare bones of the Court Statute as to the Court's internal organisa-tion and procedure and also for purposes of the development of the Court's own substantive legal philosophy, the Court does have its own *corpus* of established *jurisprudence* and its own rich, autonomous experience extend-ing, now, for seven decades back to the establishment of the old, Permanent Court of International Justice. In the International Court's approach to resolution of the contemporary political-legal conflict over recourse to numerically-limited, Special Chambers of the Court, it is right to remember that, over those seven decades, the International Court always made its decisions collegially, as a *plenum* or Full Court of fifteen judges; so that attempted analogies today from the practice of some Continental European and other tribunals that do permit usage of a multi-Senate or multi-Chamber system, may be alien to the International Court's own acquired experience and its cumulative tradition of internal organisation.

In approaching its new policy-making *rôle*, the International Court has sensibly felt free to disengage itself from some overly rigid, Municipal, national Constitutional Law *doctrines*, – now, being discarded in the more advanced Municipal, national legal systems themselves – that would insist on an absolute separation-of-powers between the different, coordinate institutions of community policy-making. Such a postulated constitutional separation-of-powers, when projected at the International level, had seemed to amount, at times, to a notion of a necessary and inevitable jurisdictional conflict between Court on the one hand, and the Security Council and the General Assembly, in the approach to World Community problem-solving. The new International judicial approach, rejecting, in passing, old-fashioned notions of *litispendence* that hardly appear persuasive or even legally relevant in a contemporary Court context, is to look to a complementarity of problem-solving competences of the different World Community organs – Security Council, General Assembly, and International Court, – and to seek and foster mutual cooperation in the devising of measures which, if they are to be successful in resolving the World Community problems involved, will necessarily have to be interdependent and interrelated. The new judicial pragmatism, in this regard, is reflected in new notions of institutional comity [*Organtreue*] within the United Nations organisation, and of obligations of mutual cooperation and also mutual restraint, *inter se*, on the part of the different, coordinate United Nations organs. It implies a common responsibility of the Court, together with the Security Council and the General Assembly, in international conflicts-resolution, particularly in situations involving Threats to the Peace, or Breaches of the Peace, or Acts of Aggression of the sort referred to in Article 39 of the United Nations Charter. Inherent in that is a further, necessary notion that has some obvious links to the American Constitutional Law-inspired "Uniting for Peace" Resolution that was adopted by the United Nations General Assembly in the Korean crisis of 1950, when Security Council-based peace-keeping action appeared threatened with constitutional-legal paralysis because of the threat of arbitrary or capricious exercise of the Big Power (Permanent Members') veto in the United Nations Security Council. That is the proposition that the Court must be fully legally competent and able to move in, if necessary, and affirmatively to fill any constitutional gap if a vacuum would otherwise result in World Community decision-making for crisis-situations.

Some questions of basic methodology and approach to the subject perhaps warrant some preliminary discussion. It is customary to differentiate or separate the work of the International Court over the, by now, almost seven decades of its existence into what is conveniently referred to as the era of the "old" Court (the Permanent Court of International Justice of the between-the-two-World-Wars period), and the era of the "new" Court (the re-named International Court of Justice) that became its lineal successor in 1946. There are, to be sure, some technical-legal distinctions – commented on in the succeeding text – that can be made in the constitutional base and establishment of the two Courts, the "old" and the "new". Yet it is readily apparent, in the empirical record of the *jurisprudence* of the two Courts, that there is no sudden, sharp break or hiatus between them in 1946 or indeed for the next several decades, in terms not merely of basic philosophy of law and judicial thought-ways and conceptions of the *rôles* and missions of the Court, but also of the character and composition of the Court and its individual judges and even of the Court's main client-States and the nature of the litigation that they choose to bring before the Court. While some basic intellectual differences and divergences within the Court's judicial ranks begin, finally, to emerge by the opening of the decade of the 1960s, it is not until the bitterly contested, single-vote-majority decision of the Court in *South West Africa. Second Phase*, in 1966, that an historical turning-point can be said to have been reached, in the Court's evolution. That case, clearly, represents a watershed decision, in that, while it was a triumph of the traditional, "classical", conception of the International Court's proper function, it also had within it the intellectual seeds of the overthrow of that earlier, long-dominant approach to the judicial process and judicial decision-making. By 1971, the erstwhile majority position in *South West Africa. Second Phase* only five years before, is completely routed and the Court is entered on a new phase which, with some dialectical, trial-and-error experimentation and testing, is confirmed and consolidated to the present day. It is in this sense that it seems more correct to classify the Court's *jurisprudence*, temporally, in terms of an earlier "classical", *Eurocentrist* era that lasted up to, and through, the year 1966, and a new, post-1966, "contemporary" Court.

A further, basic methodological question has to do with how best to explain and demonstrate the changes within the Court, in its internal composition and in judicial reasoning and judicial thought-ways and in the goal values or policies rendered by the judges in actual, concrete cases or references coming before the Court. The Court, of course, is not bound by any Common Law doctrine of Precedent, and its decisions have, in terms of the Court Statute, Article 59, "no binding force except between the parties and in respect of that particular case". Nevertheless, some Court decisions, because of their timing, or perhaps because of the intellectual quality of the judicial Opinions filed in them (whether the official Opinion of Court, or even individual Concurring or Dissenting Opinions), or because of the intrinsic political importance of the issues involved and the weight attached to them by different State actors, do clearly come to acquire the character of "leading cases", attested to, as such, in the learned *doctrines* and academic commentaries, and also in the public appraisals and critiques advanced in the United Nations General Assembly and in other international political, diplomatic, or professional-legal arenas. In the present study, the author has chosen to give most weight and authority, political and legal, to those leading cases; and to focus the detailed analysis and appraisal of the Court's own internal processes of reasoning and decision-making, and its Opinion-writing in explanation and rationalisation of the ultimate decisions, upon those very cases. While there is necessarily a certain element of the subjec-tive, – once one departs from the obvious enough point that not all of the Court's decisions over the years are of equal value or equally deserving of study – in choosing some fewer cases as worthwhile and passing over very many more in silence, I am struck by the fact that Richard Falk, in a study I had not examined until after I completed writing up the lectures, was in agreement with me as to the major choices. In this context, from the work of the "old" Court of the between-the-two-World-Wars era, only *Eastern Carelia*, and *Austro-German Customs Union*, seem particularly relevant to the contemporary International Court. In the early, post-World War II years, *Corfu Channel*, and the two *United Nations Membership* rulings, indicate the larger, inter-systemic (legal, and political) consensus within the "new" Court as to basic judicial reasoning and conceptions of the judicial decision-making *rôle*; while *United Nations Expenses* in 1962 indicates how firmly that methodological consensus can be maintained in spite of the more obvious substantive law, "policy" pressures the other way. *South West Africa. Second Phase* and *Namibia*, heralding the achievement of a "Court Revolution", and the transition from the traditional or "classical" Court to the modern or "contemporary" Court must be there, of course, as also with *Nuclear Tests*, *Western Sahara*, *Aegean Sea Continental Shelf* and other cases that demonstrate the still-remaining, empirical, trial-and-error testing that must be gone through before the contemporary Court can arrive, – as it seems finally to have done with its *Nicaragua*, 1984–1986, rulings, – at its new, activist, policy-making *rôle*. This will be exercised confidently, and with a sophisticated awareness of the complementarity of the Court's functions, in World Community problem-solving, with those of the General Assembly and Security Council, by a tribunal that is now fully representative in "regional" terms (legal-systemic, ethno-cultural, and political-ideological, as well as the more conventional geographical definition of earlier years).

A witness to the dramatic changes in dominant judicial philosophy within the Court's ranks who was also a leader in that process of internal transition from the "old" to the "new", was Manfred Lachs. First elected to the Court, in replacement of his fellow-countryman Winiarski, in the regular elections of 1966 that were held only two months after the Court's single-vote-majority decision in *South West Africa. Second Phase,* Judge Lachs is still there a generation later, having been reelected twice, each time with impressively large majorities, and with co-nominations from the main Western states as well as from the Third World and Eastern Europe. More perhaps than any other member of the Court, Judge Lachs is seen as personifying the new judicial thinking, with its renouncing of the "dead-hand control" of old *doctrines* and old *jurisprudence* developed in other, earlier times, in favour of rational contemporary solutions to contemporary problems of the World Community. On literary-stylistic and legal-argumentation grounds, it is not too difficult to identify as Judge Lachs' personal drafting the *Namibia* Advisory Opinion of 1971, with its conscious openings to the rapidly evolving juridical conscience of the World Community. At the same time, the Court's final Judgment in *Nuclear Tests,* an historically correct and necessary result, is recognisably from Judge Lachs' pen and stands as an exercise in judicial pragmatism by a Court President (as Judge Lachs then was) trying carefully to build a majority among judges still cautious, then, as to venturing on the *avant-garde* in doctrinal-legal terms. In recognition of his long-time services to the progressive development of International Law and also in celebration of professional-legal ties and personal friendship going back, now, more than thirty years, the present study is respectfully dedicated to Judge Lachs.

CHAPTER I

# Contemporary Conceptions of the Rôle of International Judicial Settlement

## 1. CHANGING NATIONAL POSITIONS ON THIRD PARTY (AND ESPECIALLY COURT-BASED) DISPUTES-SETTLEMENT

In the post-World War II era, recourse to the International Court of Justice, and also utilisation of international adjudication or arbitration generally for purposes of resolution of international conflicts and disputes between states, have been thought of as a distinctively American, United States' contribution to the theory and practice of International Law and Relations. This has resulted from the coincidence of two different factors, each resulting from the political and ideological dominance of the United States in the post-1945 system of World public order. First, a very idealistic group of U.S. "establishment" lawyers, who were not always experienced in the history of inter-State relations but whose leaders were often stalwarts of right-of-centre, Republican Party politics, began campaigning within the American Bar Association, and in the international unions of lawyers that developed from it, for acceptance by the U.S. and other states of the Compulsory Jurisdiction of the newly-renamed International Court of Justice, and more generally for adoption of the principle of neutral, Third Party arbitrament for international differences. This U.S.-based campaign, at its height during the late 1940s and in the 1950s, under the appropriately-titled (if rather open-ended), World-Rule-of-Law rubric,[1] appeared in many respects as a latter-day atonement for the non-adherence by the United States government, in the between-the-two-World-Wars era, to the jurisdiction of that first World Court, the *old* Permanent Court of International Justice. The U.S. non-participation in the work of the old Court – other than through a succession of very able individual U.S. judges who were elected, as a matter of grace by other participating states, in their personal, private, capacities as jurists and without official, U.S. government sponsorship[2] –

was a politically logical, though legally unnecessary, consequence of the
U.S. Administration's non-endorsement of the "Carthaginian" Peace Treaty
of Versailles of 1919, with which the institution of the Court was inevitably
associated in its "all spoils to the victors" peace settlement.

The non-participation by the U.S. government in the *old* Court was an
element, though only one element, in the *old* Court's being perceived,
historically, as a limited, "regional", Western European "family compact",
tribunal, with an agenda and *clientèle* confined, essentially, to the members
of the victorious military alliance of World War I and to the new
"succession" states that were the beneficiaries of the Versailles Treaty.

A second factor in the widespread tendency, after 1945, to think of
international adjudication in general and the institution of the International
Court in particular as being distinctively "American", stems from the post-
War academic phenomenon, which that most eclectic of modern U.S. social
scientists, Professor Harold Lasswell of the Yale Law School,[3] compared to
the pilgrimage of students from all over Europe to the Northern Italian
universities in the medieval Dark Ages. Aided by generous U.S. scholar-
ships and bursaries, under boldly imaginative and idealistic plans like the
Fulbright programme, there was a veritable invasion of U.S. graduate legal
and other centres, at Harvard, Yale, Columbia, Michigan, and elsewhere, by
the best and brightest of the Western European law graduates, and then by
similar quality graduates from Asia, Latin America, and other regions. The
U.S. Supreme Court, in the late 1940s and the 1950s, under the influence of
the liberal-activist, policy-oriented judges appointed by President Roosevelt
and President Truman, was then at the *apogée* of its intellectual prestige and
its political power. American Constitutional Law, with the in-built commitment to Law as a dynamic instrument of conscious social and economic
change, dominated the U.S. Law School curriculum of the time. Foreign
graduate legal students, when exposed to the evangelical U.S. Law School
message of the times that Law necessarily existed in symbiotic relation with
Society and that legal doctrines operated upon general social forces in a
continuing dialectical process, with the Courts as the prime institutional
outlet for application of those essentially dynamic theories of law, took
those same ideas home. They then transferred and applied them, in their
later careers as political leaders, foreign ministry legal advisers, or even
international arbitrators, to constitutional institutions of World government
like the United Nations General Assembly and the International Court. One
of the continuing, symbolic expressions of that earlier love-relationship
between U.S. intellectual-legal leaders and the International Court, is the
Jessup International Moot Court competition, held in Washington, D.C.,
and named after one of the most interesting (and liberal activist) of the U.S.

judges who served on the International Court, Philip Jessup,[4] who had won his spurs as an International Law professor and then as a U.S. diplomatic Ambassador-at-large. U.S. diplomatic negotiators at international codifying conferences over that same period were routinely pressing for the express inclusion of judicial settlement, as prime means of disputes-settlement, in the listing of conflicts-resolution procedures in the concluding sections of multilateral conventions and other general treaties.

All this makes more striking the latter-day *volte face* by the U.S. State Department against the International Court of Justice, manifested not merely in the official termination of the U.S. acceptance of the Compulsory Jurisdiction of the Court, in the aftermath of the preliminary judgments in *Nicaragua* v. *U.S.*;[5] but also in the U.S. Administration's evidently calculated public denigration of the International Court *qua* institution and of several of its main judicial personalities, following on the International Court's later, *Merits* judgement[6] in the same case. The U.S. State Department indicated, at the time, that henceforward the U.S. would eschew the normal jurisdiction of the Court, exercised through the *plenum* or Full Court of fifteen judges, which the U.S. Administration now stigmatised as "political",[7] in favour of recourse to the new jurisdictional device, inaugurated with the Canada-U.S. "regional" conflict in *Gulf of Maine* at the opening of the 1980s,[8] of a limited, five-member, panel or Special Chamber of the Court. The political significance of this latter-day jurisdictional ploy, facilitated by changes in the Court's Rules in the 1970s, was that according to the U.S. State Department's argument, which a majority of the Full Court of the International Court had apparently been persuaded to accept in its preliminary ruling constituting the very first such five-member Special Chamber of the Court, in *Gulf of Maine*,[9] it was the parties to a particular case, and not the Full Court itself, that would finally determine which five members of the Full Court would be selected to compose the Special Chamber, and, *ex hypothesi* and much more importantly politically, which ten members of the Full Court would necessarily be excluded or vetoed as to service on the panel.

Balancing the evident contemporary disillusionment of the U.S. Administration with the International Court, in reversal of earlier U.S. enthusiasm for the principle and the practice of judicial settlement, are contemporary Soviet attitudes to the Court. A recent study in the *Soviet Yearbook of International Law*,[10] (which, incidentally, signals the newly rediscovered elements of historical continuity between *pre*-, and *post*-October Revolution, Russian International Law *doctrines*) rightly directs attention to the pioneering contribution of great Imperial Russian jurists, of the like of Malinovsky, Kamarovsky, and de Martens, to the development of machinery for the peaceful settlement of international disputes. One might properly have added to these names the (slightly earlier in point of time) contribution of Besobrasoff of St. Petersburg, who was one of the original Founding Fathers of the *Institut de Droit International* in 1873. De Martens' impressive scientific-legal publications, ranging from his studies on the Right of Private Property in War, and on the Office of Consul and Consular Jurisdiction, to a brilliant series of monograph case-studies in the diplomatic history of international conflicts-resolution, regrettably, have been largely forgotten today. However, de Martens' applied legal-diplomacy at The Hague Peace Conference of 1899 remains well known, including not merely his distinctive proposals on *temperamenta belli*, but also his suggestions on the importance of international fact-finding and on the need for creation of international committees of enquiry, representative of the rival state parties to any international dispute, in order to establish the correct facts at the base of that dispute. More novel, at least for non-Russian students, in the current *Soviet Yearbook* survey, is the extended examination of Kamarovsky and of his draft proposals, advanced as early as 1881, for establishing a permanent international court of justice, – the more impressive because these proposals contained concrete suggestions as to the internal structure and practice of such a necessarily plural-legal or legally inter-systemic international tribunal. Contemporary Soviet scholars would accord to Kamarovsky's seminal thinking a direct influence on the formation and organisation of both the *old* Permanent Court of International Justice and also the *new* International Court of Justice, and they cite in this behalf a number of specific, detailed sections of the Statute of the Court.[11]

Researches such as these, amply rooted in Russian legal history, provide substantial intellectual-legal support, (and also legitimacy, if you wish), for President Gorbachev's imaginative new proposals for fuller utilisation of the International Court in international conflicts-resolution. These proposals mark a departure from, if not indeed heralding a direct reversal of, traditional Soviet International Law attitudes to the Court and to international adjudication, manifested as early as the early 1920s and maintained from the era of the *old* Court to that of the *new* Court where they were reaffirmed, in the 1960s, by the eloquent and persuasive then Soviet member of the Court, Judge Koretsky.[12] We shall have occasion to examine these distinctive Soviet International Law attitudes in some more detail, later. For the moment, it can be said that over most of that long time period, such essentially negative or defensive Soviet positions in relation to the Court seemed to make good sense politically in Soviet terms, granted the generally prevailing philosophical balance on the Court and Court's approach to its own *rôle* in international problem-solving; just as in the present, rather different political and social context, President Gorbachev's current initiatives in relation to the Court can be justified pragmatically as a response to radically new political conditions in the World Community as a whole and in the Soviet Union itself.

## 2. ETHNOCENTRICITY OF "CLASSICAL" INTERNATIONAL LAW INSTITUTIONS AND PROCESSES LIKE JUDICIAL SETTLEMENT

Western legal theory immediately after World War II emphasised the relativism, in cultural and ideological terms, of legal concepts and legal ideas, and of the legal institutions and processes through which they emerged. The leading philosopher of law among these scholars, Filmer Northrop of the Yale Law School,[13] drew upon the teachings of the Imperial Austro-Hungarian scholar, Ehrlich and his central concept of the community "living law"[14] – the *de facto* social attitudes, beliefs, and customs of any nation or of territorially-based ethno-cultural minorities within a larger nation – as necessarily conditioning and limiting the operational reality of positive law codes and statutes, executive-administrative decrees, and Court decisions, rendered by the State authority through its main institutions, judicial and other. Within a multi-national society, the positive law enactment of a central government could sometimes seem rendered by a distant and alien State authority, as with the Vienna-based, German, Habsburg *régime* of the Austro-Hungarian Empire in whose remote frontier province of Bukovina Ehrlich himself had passed his early professional-academic legal years. Northrop argued that every society should develop its own distinctive law and institutions, reflecting its own community "living law" – the concept of Jurisculture, in the terminology of Northrop's student, Gray Dorsey.[15] Finding confirmation for his thesis in the empirically-based researches of social scientists like Sorokin, Kluckhohn and Hoebel, Northrop went on to offer an alternative approach in building a viable system of World public order for the post-World War II era, to that projected by the U.S. State Department and the specialist legal advisers and consultants that it assembled at Yalta and other wartime conferences and above all at the San Francisco Conference in 1945 that drafted and then adopted the United Nations Charter. For the U.N. Charter, in Northrop's opinion, projected into the post-War World Community a constitutional-legal model of international organisation that drew very heavily upon the U.S. Constitution and U.S. constitutional institutions and upon the United States' own unique constitutional-historical experience. The "constitutionalising" of the post-World War II international system in this way was inspired by a generous U.S. vision of the need to submit international conflicts to rational and orderly processes of Third-Party and especially Court-based resolution that have been the historical stuff of the American legal system. Northrop countered all this by suggesting that judicial decision-making was an inherently Western approach to dispute settlement, and that it was the product of factors intrinsic to Western jurisculture and Western historical-legal experience that were not necessarily replicated in other, non-Western societies. On this view such other, non-Western societies could hardly be expected to share the post-1945 enthusiasm of U.S. professional-legal and scientific-legal groups for proselytising in behalf of universal acceptance of the Compulsory Jurisdiction of the World Court.

Northrop's position on the non-universality, in comparative law, national jurisculture terms, of judicial settlement as a solvent for community conflicts, and his argument therefrom as to the limited importance or relevance of international judicial settlement for the building of a viable post-War public order system for a necessarily increasingly pluralistic World Community, were echoed by other distinguished Western legal contemporaries – the U.S. scholar, Quincy Wright,[16] the British jurist and international civil servant, Jenks,[17] and the Dutch scholar, Röling,[18] as prime examples. The distinguished Egyptian jurist and diplomat, Boutros-Ghali,[19] also decried what he identified as an artificiality or preciosity in the legal culture of a highly-educated Arab *élite*, (usually formed by graduate legal studies in Paris or elsewhere in the West), that favoured a Western-style "rule of law". Boutros-Ghali charged that – "those ruling *élites* were impregnated with Western constitutionalism and believed that inter-Arab conflicts could be settled by an international judge", rather than by the more pragmatic forms of political accommodation common to pre-Westernised Arab legal history.

On the other hand, the contemporary Indian jurist, Anand,[20] notes the long exposure, extending over two or three centuries, of non-Western societies in Asia and Africa to Western legal culture and Western civilisation in its various Western European manifestations, through the instrument of Colonialism, political and economic, with its forced application of European notions of legal sovereignty and of European concepts and institutions of public law, generally. The long-term impact of such, originally alien, Western European, basic legal ideas and processes, on non-Western, indigenous, Colonial peoples had brought a consequent influence on the lives and legal thought-ways of those societies and their peoples, to the point where, in Anand's view, there were, today, no particular intellectual barriers for Asian and African states in accepting international adjudication or international arbitration (Western-derived as these may have been, historically) for purposes of settlement of their own international disputes today. Within Africa, while Ofosu-Amaah[21] has decried the lack of interest of the former European Colonial powers in going beyond the private law domain, or seriously exporting Public Law, including Public International Law, to their subject peoples in the era of Imperial rule, Judge Elias seems much more optimistic about the post-Decolonisation era and the influence of trans-national international private associations and foundations of judges, legal practitioners and other jurists, like the (albeit Western-based) International Commission of Jurists in Geneva and the World Peace through Law Centre in Washington, D.C., in the evolution of contemporary advanced African thinking on International Law.[22]

Finally, Judge Lachs, in a masterly philosophical overview of the historical process of "reception" of substantive-legal and processual-legal ideas from one society to another, reminds us of the trans-cultural, universalising effects of legal education, not merely in the contemporary "Global Village" but also, much earlier, in the interaction of scholars across conventional national frontiers, East and West, as far back as Medieval times.[23]

Specialists in Comparative Constitutional Law would confirm the dynamic element in legal "reception' from one society to another in pointing to the signal success of the distinctively U.S. institution of Judicial Review (of the Constitution) as "received" in Japan under the new, post-World War II, democratic constitution of 1946; and also as "received" in India under the new, post-Decolonisation, republican constitution of 1950.[24] In those countries, an archetypal U.S. constitutional-legal process has well and truly taken local root, and flourishes with an intellectual resourcefulness and vitality at least equal to the part played by judicial review in the United States constitutional system. To some extent, the institution of judicial review of constitutionality may even be said to have broken significant new ground, outside the U.S., in constitutional-legal terms. In the legal "great debate" of the immediate post-War years between, on the one hand, Western jurists like Northrop and Quincy Wright, who were commendably sensitive to the new political and legal pluralism of the new, vastly expanding World Community of their era, and their intellectually far more conservative or traditional, Western colleagues who still insisted on conceiving the World public order system in the old, pre-War, wholly Western ("Eurocentrist") political and legal terms, it may well be that both sides to the debate underestimated the capacity of indigenous, local, non-Western legal *élites* in the Colonial countries to "receive", and creatively to adapt to local circumstances and needs, distinctively Western legal institutions and legal processes. In a certain sense, Northrop and his colleagues' and students' cultural-anthropological legal hypotheses were derived from ideal-type situations, being based on models of non-Western societies in their original, legally "pure" form *before* arrival of the first European colonisers and the forced "reception" of European Imperial-legal institutions, processes and substantive ideas. The fault would not be in the Law and Society mode of legal analysis itself, nor in the key concept of the community "living law" as a limiting condition to the positive law. It may lie, rather, in the failure to recognise that any "reception" of a foreign system of positive law, – even an imposed, forcible "reception", – may itself, by its very impact and effect in modifying or changing local legal thought-ways, create a new local "living law", – at least on the part of the all-important indigenous legal *élite* who will graduate to political and legal power on the achievement of self-determination and independence from the original, parent European Colonial authority.[25] The concept of the "Global Village", applied to legal learning and legal culture as "received" and diffused throughout the World Community today, operates as an inter-nationalising, universalising force. It is a corrective to any too literal or too rigid deference to the cultural-ideological relativism or particularity of legal institutions, processes and substantive rules, in the present era of rapid and widespread interaction and interchange between different peoples and different cultures in the contemporary World Community.

## 3. THE INFLUENCE OF EVOLVING NATIONAL CONSTITUTIONAL INSTITUTIONS AND PROCESSES UPON INTERNATIONAL JUDICIAL SETTLEMENT

The post-World War II era saw not merely a revolution in the theory and practice of international relations, with the disappearance of an erstwhile Western political-military hegemony, and the downfall of Imperialism and the ending of Colonialism (at least in its "classical", Western European phase). It also produced a radical transformation in hitherto "classical", Western conceptions of Constitutional Law and Government, and the main institutions and processes for ensuring democratic constitutionalism. Of particular importance and relevance in the present context are the institutions of federalism and of constitutional review.

The emergence, as an imperative principle of the "new", post-"classical" International Law, (ranking today almost as *Jus Cogens*), of Self-Determination of Peoples,[26] had implications that carried over from International Law to municipal, national law. It implied a new sensitiveness on the part of national governments in what were so often (for reasons of past history or else of present Decolonisation) multi-national states, to claims to ethno-cultural particularism and constitutional self-realisation along cultural, linguistic, religious, or similar grounds, when advanced by geographically-concentrated minority communities or groups existing within the legal frontiers of the state. The constitutional-legal consequences, in terms of practical, institutionally-based follow-up, would be considerable for those post-Westphalia, Western European nation-states with their inherited, too often unbridgeable gaps or conflicts between the pursuit of geopolitical "natural frontiers" on the one hand and the desires to maintain a unified, integrated and necessarily homogeneous, national community.

The impact, long-range, on the new, post-Decolonisation, "succession" states in Asia and Africa would also be marked. The institutional devices for reconciling national unity or at least minimum national cohesiveness with increasingly clamant claims to ethno-cultural particularity were to be sought in constitutional forms of an increasing legal-scientific and technical sophistication, from the often costly, trial-and-error experience of Comparative Constitutional Law. Federalism[27] or, more loosely, plural-con-stitutionalism, was increasingly seen as resting on a constitutional balance or equilibrium of forces, transcending the old-fashioned concept of the Separation of Powers derived from Montesquieu. This latter too often had ended up in a rigid, *a priori* division of governmental decision-making authority into separate, watertight compartments of power and competence, that were artificially separated from each other and considered incapable of being mutually complementary or of operating at the same time. The new concept was, rather, one of countervailing power, and of the need for avoiding any concentration of all state authority in the one constitutional institution or arena. It also involved recognising that all organs of state authority share responsibility for community problem-solving on major tension-issues; and that they may, therefore, sensibly operate simul-taneously and not necessarily sequentially, and that their mandate involves mutual cooperation and not any necessary or inevitable conflict *inter se*. The major expression of the new constitutional-legal thinking found itself in the notion of Federalism, and hence of federal constitutional law, as being *process* and not any static body of rules and processes that had jelled, once and for all, in some bygone age. This involved the further notion that the positive law, so far from being rigid and immutable, existed in a continuing, dynamic relation with the society for which it had first been developed, and that it should continue to evolve in true dialectical fashion, in response to rapidly changing societal conditions and demands. As a correlative to the new Federalism, and as its main institutional outlet, we have the Special Constitutional Court as it developed in Continental

Western Europe in the post-World War II period.

The Special Constitutional Court, as constitutional art-form, emerged in the early post-War years. Its ties of historical consanguinity to the U.S. Supreme Court are clear enough. For the U.S. Court, especially since the reforms effected by the Judiciary Act of 1925 with the discretionary control over the Court's own jurisdiction that that conferred, has become for all practical purposes a tribunal specialised in constitutional law. Its reputation and record, as a liberal activist, policy-making court, has been perhaps the most widely "received" American legal image for other contemporary legal systems. The Special Constitutional Court, as master constitutional institution, was incorporated in the Bonn (West German) Basic Law of 1949,[28] itself established as a provisional constitution for the newly-created state of West Germany, formed out of the three Western powers' Zones of Military Occupation in Germany. The three Western powers had posited return of legal sovereignty to the new West German state on the condition of the adoption of a new, democratic constitutional system for the new West German state. The wholly German, West German Parliamentary Council, which drafted up what became the Bonn charter, drew upon a number of intrinsically German legal sources and also some past German liberal democratic constitutional experience. While the Parliamentary Council's members were certainly familiar with the distinguished Austrian-German jurist, Kelsen, and his work on the Austrian Constitution of 1920 and the limited Constitutional tribunal therein established, the influence of U.S. general constitutional ideas is also unmistakable, even without any overt pressures from the American Military Government and its roster of distinguished academic and technical constitutional advisers, like the distinguished German-born Harvard professor, Carl Friedrich.[29] Beyond that, the Special Constitutional Court (*Bundesverfassungsgericht*) created in 1951 in terms of the Bonn Basic Law (Constitution) of 1949, was fortunate in having, in the first group of judges elected to its ranks, several jurists who were well-experienced, by forced refuge abroad during the Hitler years, in Anglo-American jurisprudence. Among these, the scholar-jurist Judge Gerhard Leibholz,[30] and Vice-President Katz, stand out. Their continuing influence on the new Court – in Leibholz' case, for the Court's first two decades until his retirement in 1971, and in Katz' case for the first decade until his death in 1961 – is apparent, not merely in the Court's *jurisprudence* but also, and more importantly long-range, in the Court's internal organisation and approach to decision-making, and in the Court's habits of reasoning and thought-ways as they evolved over the years. From a traditional, Civil Law-style tribunal, respecting the Continental Civil Law canons of collegiality, anonymity, and specialisation, the West German

Court developed into something new and *sui generis*, drawing upon the best of U.S. Supreme Court experience but also retaining its own distinctively Civil Law elements and thus serving in its turn – more easily than the Common Law-based U.S. Supreme Court could have hoped to have done itself – as model or paradigm for democratic constitution-makers in still other, Civil Law-based countries.

While the direct "reception" of American constitutionalism is dominant in the emergence, post-War, as *de facto* Special Constitutional Courts, of the Japanese and the Indian Supreme Courts, it is the West German *Bundesverfassungsgericht* that provides the intellectual-legal inspiration and model for the subsequently developed Special Constitutional Courts of legal systems as diverse as those of Socialist Yugoslavia, the short-lived bi-national Republic of Cyprus, post-Franco Spain, post-Salazar Portugal, and even the new, quasi-federal, Belgian state (with its *Cour d'Arbitrage* established in 1980). There may be room for disagreement among legal scholars as to how much, if at all, indigenous Continental European intellectual influences of a neo-Kelsenian variety,[31] rather than any "received" American constitutional ideas, contributed to these Continental European developments outside West Germany itself. The case for neo-Kelsenism would be at its strongest with the Italian Constitutional Court; but once it has been decided that the principle of Constitutional Review should be institutionalised in Court form, the recourse to the (ultimately U.S.-influenced) *Bundesverfassungsgericht* for working models for Court organisation and Court process is inescapable.

An alternative, also distinctively Continental European model, that owes no apparent major debts to Kelsen, is that deriving from post-War France, under the Constitution of the Fourth Republic of 1946, and, much more substantially, under the Constitution of the Fifth Republic of 1958, with its special *Conseil constitutionnel*.[32] An institutionalised system of review and testing of the constitutionality of legislation, to be exercised by a standing committee of the legislature, much in the fashion of the *Comité constitutionnel* under the Fourth French Republic, should present no special intellectual-legal problems of reconciliation with Rousseau-ist constitutional notions of the sovereignty of the elected legislature; or, for that matter, with Marxist-Leninist constitutional notions of all-power to the Supreme Soviet (legislature). The Chinese constitutional theorist, Dong Chen Mei,[33] was able to argue, in 1988, – convincingly in terms of then existing legal orthodoxies, – both for the creation of a special Review Organ for Unconstitutionality; and also, in the design and choice of such a body, for eschewing the U.S. *judicial* review model in favour of the earlier, Continental European-favoured model of determination of constitutionality of laws and decrees through their examination or approach by *legislative* organs. The suggestion advanced, then, by this Chinese scholar was that the Chinese National People's Congress and its Standing Committee should exercise just such a function. Whatever the modalities, the commitment to the general principle of an institutionalised constitutional review is clear.

In the case of the Soviet Union, special factors, and particularly the prospects of a permanent political minority status for any Soviet judge or judges within the ranks of the old Permanent Court of International Justice and also the successor International Court of Justice, with predictable effects in terms of the composition of voting majorities within the Court, produced the long-standing Soviet Government policies of neither accepting the Compulsory Jurisdiction of the World Court nor hazarding the Soviet's own vital interests by way of special agreements for reference of cases to the Court. When allied to Vyshinsky's powerful philippic, first formulated for purposes of Soviet internal, Municipal, constitutional law, against judicial legislation in any form[34] – which Vyshinsky himself related, in part, to the lessons that he thought to be derived from the U.S.' own unfortunate historical experience with the conservative "Old Court" majority on the U.S. Supreme Court prior to the President Roosevelt-inspired "Court Revolution" of 1937, – this resulted in a very powerful weight of Soviet scientific-legal *doctrines* denying any policy-making, law-making *rôle* for adjudication, whether national or international. A significant *rôle* reversal or change of attitude seems presaged today by the new Soviet interest in constitutional review, manifested in President Gorbachev's public praise of the International Court of Justice, and in his quite specific proposal, in his address of 7 December 1988, that all states agree to recognise the binding jurisdiction of the International Court with respect to the interpretation and application of human rights agreements. This concrete suggestion was immediately acted upon by Decree of the Presidium of the Supreme Soviet of the U.S.S.R., which accepted the Compulsory Jurisdiction of the International Court in respect to six specific international Conventions in the human rights field.[35] Parallel to this new Soviet initiative at the international level, there is, in Soviet internal, constitutional law writings, a new attention to the principle of constitutional review, especially when it should involve control of normative acts by courts.[36] President Gorbachev's own constitutional reform projects within the Soviet Union itself include suggestions for constitutional review, though rather more along the lines of the earlier (Fourth Republic) French system of review by a Constitutional Committee, than the United States Court-based model.[37] If we remember that the first openings to a legislature-based system of constitutional review, under the Fourth French Republic, led on logically and inevitably to a form of qualified review by an independent constitutional tribunal under the Fifth French Republic and one whose jurisdictional base has since been broadened considerably and facilitated by later constitutional amendment, then the opportunity for further *Perestroika*, within the new "Gorbachev Constitution", by way of judicially-based review of constitutionality, is there.[38]

Enough has been said to indicate that, in terms of contemporary comparative legal science and comparative jurisculture, the principle of judicial settlement of disputes is no longer – if it ever was, – an esoteric, "Western", even purely U.S., constitutional notion. Together with the larger concept of constitutional review, judicial settlement of disputes is now generally accepted as a necessary, cardinal aspect of democratic constitutionalism, to be effectuated and entrenched in concrete, institutionally-based terms. That helps to explain judicial settlement's new-found popularity at the international relations level, and also the International Court's new *clientèle* of Third World States[39] that once had spurned the Court as being dominated by Western states and as implementing, in consequence, a *jurisprudence* that favoured the Western political interests and the maintenance of the *status quo* in International Law. It also renders doubly ironic the U.S. Administration's current, seeming turning of its back on the International Court and on international adjudication generally, in view of all the past impressive historical record of sustained intellectual-legal support and political proselytising by U.S. political leaders and U.S. professional and academic jurists, in behalf of the principle of judicial settlement of international disputes.

## NOTES

1. See, for example, *The Four Steps at Athens toward World Peace through Law*, (World Peace through Law Centre, Washington, D.C.), (1963), pp. 2–3.
2. Among such distinguished U.S. jurists who were elected to the old Permanent Court in their personal capacities, were Charles Evans Hughes, who was, successively, Justice of the U.S. Supreme Court, unsuccessful Republican Party candidate for U.S. Presidency in 1916, and U.S. Secretary of State, prior to his election to the P.C.I.J., and who was later, immediately on his retirement from the P.C.I.J., appointed as Chief Justice of the U.S. Supreme Court (1930–1941); and also Frank Kellogg, who was U.S. Secretary of State and co-father of the Kellogg-Briand Pact of 1928, and who succeeded Hughes as judge on the P.C.I.J.
3. See, for example, Lasswell, *The World Revolution of Our Time. A Framework for Basic Policy Research* (1951); Lasswell (with McDougal), "The identification and appraisal of diverse systems of Public Order", *American Journal of International Law* vol. 53 (1959), p. 1.

4. See, for example, his strong Dissenting Opinion in *South West Africa. Second Phase. Judgment*, I.C.J. Reports 1966, p. 6, at p. 323.

5. *Military and Paramilitary Activities in and against Nicaragua (Nicaragua v. United States of America), Provisional Measures, Order of 10 May 1984*, I.C.J. Reports 1984, p. 169; *Jurisdiction and Admissibility, Judgment*, I.C.J. Reports 1984, p. 392.

6. *Merits, Judgment*, I.C.J. Reports 1986, p. 14.

7. See Statement of Department of State on U.S. Withdrawal from Nicaragua Proceedings, 18 January 1985, reprinted in "Contemporary Practice of the United States", *American Journal of International Law* vol. 79 (1985), pp. 438, 441.

8. *Delimitation of the Maritime Boundary in the Gulf of Maine Area (Canada v. United States of America), Constitution of Chamber, Order of 20 January 1982*, I.C.J. Reports 1982, p. 3.

9. But see, however, the Declaration of Judge Oda, *ibid.*, p. 10; the Dissenting Opinion by Judge Morozov, *ibid.*, p. 11; and the Dissenting Opinion by Judge El-Khani, *ibid.*, p. 12.

10. Starodubtsev, "Problemi mirnikh sredstv razreshenia mezhdunarodnikh sporov v trudakh russikh dorevolutsionnikh uchenikh", *Sovetskii Ezhegodnik Mezhdunarodnogo Prava* [1987] p. 260.

11. Starodubtsev, *ibid.*, (citing Statute of the International Court of Justice, Articles 2, 3, 25, 36, 39, 42–44, 46, 48–54).

12. See, for example, *Certain Expenses of the United Nations, Advisory Opinion*, (Dissenting Opinion of Judge Koretsky), I.C.J. Reports 1962, p. 151, at p. 268.

13. See, for example, Northrop, "The Complementary Emphases of Eastern Intuitive and Western Scientific Philosophy", in *Philosophy: East and West*, (Moore ed., 1944); Northrop, *The Meeting of East and West. An Inquiry concerning World Understanding* (1950).

14. Ehrlich, *Grundlegung der Soziologie des Rechts* (1913). And see Northrop, "Naturalistic and Cultural Foundations for a more Effective International Law", *Yale Law Journal*, vol. 59 (1950), p. 1430; Northrop, "Contemporary Jurisprudence and International Law", *Yale Law Journal*, vol. 61 (1952), p. 623.

15. Dorsey, *Jurisculture. Greece and Rome* (1989). And see also Dorsey, "Two Objective Bases for a World-Wide Legal Order", in *Ideological Differences and World Order* (Northrop, ed.) (1949).

16. Quincy Wright, "Asian Experience and International Law", *International Studies* (New Delhi), vol. 1 (1959), p. 84.

17. Jenks, *The Common Law of Mankind* (1958); Jenks, *The Prospects of International Adjudication* (1964).

18. Röling, *International Law in an Expanded World* (1960).

19. Boutros-Ghali, "The Arab League 1945–1970", *Revue Egyptienne de Droit International*, vol. 25 (1969), p. 67.

20. Anand, "Attitude of the 'New' Asian-African Countries towards the International Court of Justice", in *Studies in International Adjudication* (1969), p. 53; Anand, "Rôle of International Adjudication", in *The Future of the International Court of Justice* (Gross, ed.) (1976), vol. 1, p. 4.

21. Ofosu-Amaah, "Regional Enforcement of International Obligations", *Zeitschrift für ausländisches öffentliches Recht und Völkerrecht*, vol. 47 (1987), pp. 80, 84. And see also *African International Legal History* (Mensah-Brown (ed.)) (1975).

22. Elias, *Africa and the Development of International Law* (2nd rev. ed., Akinjide), (1988), pp. 29–30.

23. Lachs, *The Teacher in International Law (Teachings and Teaching)* (1982).

24. See, generally, the present author's *Supreme Courts and Judicial Law-Making. Constitutional Tribunals and Constitutional Review* (1986); *Federalism and Supreme Courts and the Integration of Legal Systems* (McWhinney and Pescatore, eds.) (1973); *Verfassungsgerichtsbarkeit in der Gegenwart. Länderberichte und Rechtsvergleichung* (Mosler, ed.) (1962).

25. Common exposure of national legal *élites*, from many different cultures, to graduate education with the same small group of legal teachers in a few major World legal centres, yields the current phenomenon of an increasing homogenisation of an international legal *élite*, transcending conventional political-territorial frontiers. See Julius Stone, "A Common Law for Mankind?", *International Studies* (New Delhi), vol. 1, p. 430.

26. Calogeropoulos-Stratis, *Le droit des peuples à disposer d'eux-mêmes* (1973); Doehring, *Das Selbstbestimmungsrecht der Völker als Grundsatz des Völkerrechts (Referat und Diskussion der 13. Tagung der Deutschen Gesellschaft fur Völkerrecht)* (1974); Ermacora, *Die Selbstbestimmungsidee. Ihre Entwicklung von 1918–1974* (1977).

27. See, generally, *Studies in Federalism* (Bowie and Friedrich, eds.) (1954).

28. See, for example, the present author's *Föderalismus und Bundesverfassungsrecht* (1961); *Constitutionalism in Germany and the Federal Constitutional Court* (1962).

29. See, generally, Friedrich, *The Impact of American Constitutionalism Abroad* (1966); Friedrich, *Limited Government. A Comparison* (1974); *Studies in Federalism* (Bowie and Friedrich, eds.) (1954).

30. Leibholz, *Die Gleichheit vor dem Gesetz* (1st ed., 1925; 2nd rev. ed., 1959); and see, generally, *Die moderne Demokratie und ihr Recht. Festschrift für Gerhard Leibholz* (Bracher *et al.*, eds.) 2 vols. (1966).

31. Compare Cappelletti, (book review), *American Journal of International Law*, vol. 82 (1988), pp. 421, 422.

32. Favoreu and Philip, *Le Conseil constitutionnel* (1978); Luchaire, *Le Conseil constitutionnel* (1980).

33. Dong Chen Mei, "Viewing the Chinese Review Organ for Unconstitutionality Worldwide", in *Law in East and West: Recht in Ost und West* (Nakamura, ed.) (1988), p. 463.

34. Vyshinsky, *The Law of the Soviet State* (English transl., 1954), p. 56 *et seq.*

35. As re-published in *American Journal of International Law*, vol. 83 (1989), p. 457.

36. Tumanov, "Sudebnii Kontrol za konstitutsionnostu normativnikh aktov", *Sovetskoe Gosudarstvo i Pravo*, (1988) (no. 3), p. 10.

37. Compare Hazard, "The Gorbachev Era in the USSR", *Syracuse Journal of International Law and Commerce*, vol. 16 (1988), p. 1.

38. President Gorbachev's most recent constitutional reform proposals in fact reveal a progression to a German-style Special Constitutional Court. See "Gorbachev legt den Entwurf eines Unionsvertrags vor: eine 'Union der Souveränen Sowjetrepubliken' angestrebt," *Frankfurter Allgemeine Zeitung*, 27 November 1990.

39. See the comments, to this effect, variously, by Judges Nagendra Singh, de Lacharrière, and Lachs, in *Judging the World* (Sturgess and Chubb, eds.) (1988), pp. 453, 457, 468.

## CHAPTER II

# The Contemporary International Judicial Process.
# Law and Logic, and the "Law" / "Politics" Dichotomy

## 1. JUDICIAL POSITIVISM AND THE LIMITS OF LEGAL LOGIC:
### *South West Africa, Second Phase, (1966), Namibia (1971)*

There are some few, land-mark decisions that stand out in the history of any tribunal, as either marking the end of an historical era in Court *jurisprudence*, or else presaging new and radically different trends in judicial policies for the future. This is understandable enough in the case of a Common Law or Common Law-influenced court, since the Common Law doctrine of precedent admits of the existence of *locus classicus* decisions; but it is also true with Civil Law courts where the authoritative text-writers seem very readily, and quickly, to establish their own consensus as to which Court decisions are worthy of notation and analysis in depth, in the learned *doctrines*, as heralding significant change to the *jurisprudence constante*. With Common Law-influenced tribunals, it may well be the public reaction to a judgment and the public perception of its political impact, rather than the *opinio iuris*, that supplies the dynamic, dialectical, law-in-the-making element. Charles Evans Hughes, a sometime Justice of the U.S. Supreme Court, and then, briefly, a Judge of the old Permanent Court of International Justice in The Hague, before his resignation to take up the Chief Justiceship of the U.S. Supreme Court, identified certain land-mark decisions in the work of the U.S. Supreme Court, on the basis of their negative public impact at the time of their first publication, and then the immense political reaction that they brought in their wake. Hughes characterised such decisions as being among the U.S. Supreme Court's "great, self-inflicted wounds";[1] and he cited, as prime example, the decision in the *Dred Scott* case,[2] which was rendered just before the American Civil War, and which, unnecessary as it may have been in strictly legal terms and decided apparently without any judicial regard to its direct political consequences, is

16

considered by very many historians to have hastened the onset of that great military conflict.

The International Court of Justice ruling in *South West Africa, Second Phase*, in August, 1966,[3] on many views, falls into that category of a legally unnecessary and, in its immediate impact, politically disastrous decision. Nevertheless, because of the public reactions that it provoked, it may have hurried the Court into a long-overdue review and examination of its own *rôle* in relation to other, coordinate institutions of World Community policy-making like the U.N. General Assembly and Security Council, and, also of the Court's own special responsibilities for the "progressive development of International Law" in an era of transition and fundamental and rapid change in the World Community.

The issue of the legal status of the old League of Nations Mandate, now United Nations Trust Territory, over the former German Colony of South West Africa (Namibia), had been before the U.N. General Assembly in various forms since the opening of the 1950s. What had triggered the U.N. General Assembly's interest had been the accentuation of the original Mandatory state, South Africa's, racially discriminatory policies within its own frontiers, with the election in 1948 of an ultra-Nationalist, white minority government committed to application of policies of racial separation (*Apartheid*) within South Africa itself and, by extension, also within the Mandate/Trust Territory of South West Africa (Namibia). The continuing refusal of the white minority government of the Republic of South Africa to discuss the matter within the United Nations parliamentary arenas, or even to acknowledge the jurisdiction of the U.N. Trusteeship Council over South West Africa (Namibia), led to the tactical decision by states opposed to the *Apartheid régime* in South Africa to try to transfer the issue to the international judicial arena. Eventually, after a series of trial ventures before the International Court, two African states, Ethiopia and Liberia, whose designation as plaintiffs in the matter was politically logical in so far as they had been members of the original international legal authority, the League of Nations, that had conferred the Mandate on South Africa, had been able to persuade the International Court of Justice, in 1962,[4] by a single vote majority (eight-to-seven) to accept jurisdiction over their legal complaint against the Republic of South Africa. On this basis, the Court entered upon hearings on the substantive legal issues of the compatibility of racial separation (*Apartheid*), in its purported extension to the Mandate/Trust Territory, with International Law. In 1966, however, the International Court of Justice now ruled, by a single vote majority (eight-to-seven) once again, that it had no jurisdiction to rule on the substantive legal issues involved.[5] The composition of the International Court and the bench of the

Full Court sitting on the case, had changed somewhat between 1962 and 1966, and this is the immediate political explanation and legal justification for the seeming *volte face* from the first, 1962, ruling to the second, 1966, ruling. "Death, disease, and disablement", as it was remarked wryly at the time, played a not altogether fortuitous part in the Court switch between the two decisions. One of the judges from the earlier, 1962 decision, who had been with the Court majority in that decision, Judge Badawi (Egypt), had died in 1965, and his successor, Judge Ammoun (Lebanon), who would predictably have voted the same way as Judge Badawi, took his place on the Court too late to participate in the Court hearings and therefore also in the final Court vote for the 1966 decision. A second judge, who had been in the Court minority in the earlier, 1962 decision, Judge Bustamante y Rivero (Peru), was ill throughout the hearings for the 1966 decision, and took no part in the final Court vote in 1966. A third judge, Sir Mohammed Zafrullah Khan (Pakistan), elected to the Court in 1964, was persuaded by the Court's President, Sir Percy Spender (Australia), to recuse himself for the 1966 case, on the basis that he had participated, as national Delegate to the U.N. General Assembly, in earlier General Assembly debates on South West Africa. The Court President, Sir Percy Spender, as himself a Common Law-trained jurist, took the strict English Common Law attitude to judicial disqualification for "interest", and evidently relied upon the Court Statute[6] for purposes of pressing the point upon Judge Zafrullah Khan. Since, in political-legal terms, the absent votes of Judge Ammoun and of Judge Bustamante y Rivero would presumably have cancelled each other out, Judge Zafrullah Khan's vote would clearly have been crucial in the final outcome; and once he had been disqualified the particular outcome of the 1966 decision was inevitable and predictable in advance, on the basis of the 1962 Court vote. The 8-to-7 Court vote from 1962, in favour of exercising jurisdiction to hear the case, was immediately converted – with the subtraction of Judge Ammoun, Judge Bustamante y Rivero, and Judge Zafrullah Khan – into a 6-to-6 tie vote in 1966. With the two *ad hoc* judges, named by the rival parties, added and, predictably, cancelling each other out, this became a 7-to-7 tie vote; and the deadlock was able legally to be broken by the Court President, Sir Percy Spender's, exercising his right, under the Court Statute,[7] to cast a second, tie-breaking vote in the case, making it now an 8-to-7 decision that effectively countermanded the thrust and intention of the 1962 Court decision. The *rôle* of the Court President, Sir Percy Spender, in producing that Court *volte face*, as between 1962 and 1966, through his initiative in inducing Judge Zafrullah Khan's self-disqualification, has been strongly criticised; and it was undoubtedly part of the hidden agenda, at the U.N. General Assembly only several months later, at the time of the regular, triennial elections for the Court, when Spender's co-national, Sir Kenneth Bailey, a distinguished U.N. diplomat and jurist in his own right, was defeated in his bid to be elected in Spender's seat on the Court.

The legal *rationale* for the Court's single-vote-majority decision in 1966, distinguishing it from the single-vote-majority decision the other way in 1962, has to be that while the two plaintiff states, Ethiopia and Liberia, had *locus standi* and a sufficient legal "interest" to raise the substantive legal issue of extension of the *Apartheid régime* to South West Africa (Namibia), (the 1962 ruling), they did not have a sufficient legal "interest" to receive a decision on that substantive issue (the 1966 ruling). As a judicial "distinction" explaining and justifying the Court's exercise of jurisdiction in 1962 and its refusal to exercise jurisdiction in 1966, it would, as the Canadian Prime Minister of the day, Lester Pearson, remarked, have baffled the intellectual ingenuity of the Mediaeval Schoolmen skilled in arguing, as in the legendary debate between St. Thomas Aquinas and Duns Scotus, as to how many angels could sit on the point of a needle. The distinction was, understandably enough, bitterly assailed, in the U.N. General Assembly and elsewhere, as turning on "political" and not on "legal" considerations. According to this particular argument, the distinction had been adopted by a "Western", or at least Western-dominated tribunal, as a legal device for protecting a racist, white minority *régime* in a still-surviving remnant of the Western European Colonial system, from scrutiny and review by the organised World Community, applying contemporary World Community standards. The charge of "political" decision, levelled against the Court immediately after the *South West Africa. Second Phase* judgment of 1966, came predominantly from newly-independent, self-governing, former Colonial, Third World states. With a significant change in the identity of the persons making the complaint, it is not intrinsically different from that later charge levelled by the U.S. State Department against the International Court in the bitter U.S. reaction to the Court's *Nicaragua* rulings in the period 1984–1986.[8] The players may be quite different, but the substantive content of the charge remains the same. Yet, in respect to each case – that of 1966, and that of two decades later – it may be suggested that the explanation for the Court's actions lies not in any purely subjective individual judicial attitudes or *ad hoc* individual judicial reactions to casual political events; but rather in readily identifiable and predictable elements of national legal culture on the part of the leading judicial personalities involved. We might include, here, particular national conceptions of the nature of the judicial process and the relevance and limits of legal "logic" in judicial decision-making; and also of the social responsibilities of the judge, *qua* community decision-maker, in adjusting or re-making old positive law so as to respond to long-range trends and directions in society and in the complex of competing interests pressed within society at any time.

In the *jurisprudence* of the International Court in the first two decades of the post-War era, the influence of legal positivism, and of what might be called the more traditional conceptions of the judicial process, is dominant. The Court's membership, for much of this period, reflecting the numerically rather limited United Nations of that particular earlier time era and the equally restricted, pre-Decolonisation World Community to which that U.N. membership itself corresponded, was dominated by Western jurists. The few non-Western judges on the International Court were themselves usually the product of advanced academic and professional-legal training in Western European legal institutions. It is known that the official Opinion of Court in *South West Africa. Second Phase*, signed by Sir Percy Spender in his capacity of Court President and member of the Court majority in the case, was also heavily influenced, in its reasoning and elaboration and in its actual literary drafting, by the British judge on the Court, the long-time Legal Adviser to the British Foreign Ministry, Sir Gerald Fitzmaurice. Sir Gerald had had the best of classical language training, prior to his legal studies, and his professional-legal work, as evidenced both in international diplomatic-legal conferences and also in scientific-legal bodies like the *Institut de Droit International*, was always characterised by an extreme clarity and precision of expression, and a rigorous avoidance of any exaggerations of language or style or the resort to legal hyperbole. In particular, Fitzmaurice's opinions were consciously free from any discussion of "policy", or of philosophical or value considerations inherent in legal decisions. He was, in all respects, not merely committed to a "logical", value-neutral conception of law that was deliberately restricted to the exegetical approach to legal texts and documents, but also armed by his education and professional experience with the formidable intellectual-legal skills and techniques necessary to render such analytical-logical approach in a technically sophisticated and persuasive, pure form. Fitzmaurice's basic philosophy of law, in fact, resembled very much the late-19th century abstract perfectionism of the German Civil Law Pandectists, so accurately rendered by von Ihering with the (not necessarily pejorative) concept of the *BegriffsHimmel*. Fitzmaurice's intimate collaborator in *South West Africa. Second Phase* and the actual signatory to the final Court judgment, Judge-President Spender, had been in his immediate pre-judicial career in Australia a successful national Foreign Minister and then diplomat; but his main professional-legal competence had been attained as a Barrister practising in the highly refined, analytical-legal world of the Equity Bar. The twinning of Spender and Fitzmaurice for purposes of the 1966 International Court majority opinion and its elaboration and drafting, was natural enough; and the final formulation reflects in full measure the fine professional-legal skills of both men. The Court majority opinion is, as Professor Harold Laski once remarked of Hans Kelsen and his Pure Theory of Law, "an exercise in logic, but not in life". Its logic and reasoning are impeccable and beyond effective intellectual counter, if only you are prepared to concede its (necessarily extra-legal) starting point or basic premise: that the particular issue before the Court can be, and should be, absolutely divorced from its social context for purposes of the Court's ruling. The critical historical-legal assessment of the Court majority judgement in *South West Africa. Second Phase*, denying the Court's jurisdiction to rule on the substantive legal issues, must properly be directed to its basic premise, and to the particular philosophy of law (legal positivism) and to the particular conception of the *rôle* of the judge (absolute divorcement between Law and Society) inherent in it.

The antonym to the Spender-Fitzmaurice majority formulation in *South West Africa. Second Phase* in 1966 is best supplied, and most strikingly, in the Dissenting Opinion of the then U.S. judge on the Court, Philip Jessup.[9] This may seem a little surprising in the context of the U.S. State Department's later-to-be-made, strong criticisms of the International Court's rulings on *Nicaragua*, in its various phases, in the period 1984–1986; but it is not all surprising in the context of the mid-1960s when Jessup was filing his rightly celebrated Dissenting Opinion to the Court majority judgment. For it was the U.S. Law Schools, above all, that were then the intellectual leaders in the battle against Legal Positivism and the so-called "black-letter" tradition of law. A central thrust of the U.S. Law Schools' teachings was the call for a more Realist jurisprudence, which would, on a properly empirical basis, identify the competing social interests involved in any problem-situation before the courts, and try to achieve an acceptable balance in community terms, between those interests, for purposes of final decision-making. Among the American Legal Realist-inspired scientific studies were those emphasising the indeterminacy of the judicial process and the limits to legal logic as a practical guide to the analysis of past Court *jurisprudence* and to explaining just how decisions were arrived at in the particular cases. It was the great Mr. Justice Holmes of the U.S. Supreme Court, after all, who had warned U.S. law professors and legal practitioners of the inarticulate major premises,[10] social and economic in nature, and far more controlling in any case than traditional legal logic, that, in Holmes' own view, effectively determined the Court decision in any case. An equally persuasive U.S. scholar-judge, Mr. Justice Cardozo, had, very early, explored the nature of the judicial process and tried to identify the opportunities, therein, for the creative, inductive judicial leap beyond any unimaginatively mechanical restatement of the old law and into the making of new law. The U.S.-influenced Australian jurist, Julius Stone, would later, in masterly scientific-legal *exposé*, demonstrate the fallacies of the logical form inherent in traditional legal reasoning,[11] and the consequent indeterminacy and unpredictability of the judicial process when its analysis was artificially divorced from the complex of social and economic interests to which all positive law decisions must inevitably respond.

Judge Jessup, in his Dissent in *South West Africa. Second Phase*, rejected the notion that words are timeless absolutes that have a constant legal meaning that survives even radical changes in the background societal conditions against which they first emerged. Judge Jessup is reaching out here – though he does not expressly acknowledge it – to the doctrine of Intertemporal Law:[12] that legal concepts are formed in their own special space-time contexts, in response to particular interests pressed in particular societies at particular times. But Judge Jessup would then reject the essentially static, conservative approach to International Law that some of its main academic-scientific proponents had advanced when they sought to limit the task of legal interpretation to finding an original meaning and then applying it mechanically today. Instead, Jessup applied a dynamic, evolutionary approach to past *jurisprudence*. He took judicial notice of the passage of time since the international legal category of the old League of Nations Mandate was first conceived and, in consequence, was able to take notice, over that time period, of the "accumulation of expressions of condemnation of *Apartheid*" as "proof of the pertinent contemporary international standard."[13] Applying this consciously developmental approach to legal interpretation, Judge Jessup broke sharply with the Court majority in its refusal to exercise jurisdiction to rule on the substantive legal issues involved in *South West Africa. Second Phase*.

The inspired judicial Dissenting Opinion of today that seeks to develop the positive law dialectically in accord with changing history is so often the judicial orthodoxy of tomorrow or the day after tomorrow. Within five years of the *South West Africa. Second Phase*, single-vote-majority ruling, the International Court was given a second chance on the same issue. By lop-sided, 13-to-2 and 11-to-4 votes on the substantive legal issues, the Court proceeded essentially to reverse the 1966 ruling, in the 1971 Advisory Opinion in *Namibia*.[14] The opening of the new Court majority in *Namibia* to the notion of International Law in its modern, progressive or generic interpretation conception, is clear:

"... The Court is bound to take into account the fact that the concepts embodied in Article 22 of the [League of Nations] Covenant ... were not static, but were by definition evolutionary, as also, therefore, was the concept of the 'sacred trust'. The parties to the Covenant must consequently be deemed to have accepted them as such. That is why, viewing the institutions of 1919, the Court must take into consideration the changes which have occurred in the supervening half-century, and its interpretation cannot remain unaffected by the subsequent development of law, through the Charter of the United Nations and by way of customary law. Moreover, an international instrument has to be interpreted and applied within the framework of the entire legal system prevailing at the time of interpretation. In the domain to which the present proceedings relate, the last fifty years, as indicated above, have brought important developments. These developments leave little doubt that the ultimate objective of the sacred trust was the self-determination and independence of the peoples concerned. In this domain, as elsewhere, the *corpus iuris gentium* has been considerably enriched, and this the Court, if it is faithfully to discharge its functions, may not ignore."[15]

It was left to Judge Fitzmaurice, the principal intellectual architect of the *South West Africa. Second Phase* single-vote-majority decision of 1966, and now reduced to the condition of lonely judicial survivor in *Namibia*, 1971, to sound a lament for the purely "logical", strict-and-literal approach to the judicial process now, seemingly, lost on the Court.[16] Judge Fitzmaurice recurred for purposes of his Dissent to the strictures of the one-time U.S. judge on the old Permanent Court of International Justice, Manley Hudson, on the necessity for the Court to keep – "within the limits which characterise judicial action"; to act – "not as an 'academy of jurists' but as a responsible 'magistrature'".[17]

## 2. COMPETING THEORIES OF JUDICIAL INTERPRETATION.
THE JUDICIAL ACTIVISM/JUDICIAL SELF-RESTRAINT CONTINUUM[18]:
*Nuclear Tests* (1973, 1974)

The conflict, within the International Court, over theories of interpretation and the conception of the judicial function and the proper approach to jurisdiction, is sometimes rendered, – inaccurately, it may be suggested – in terms of the classical, Positivism/Natural Law antinomy. The commitment of classically-trained jurists like Sir Gerald Fitzmaurice, and the great judges of the old Permanent Court, to the Positivist credo is clear enough, with their insistence on a divorcement, for purposes of decision-making, of Law from Society, and on the application of a purportedly value-neutral, "logical" approach to cases coming before them. In his typology of legal systems, Max Weber located what he identified as the logico-formal-rational approach to Law and legal reasoning, in Western, liberal-democratic, society, founded as that society was on the rise of commerce and emphasising, at the *apogée* of its *laissez-faire*, non-interventionist period, business efficacy and the pursuit of clarity, certainty, and consistency in legal rules and legal processes, to the exclusion of other values. The professional-legal skill groups making up the legal *élites* in those Western systems at the close of the 19th and beginning of the 20th centuries, had rationalised and streamlined the constitutional law-making processes within their own states, so that changes in the positive law felt to be necessary in realisation of the business efficacy, legal certainty imperatives could always be effected through executive-legislative power, without any need for recourse to judicial power or concepts of Court-based social engineering. It is in this societal context that the concept of judicial neutrality in relation to the great social and economic issues of the day is rendered into a canon of judicial behaviour, if not indeed raised to the level of constitutional dogma.[19] Since the World Community of the same time-era is that numerically restricted, Western or Western European "family compact" group of states that remained dominant in international relations until World War II, it is not surprising that ultra-positivist legal theories perfected in Western and Western European internal, Municipal law, should be carried over, without too many second thoughts, into international legal theory. The inherently "Eurocentrist" quality of legal positivism and of the limited, "logical" conception of the judicial process and the judicial function, when carried over or "received" into International Law, stands out in historical terms.

The intellectual reaction to legal positivism within the International Court, from the mid-1960s onwards, manifest in the minority judicial positions in *South West Africa. Second Phase* in 1966 and in the new majority judicial positions proclaimed in *Namibia* in 1971, flows not so much from Natural Law or from postulated *a priori* absolute values supposed to be inherent in Law itself, as from considerations of historical relativism and the conception of law and legal rules as needing to be continuingly developed and up-dated and changed as international society itself evolves. That is certainly the thrust of Judge Jessup's brilliant Dissenting Opinion in *South West Africa. Second Phase*, and of the Opinion of Court in *Namibia*, 1971. The notion of International Law and International Society existing in symbiotic relationship with each other owes a great deal to the earlier Continental European, and later North American, social utilitarian, sociological schools of law which had, equally, in their purposefully functional or instrumental emphasis, strong elements of neo-Hegelian, historically determinist thinking. The ultra-positivist approach, for most practical purposes, disappeared from the International Court with Judge Fitzmaurice's strongly-worded farewell Dissent in *Namibia*, 1971. The subsequent intellectual differences among the judges, in terms of basic theories of legal interpretation and the approach to the judicial process generally, seem increasingly to go to questions of degree and of timing of judicial interventionism in particular problem-situations, and of the availability of alternative, non-judicial, (legislative/executive) controls, and of the complementarity or congruence of judicial action with these. We enter, then, into the highly pragmatic, functionally-oriented considerations weighing upon ultimate decision-making and its course that we observe in Comparative Law, represented in a number of major Municipal, national systems of jurisprudence, in the judicial activism/judicial self-restraint continuum.

Concrete applications, in the immediate aftermath of the *Namibia*, 1971, ruling, of the new Court majority pragmatic consensus on the nature and limits of the international judicial process, sometimes involve highly controversial decisions that can hardly be explained or rationalised by reference to an overly simplistic, classical Positivism/Natural Law dichotomy. In the first flush of the remarkable Court *volte face* of 1971, from the earlier, 1966, neo-positivist holding in *South West Africa. Second Phase*, the French *Nuclear Tests* litigation[20] might have seemed tailor-made for some high-level judicial interventionism and the enunciation of "new", Imperative Principles of International Law flowing from the preceding decade and more of highly successful and highly publicised international law-making through both the legislative (U.N. General Assembly Resolutions) and the executive (Treaties, Multilateral Conventions) routes. The Antarctic Treaty of 1959 effectively de-nuclearising that ecologically especially fragile region; the Moscow Partial Test Ban Treaty interdicting most categories of nuclear test explosions; the Moon Treaty of 1967 extending the Antarctic Treaty key principles into Outer Space; the Non-Proliferation Treaty of 1968 and a number of lesser accords,[21] when taken together and in sequence, all pointed to a particular, evolving juridical conscience, manifested in a catalogue of step-by-step positive law enactments. Such new, evolving juridical conscience would involve not merely the banning of nuclear weapon testing and perhaps nuclear weapons themselves, but also accepting that the earth's natural environment constitutes a rapidly diminishing "common heritage of Mankind" that urgently needs protection in World Community terms; and that the concept of "good neighbourliness"[22] urgently requires today some tempering of classical International Law's unbridled concepts of state sovereignty out of deference to other states' desires to live in peace and free from unwanted radioactive fall-out from nuclear test explosions.

The immediate political origins of the *Nuclear Tests* cases seemed promising for just such a venture in judicial policy-making and "new" International Law on the part of the International Court. Newly-elected social-democratic governments in "Western" states located in the South Pacific region were seeking to outlaw high-level nuclear test explosions conducted by another "Western" state, France, in one of France's remaining Colonial remnants in the South Pacific, but with an adequately evidenced and demonstrated fall-out of radio-active materials from those nuclear test explosions being carried through the upper atmosphere to other Southern hemisphere states. There was one immediate and obvious positive law problem: the French Government, politically committed as it was to establishment of President de Gaulle's independent nuclear *force de frappe*, had never signed or adhered to the Moscow Partial Test Ban Treaty of 1963. But that should not be an insuperable substantive law barrier, granted the near universality of national adherences to the Moscow Treaty and also the new disposition, evidenced within the Court in *North Sea Continental Shelf* in 1969,[23] to hold that the provisions of multilateral conventions that are generally adhered to and ratified, may become legally binding and normative even in relation to non-signatories, through their entry into the corpus of general, customary International Law. An additional legal complication to the *Nuclear Tests* cases before the Court was that the French Government denied the Court's jurisdiction in the first place, on the legal argument that the latest French acceptance of the Compulsory Jurisdiction of the Court under Article 36(2) of the Court Statute, made in 1966, expressly excluded from the French acceptance of jurisdiction – "disputes concerning activities connected with national defence". On this legal basis, the South Pacific nuclear tests being ultimately directed towards French national defence, the French Government contended that they were *ipso facto* excluded from the International Court's jurisdiction, with the consequence that the Court would have no legal competence to proceed with the Australian and New Zealand Governments' complaints. In essence, on the French view, there was no valid legal dispute of which the International Court could take cognisance. The French Government refused to enter a formal appearance before the Court, confining its response to the Australian/New Zealand legal complaints to a letter to the Court formally invoking the "national defence" reservation to jurisdiction and submitting that the complaints against it should be removed from the Court's list. Thereafter, the French Government, in denying Court jurisdiction, took no further part in the Court proceedings; though the French Government did, contemporaneously with the Court hearings, publish a White Paper[24] setting out the French position on the facts and the law of the then pending Court proceedings, the White Paper in very many respects approaching the character of the *factum* or extended written brief normally presented by parties to a case before the International Court. The then French member of the International Court, Judge Gros, as a regularly elected judge of the Court, sat on the case and participated fully in the Court's interim and final judgments, thereby allowing the two complainant states (who were un-represented on the regular bench of the Court) to name their own *ad hoc* judge to balance the French judge's presence.

## 3. PRELIMINARY AND MERITS JURISDICTION:
### *Nuclear Tests* (1973, 1974)

If there were no Court jurisdiction in the first place, there should, presumably, be no Court jurisdiction to issue Interim Measures pending final determination of the case. Otherwise, the Court would be, as it was said, "hoisting itself by its own bootstraps" into jurisdiction. On the other hand, to allow a mere denial of jurisdiction by any one party to end the matter, then and there, would surely create a legally intolerable situation. The simplest and most direct solution for the Court would be to rule on the jurisdictional issue forthwith, and then, if the Court's finding were indeed that jurisdiction existed, to proceed to at least preliminary examination of the substantive-legal issues, with the right to grant Interim relief measures at any time.

This part of the Court's Interim Order of 1973[25] and of the supporting judicial opinions, in *Nuclear Tests*, is not completely satisfying. For, on its face, the jurisdictional issue didn't seem particularly complex or to require unusual time for decision. It may be suggested that it called either for a strict application of the Court Statute, with its stress on the consensual aspect of adherence by states to the Compulsory Jurisdiction, and a conclusion then, presumably, on the facts of the instant case, against jurisdiction; or else a clear policy decision by the Court and accompanying Court explanation of why it was deemed desirable to adopt a flexible, inclusive approach to jurisdiction and to extending the Court's competence – *ut res magis valeat quam pereat*.

None of the majority judicial opinions filed in support of the Court's 1973 Interim Order treat directly of this point. Instead, those majority opinions proceed directly to the issue of the need to grant Interim Measures, without canvassing in depth the preliminary, procedural, adjectival law issue of whether jurisdiction exists in the first place – the necessary condition precedent to any ruling on the substantive-legal issues. The analysis of the *rationale* of the Court's holding on the 1973 Interim Order is, however, complicated by the fact that it is a close, 8-to-6 decision, with two of the Court's regular bench, President Lachs and Judge Dillard, not participating because of illness, and the identities of three of the majority judges and two of the minority judges remaining unknown; though no less than nine opinions were written and filed in the case (the Opinion of Court signed by Vice-President Ammoun, three Concurring Opinions by majority judges, one Concurring Opinion by the *ad hoc* (Australian) judge, and four Dissenting Opinions). The obvious conclusion from all this must be that the internal differences on the Court, among the individual judges, were marked and deeply-felt; and this, together with the unfortunate absence through illness of President Lachs, explains the fact that five of the judges failed to indicate just how they had voted, and also that the Opinion of Court fails to offer explicit reasons in support of the Interim Order ruling. Whatever ruling the Court may choose to make – strict-and-literal interpretation and consequent self-denying ordinance as to any, even preliminary, substantive-law rulings, or a more pragmatic, permissive approach pending final determination of the jurisdictional issues – legal and policy dilemmas will remain. Not surprisingly, the Court has continued with the "bootstrap" approach to preliminary jurisdiction, and its ability to decree Interim Measures and to make whatever findings on the substantive issues involved it chooses to deem necessary to that.

To return, however, for the moment, to *Nuclear Tests*, the final Judgment of the Court, in 1974,[26] is also addressed to questions, essentially, of procedural, adjectival law. It is a decision against the exercise of jurisdiction to rule on the substantive International Law questions – the "new" International Law possibilities thrown up by the case and by the *factum* filed in support of the legal complaints against France's nuclear tests in the South Pacific. Once again, as with the Interim Order, the Court is closely divided. With President Lachs and Judge Dillard now returned to the bench, and Vice-President Ammoun this time being absent, the Court, with the *ad hoc* Australian judge, now counted fifteen judges; and it was a 9-to-6 majority, again in a multiple-opinion decision (the Opinion of Court signed by President Lachs, and four other, Concurring Opinions; plus one four-judge, joint Dissenting Opinion and two other individual Dissents). But the nub of the majority position is clear: the original dispute between the two complainant states, Australia and New Zealand on the one hand, and France, had become moot because of supervening facts affecting France's legal position. There was, in consequence, no basis for the Court's purporting to exercise jurisdiction further in the matter. On the basis of statements and declarations, made at the highest level of political authority in France – by President Giscard d'Estaing himself, and by the French Foreign Minister and the French Minister of Defence[27]–and made in systematic and sustained and repeated fashion from June, 1974, onwards, indicating the termination of any further, above-the-ground nuclear tests on the part of France in the South Pacific, the Court majority concluded that the original dispute no longer existed. As noted in the official Opinion of Court signed by President Lachs:

"The Court has in the past indicated considerations which would lead it to decline to give judgment. The present case is one in which 'circumstances that have arisen render any adjudication devoid of purpose'.[28] The Court therefore sees no reason to allow the continuance of proceedings which it knows are bound to be fruitless. While judicial settlement may provide a path to international harmony in circumstances of conflict, it is none the less true that the needless continuance of litigation is an obstacle to such harmony.

"Thus the Court finds that no further pronouncement is required in the present case. It does not enter into the adjudicatory functions of the Court to deal with issues *in abstracto*, once it has reached the conclusion that the merits of the case no longer fall to be determined. The object of the claim having clearly disappeared, there is nothing on which to give judgment".[29]

The reasoning and internal logic of the Opinion of Court are impeccable, and are in accord with what we may also call an "American" approach to constitutional jurisdiction, according with the celebrated maxims in this regard laid down by Justice Brandeis of the U.S. Supreme Court – no legal positivist, but a jurist who, nevertheless, was fully conscious of the Court's obligations of self-restraint in the exercise of any policy-making *rôle*.[30]

The imaginativeness and flexibility with which the Court majority used, and extended, the concept of unilateral state acts – here Unilateral Declarations of Intention[31] – and the ability of those unilateral state acts to create binding legal obligations, without any necessary degree of formality in those state acts in order to confer juridical force upon them,[32] accompanies the judicial self-restraint expressed in the Court's final decision not to enter upon the substantive-legal questions involved in the case.

## 4. ADVISORY OPINION JURISDICTION:
### *Western Sahara (1975)*

The Advisory Opinion jurisdiction of the International Court has its constitutional base in Article 96(1) of the United Nations Charter, which authorises the Court to render an advisory opinion "on any legal question" at the "request" of the General Assembly or the Security Council. The Court Statute re-affirms that jurisdiction in its own Articles 65 and 66.

Comparative Municipal, national law experience is somewhat ambiguous as to the merits of an Advisory Opinion jurisdiction. It is well known that the United States Supreme Court, in its very earliest days, refused to give an advisory opinion at the request of President Washington, and this has both guided and controlled U.S. judicial practice since that time and also heavily influenced other countries that have looked to U.S. Constitutional Law for guidance and to the U.S. Supreme Court as *rôle* model. The contemporary U.S. policy argument – elevated almost into a legal "act of faith", – against any such Advisory Opinion jurisdiction is that it conduces to purely abstract rulings remote from the concrete, empirically-based fact-record that is a necessary part of the case/controversy jurisdiction.[33] On the other hand, the Supreme Court of Canada, resting as it does on a twin, English Common Law and French Civil Law, legal base, has, from the beginning possessed, and also actively exercised, an Advisory Opinion jurisdiction. The West German Special Constitutional Court (*Bundesverfassungsgericht*), which has become the prime model for the post-World War II constitutional tribunal now widely adopted in a number of politically and legally diverse countries, had, under the Court Statute as originally enacted in 1951, the power to give an Advisory Opinion "on a determinate constitutional question" on either the common motion of the two Houses of the federal legislature and the federal Cabinet or else the motion of the federal President alone.[34] After the unhappy experience of the recourse to this Advisory Opinion jurisdiction by the federal President, – in the West German political controversy of 1952-4 over the issue of West German adherence to the then proposed European Defence Community, – at the same time as two other, separate, constitutional processes on the same issue were launched before the Court by the rival political parties in the federal legislature, the Advisory Opinion jurisdiction was abolished in 1956.[35]

In the Advisory Opinion on *Western Sahara*, in 1975,[36] the Court had, first of all, to resolve the preliminary, procedural question of whether to render an Advisory Opinion at all. This question broke down into two separate points: *first*, the nature of the Court's Advisory Opinion jurisdiction, and the argued importance of not confusing Advisory Opinion jurisdiction with jurisdiction as to contentious proceedings or allowing it to be used as a cover for the same; and, *second*, the nature of a "legal question" and the argued importance of not allowing the Court to be drawn into discussion of abstract, philosophical issues, or else to venture upon high political issues where the Court's intervention, again according to the argument, might impede or delay eventual political or political-legal solutions. The Court decided these two preliminary, jurisdictional questions by lop-sided judicial majorities of 13-to-3 and 14-to-2 respectively, but once again, in a bench of sixteen judges (including an *ad hoc* judge) in a multiple-opinion ruling (the Opinion of Court signed by President Lachs, plus three separate Declarations by majority judges, six separate Concurring Opinions, and one Dissenting Opinion). The *first* preliminary point, going to the Court's exercise of jurisdiction, involved re-examination of the old Permanent Court's ruling in *Status of Eastern Carelia*, in 1923,[37] when the Court had there declined to exercise Advisory Opinion jurisdiction on the apparent principle that a state – in that instance, the Soviet Union – couldn't be compelled, without its consent, to submit its disputes with other states – in that instance, Finland – to the Court's jurisdiction. In essence, in *Western Sahara*, Spain had claimed that the moving parties, Morocco and Mauritania, were attempting to achieve indirectly, through the Advisory Opinion route, what they could not achieve directly through Contentious proceedings because of Spain's lack of consent to such Contentious jurisdiction of the Court. The Court, in *Western Sahara*, however, distinguished and limited the old Permanent Court's declining of Advisory Opinion jurisdiction in *Eastern Carelia* in 1923, on the basis that in that earlier matter one of the states concerned, the Soviet Union, was neither a party to the Court Statute nor, at the time, even a Member of the League of Nations:

"... Lack of competence of the League [of Nations] to deal with a dispute involving non-member States which refused its intervention was a decisive reason for the Court's declining to give an answer. In the present case, Spain is a Member of the United Nations and has accepted the provisions of the Charter and [Court] Statute; it has thereby in general given its consent to the exercise by the Court of its advisory jurisdiction."[38]

The Opinion of the Court in *Western Sahara* went beyond this distinguishing of the old Permanent Court's restrictive approach to Advisory Opinion jurisdiction. The Court cited, with approval, its own earlier ruling in *Interpretation of Peace Treaties with Bulgaria, Hungary and Romania, First Phase* in 1950,[39] in which it had also had to consider the continued relevance, today, of the old Permanent Court's 1923 *Eastern Carelia* holding. As the Court had said in *Peace Treaties*, in 1950, there was a –

"confusion between the principles governing contentious proceedings and those which are applicable to Advisory Opinions.

"The consent of States, parties to a dispute, is the basis of the Court's jurisdiction in contentious cases. The situation is different in regard to advisory proceedings even where the Request for an Opinion relates to a legal question actually pending between States. The Court's reply is only of an advisory character; as such, it has no binding force. It follows that no State, whether a Member of the United Nations or not, can prevent the giving of an Advisory Opinion which the United Nations considers to be desirable in order to obtain enlightenment as to the course of action it should take. The Court's opinion is not given to the States, but to the organ which is entitled to request it; the reply of the Court, itself an 'organ of the United Nations', represents its participation in the activities of the organisation, and, in principle, should not be refused."[40]

The *second* preliminary point, going to the Court's exercise of jurisdiction in *Western Sahara*, related to the interpretation of the actual definition of the Court's Advisory Opinion jurisdiction, in the United Nations Charter itself as well as in the Court Statute. Article 96 of the U.N. Charter authorises the giving of an Advisory Opinion – "on any legal question", as does Article 65 (1) of the Court Statute.

The Spanish Government's contention, in *Western Sahara*, was that the two substantive-legal questions now referred by the U.N. General Assembly to the Court – whether the Western Sahara territory was *terra nullius* at the time of the purported acquisition of legal title to it by Spain, and also the nature of the legal ties existing between Western Sahara and the Kingdom of Morocco and the Mauritanian entity – were "not legal, but are either factual or are questions of a purely historical or academic character".[41]

The Opinion of Court in *Western Sahara* had, however, little difficulty in rejecting this argument. Citing its *Namibia*, 1971,[42] holding, the Court affirmed that – "a mixed question of law and fact is none the less a legal question"[43] within the meaning of Article 96 of the U.N. Charter and Article 65 (1) of the Court Statute. The Court also, on the basis of its 1948 ruling in *Conditions of Admission of a State to Membership in the United Nations (Article 4 of the Charter)*,[44] rejected the further Spanish Government contention that it should not deal with a – "question couched in abstract terms". The Court pointed to its dictum, in that 1948 ruling, that the Court – "may give an advisory opinion on any legal question, abstract or otherwise".[45] In rejecting, in this way, the restrictive view that had been contended for, as to the scope of its Advisory Opinion jurisdiction,[46] the Court recorded its conclusion, on the facts of *Western Sahara*, that the matters on which the U.N. General Assembly now sought its opinion were – "for a practical and contemporary purpose".[47]

The Court went on to reject, *seriatim*, several further objections advanced to its exercising the Advisory Opinion jurisdiction.

One such further objection was that the proceedings were "devoid of purpose" since the United Nations had already affirmed the nature of the Decolonisation process applicable to Western Sahara, according to the U.N. General Assembly's famous Resolution 1514 (XV) of 1960, establishing the master International Law legal norms on Decolonisation. The International Court's response, here, was that the principles and techniques to be followed to achieve Decolonisation had not been finally settled among the wide range of alternative legal solutions open compatibly with self-determination and national unity and territorial integrity.[48]

A further objection was that the actual questions posed by the U.N. General Assembly in the request to the Court for Advisory Opinion were – "academic and legally irrelevant".[49] The Court's express counter to this objection was that, while U.N. General Assembly Resolution 1514 (XV) of 1960 provided the basis for the process of Decolonisation since 1960, it was complemented by General Assembly Resolution 1541 (XVI) of 1961 which opened up a choice of options, for the future, for erstwhile non-self-governing territories: emergence as a sovereign independent State; free association with an independent State; or integration with an independent State.[50] In the Court's Opinion, the Advisory Opinion to be rendered in the present proceedings would – "furnish the General Assembly with elements of a legal character" relevant to its further treatment of these alternative possibilities.[51]

## 5. PRELIMINARY AND MERITS JURISDICTION RE-VISITED:
### Aegean Sea Continental Shelf (1976, 1978)

After this clear, categorical affirmation of a plenary, unqualified Advisory Opinion jurisdiction, untrammelled by any attempt to read it down by, in effect, assimilating it to ordinary case/controversy restrictive criteria, the Court had occasion, once more, in Aegean Sea Continental Shelf, Interim Protection, in 1976,[52] to return to the issues of Preliminary and Merits jurisdiction that had so troubled it in Nuclear Tests in 1973 and 1974. Although the Court, in refusing to grant a Greek Government request for the indication of Interim Measures of protection in its continuing dispute with Turkey over ownership and exploitation of the Aegean Sea's Continental Shelf, did so by a 12-to-1 vote, with only the Greek ad hoc judge dissenting, there were no less than ten judicial opinions filed in that case (the Opinion of Court signed by President Jiménez de Aréchaga, eight separate Concurring Opinions, and the single Dissenting Opinion filed by the Greek ad hoc judge). The Turkish Government's reply to the Greek

Government's application to the Court and request for Interim Measures had been, (echoing arguments advanced by the French Government in its White Paper published in connection with the *Nuclear Tests* litigation), to deny Court jurisdiction under the General Act for the Pacific Settlement of International Disputes of 1928 that had been particularly relied upon by Greece, by denying its continued applicability as treaty in force between Greece and Turkey; and also to contend that, even if the General Act of 1928 were still in force and applicable, the matters now submitted by Greece fell within the terms of reservation and exception to Court jurisdiction set out in Greece's 1931 instrument of accession to the Act.[53]

The official Opinion of Court in *Aegean Sea Continental Shelf, Interim Protection* dealt with the Greek arguments on Court jurisdiction, and the Turkish reply thereto, elliptically and almost by indirection:

"... It is not necessary for the Court to reach a final conclusion at this stage of the proceedings on the questions thus raised concerning the application of the 1928 Act as between Greece and Turkey, and it will therefore examine the request for the indication of interim measures only in the context of Article 41 of the Statute."[54]

Does the Court power to grant Interim Measures in any case presuppose that the Court will have jurisdiction, anyway, upon the Merits of the case? Should the exercise of any power to grant Interim measures be predicated upon a prior Court finding of jurisdiction on the Merits? Three of the judges making up the Court majority in *Aegean Sea Continental Shelf, Interim Protection* thought so (Judges Morozov, Mosler, and Tarazi), and each denied categorically, in separate Concurring Opinions, that Article 41 of the Court Statute (the Court power to indicate Provisional Measures) could constitute in itself an independent source of jurisdiction separate and distinct from the Court's general jurisdiction as established under Articles 36 and 37 of the Statute. We may add to these three majority judges Judge Ruda who, in his own Concurring Opinion, denied any power in the Court to consider Interim measures without its first deciding its own basic competence on the Merits, at least *prima facie*; and Judge Lachs who stressed, in his own Separate Opinion, the obligation of the Court to consider the general jurisdictional issue and to make clear its own provisional views; plus, finally, two judges among the majority who did not file Separate Opinions in *Aegean Sea, Interim Protection* to this effect, but who did take a similar position, clearly and unequivocally, in *Nuclear Tests* (Judges Forster and Gros). We are thus left with a majority of seven judges out of the twelve adhering to the official Opinion of Court in *Aegean Sea, Interim Protection* who must be in disagreement with the Opinion of Court's basic approach of escalating to jurisdiction to grant Interim measures without any prior finding, at least *prima facie*, of jurisdiction on the Merits. The mystery of the *ratio decidendi* of *Aegean Sea, Interim Protection* is deepened if we consider that two more among the majority judges filing individual Separate Opinions also appear to have rallied to the need for demonstration of at least *prima facie* jurisdiction on the Merits before any Court exercise or grant of Interim Measures (President Jiménez de Aréchaga who regarded it as "devoid of sense" to act otherwise,[55] even though believing Article 41 of the Court Statute to constitute an autonomous grant of jurisdiction; and Judge Nagendra Singh who insisted on a higher degree of satisfaction than the positive but cursory test of *prima facie* jurisdiction and who saw, as the acid test, that judgment should be within clear prospect. Even Judge Elias who, alone among the eight majority judges filing Separate Opinions, seemed not to be troubled by any necessity to decide the question of jurisdiction on the Merits before going on to rule under Article 41, nevertheless declared that the preliminary jurisdictional issue required urgent and serious re-thinking.

The power of the Court to address its own jurisdiction at a Preliminary stage – the *compétence de la compétence* – is normally related to Article 36(6) and also Article 53 of the Court Statute. Article 36(6) says only that –

"In the event of a dispute as to whether the Court has jurisdiction, the matter shall be settled by the decision of the Court."

Article 53 is confined to the special situation –

"whenever one of the parties does not appear before the Court, or fails to defend its case",

– where the Court, before acting upon a request from the other party to decide in its favour, must –

"satisfy itself, not only that it has jurisdiction ... but also that the claim is well founded in fact and law."

It is elementary that the Rules of Court cannot override or contradict the Court Statute; or, *a fortiori*, override Chapter XIV (Articles 92-96) of the United Nations Charter constituting the Court. The Court Statute itself specifies, in its Article 30, that –

"the Court shall frame rules for carrying out its functions. In particular, it shall lay down rules of procedure".

At issue in the present case is the meaning of the provisions, in the Rules of Court, as to "Preliminary Objections", and specifically Article 79 of the 1978 Revised Rules of Court, itself a replacement of Article 67 of the 1972 Revised Rules, which had amended the earlier dispositions as to "Preliminary Objections" contained in Article 62 of the 1946 Rules. Article 62(5) of the original, 1946 Rules, had specified:

"After hearing the parties the Court shall give its decision on the objection or shall join the objection to the merits. If the Court overrules the objection or joins it to the merits, it shall once more fix time-limits for the further proceedings."

The amendment in the 1972 Revised Rules, re-numbered as Article 67(7), and later reproduced as Article 79(7) of the current, 1978 Revised Rules, runs:

"After hearing the parties, the Court shall give its decision in the form of a judgment, by which it shall either uphold the objection, reject it, or declare that the objection does not possess, in the circumstances of the case, an exclusively preliminary character. If the Court rejects the objection or declares that it does not possess an exclusively preliminary character, it shall fix time-limits for the further proceedings."

As a matter of the ordinary rules of interpretation, it would appear clear that the deletion, as between the 1946 Rules and the 1972/1978 Revised Rules, of an earlier explicit mandate to join Preliminary objections to the Merits, could not deprive the International Court of its inherent power to do just that. It is submitted that the Court's *jurisprudence*, since the 1972 Revisions, vindicates the Court's pragmatic disposition, in fulfillment of its general problem-solving function, to avoid any attempt at overly abstract or precious separation, in successive or staged proceedings, of preliminary, jurisdictional issues from the substantive issues in the cases coming before the Court.

In *Nuclear Tests*, as noted, the Court majority's broadly facultative approach to its own jurisdiction and its disinclination, in spite of the then recently adopted, 1972 amendments to the 1946 Rules of Court, to bifurcate its decision-making temporally, into successive, Preliminary/Merits phases, is emphasised by the various anguished individual judicial Opinions, whether Separate Opinions or Dissenting Opinions, addressed to the point in the Court's *Judgment* of 20 December 1974. As the Opinion of Court noted:

"the Court possesses an inherent jurisdiction enabling it to take such action as may be required, on the one hand to ensure that the exercise of its jurisdiction over the merits, if and when established, shall not be frustrated, and on the other, to provide for the orderly settlement of all matters in dispute, to ensure the observance of the 'inherent limitations on the exercise of the judicial function' of the Court and to 'maintain its judicial character.'"[56]

As the Court's judgment went on. –

"Such inherent jurisdiction, on the basis of which the Court is fully empowered to make whatever findings may be necessary for the purposes just indicated, derives from the mere existence of the Court as a judicial organ established by the consent of States, and is conferred upon it in order that its basic judicial functions may be safeguarded."[57]

There is, further, no warrant, in the language of the 1972 Revised Rules of Court (now the 1978 Revised Rules), or in the *jurisprudence constante*, for seeking to limit this broadly facultative Court approach to issues of jurisdiction and admissibility and to using the Court's inherent power to join Preliminary (jurisdictional and admissibility) issues to the Merits and to carry them over for decision at the subsequent Merits stage, to proceedings relating to requests for Interim Measures. The last word in the particular matter might well be left to Judge Lachs, in his Declaration annexed to the Court's ruling in *Border and Transborder Armed Actions (Nicaragua v. Honduras), Jurisdiction and Admissibility, Judgment,* in 1988, where the Full Court ruled unanimously in favour of jurisdiction and admissibility:

"… This Court has to exercise the utmost care to discourage attempts to resort to it in any case lacking a proper jurisdictional foundation, but at the same time not to deny States their right to benefit from its decisions where such a foundation does exist."[58]

The resolution of that antinomy, in line with the discernible historical development in the Court's *jurisprudence* in its modern, post-*South West Africa. Second Phase* era, favouring a facultative approach to Court exercise of jurisdiction where the matter is put in contest is provided by Judge Lachs' policy *dictum* in the same case:

"Sometimes the mere opening of the door may bring about a solution to a dispute".[59]

## 6. THE LAW/POLITICS DICHOTOMY, AND THE "POLITICAL QUESTIONS" EXCEPTION TO JURISDICTION: *Nicaragua v. U.S.*, (1984, 1986)

In May, 1984, the International Court granted an Interim Order rejecting the U.S. Government's request for termination of the proceedings before the Court initiated by the Government of Nicaragua's legal complaint against the U.S. and also for removal of that complaint from the list of the Court's cases.[60] At the same time, and pending a final decision in the case, the International Court ordered the U.S. Government to –

"immediately cease and refrain from any action restricting, blocking or endangering access to or from Nicaraguan ports, and, in particular, the laying of mines."

These parts of the Court's Interim Order were rendered by unanimous vote of the judges. An addendum to the Court's Order, however, was adopted by

14-to-1, with the U.S. judge on the Court dissenting. That Addendum read:

"The right to sovereignty and to political independence possessed by the
Republic of Nicaragua, like any other State of the region or of the world,
should be fully respected and should not in any way be jeopardised by
any military and paramilitary activities which are prohibited by the
principles of international law, in particular the principle that States
should refrain in their international relations from the threat or use of
force against the territorial integrity or the political independence of any
State, and the principle concerning the duty not to intervene in matters
within the domestic jurisdiction of a State, principles embodied in the
United Nations Charter and the Charter of the Organisation of American
States."

In November, 1984, the International Court, after finding, by an 11-to-5
vote, that it did indeed have jurisdiction in terms of Article 36 (2) and (5) of
the Court Statute, and also in terms of the U.S.-Nicaragua Treaty of
Friendship, Commerce, and Navigation of 1956, then went on to rule, by a
15-to-1 vote (with the U.S. judge again dissenting) that it had jurisdiction to
go on to the *Merits* stage and so to proceed to the hearing of the substantive
International Law issues involved in the Nicaraguan complaint against the
U.S. The Court, at the same time, directed that its Interim Order of early
1984 and the Provisional Measures indicated in it, should remain in force
pending the final judgment on the Merits.[61]

It was at this stage that the U.S. Government announced, in January,
1985, that the U.S. would not participate any further in the case, and that it
would reconsider the U.S. acceptance of the Compulsory Jurisdiction of the
Court.[62] In a rapidly developing sequence of events, the Court went on, in
April, 1985, to hear the Nicaraguan arguments on the *Merits*, without the
U.S.; and then, on 7 October 1985, the U.S. deposited formal notice of the
termination of the U.S. Declaration of 26 August 1946, as modified in
1984, accepting the Compulsory Jurisdiction of the Court under Article 36
(2) of the Court Statute, the termination to take effect after the expiration of
six months.[63] In June, 1986, the Court announced its judgment on the
*Merits*, in which, by a 12-to-3 vote on the main issues, the Court upheld the
substance of the Nicaraguan legal charges against the U.S. government.[64]

The text of the U.S. Government statement accompanying its announcement of January 1985, that the U.S. would not participate in any further
proceedings before the Court on the Nicaraguan complaint, declared that
those proceedings constituted a –

"misuse of the Court for political purposes ... the Court lacks jurisdiction
and competence over such a case. The Court's decision of November 26,
1984, [*Jurisdiction and Admissibility*.] finding that it has jurisdiction, is

contrary to law and fact …

"The conflict in Central America … is not a narrow legal dispute; it is an inherently political problem that is not appropriate for judicial resolution. The conflict will be solved only by political and diplomatic means-not through a judicial tribunal. The International Court of Justice was never intended to resolve issues of collective security and self-defence and is patently unsuited for such a rôle".[65]

In posing a dichotomy, legal dispute/political dispute, with only the first of these, according to the U.S. Government's contention, being proper for judicial settlement, the U.S. Government also charged the International Court with making –

"a marked departure from its past, cautious approach to jurisdictional questions. The Court's decision [of November 26, 1984, on *Jurisdiction and Admissibility*] raises a basic issue of sovereignty. The right of a state to defend itself or to participate in collective self-defence against aggression is an inherent sovereign right that cannot be compromised by an inappropriate proceeding before the World Court … The decision of November 26 represents an over-reaching of the Court's limits, a departure from its tradition of judicial restraint, and a risky venture into treacherous political waters."[66]

This is a theme recurred to by a number of U.S. academic critics of the International Court in the aftermath of the 1984 Preliminary rulings, and the later, 1986 *Merits* judgment, in *Nicaragua* v. *U.S.*, – most eloquently, perhaps, by the distinguished ex-Dean of the Yale Law School and Under Secretary of State in the U.S. State Department under President Lyndon Johnson, Eugene Rostow. In a vigorously assembled and brilliantly argued attack on the International Court, published in the *American Journal of International Law* in January 1987,[67] Rostow replicated the position that a then former U.S. Secretary of State, Dean Acheson, had first advanced, years earlier, in the immediate aftermath of the Cuban Missile crisis of October, 1962.[68] Acheson's argument then, and Rostow's argument now, was that there are political-legal "No-Man's Lands", involving what states (or at least superpowers) may choose to consider as touching their own vital interests, into which the International Court (and also other international institutions) will venture only at their extreme legal, and political, peril. As far as the International Court would be concerned, it amounts to postulating a zone of non-justiciability, that is itself posited upon a "law"/"politics" dichotomy that post-Legal Realist U.S. legal theory, and also the main current of U.S. Municipal, national *jurisprudence* flowing from that, would reject today as quite unfounded when it is formulated, as now, in absolutist, *a priori* legal terms.

There is, to be sure, a category of "political questions" or of issues deemed not to be proper or ripe for Court interventionism, that is amply represented in U.S. constitutional history and also, under various alternative synonyms, in Comparative Constitutional Law in other Municipal, national legal systems.[69] These concepts amount to special constitutional-legal devices for legally immunising Courts against the necessity of making pronouncements, on demand, as to the wisdom or un-wisdom of particular exercises in executive or legislative authority. So far as they continue to be availed of by Courts today, we would describe them, in contemporary terms, as convenient instruments of judicial self-restraint and deference in regard to countervailing executive-legislative power. The exact contours and reach of the doctrine of "political questions" are not clear. There is no generally accepted or intellectually very satisfying abstract, *a priori* definition of "political questions": the legal category, whether *sub nomine* as in U.S. constitutional law, or else under some such rubric as "*Acte de Gouvernement*" in the French Civil Law system, developed historically on a case-by-case basis, with very little serious or sustained attempt at a comprehensive, overarching conceptualisation or synthesis. The practical consequences, however, are clear, since once the Courts should accept its applicability in a particular case, they will not further intervene or carry a problem through to decision.

Surveying the empirical record, in Comparative Constitutional Law, of Court decisions where the "political questions" exception to jurisdiction, or its verbal equivalents, have been successfully invoked, some key judicial policies emerge experientially. The problem-areas concerned have fallen into three main groups: problems going to the *Grundnorm* or ultimate source of legal authority and power in the state or system; intra-governmental, inter-institutional conflicts – what, in German constitutional law terms, is called *Organstreitigkeiten*; and, finally, a particular group of problems going to the legitimacy of political authority (and thus to claims by executive-legislative power for deference and self-restraint on the part of judicial power), and involving the fairness of the electoral and political representation systems as a whole.

The judicial policies invoked by Courts in justification, then, for applying a "political questions" exception to their exercise of jurisdiction have concerned, first of all, the alleged technical difficulty of certain types of subjects, – such as electoral cases[70] – which have been argued as being beyond the special competence of Courts to comprehend or, even if comprehended, to resolve in practical terms. Yet it is precisely in electoral cases that, over a number of different Municipal, national legal systems, this technical objection to justiciability has come to be seen as a false one and easily countered, in any case, by intellectually sophisticated and flexible, and also politically determined, Municipal, national judges. It is precisely in regard to this type of electoral case, which is so important to the fair and proper functioning of the political processes as a whole, that the arguments for judicial interventionism have been seen as far outweighing any incidental embarrassments for the judges. And so the "political questions" exception, in this particular area at least, has largely been discarded today in Comparative legal science.

In the international judicial arena, the technical objection to Court exercise of jurisdiction is sometimes advanced on the argument that the facts in particular problem-situations are too complex and difficult, or too remote from the forum, to be comprehended through the ordinary judicial process. Such an argument was advanced, unsuccessfully, in *Western Sahara* in 1975,[71] where the International Court had little difficulty both in finding a plethora of different factual sources and records available to it and also in concluding that the judges' own specialised professional training and experience, *qua* judges, rendered them the intellectually most competent people to resolve any fact-finding dilemmas. In *Nicaragua* v. *U.S.*, the U.S. Government also raised, unsuccessfully, at the Preliminary stage hearings, the dilemma of judicial fact-finding; but with a problem-situation as public and well-publicised as the U.S. Government's material aid and support to the so-called *Contra* rebels who were operating, from secret bases in other, neighbouring countries against the *de jure* government of Nicaragua, the concept of judicial notice, well known and amply applied in a number of different Municipal, national legal systems, proved more than sufficient to apprise the International Court judges concerning the legally-impugned U.S. Government actions.[72]

A second main judicial policy, basing application of the "political questions" exception to jurisdiction and justiciability in Comparative legal science, has to do with separation-of-powers style considerations going to the respect and deference that Courts are thought to owe to other, coordinate, popularly-elected, executive and legislative institutions of government.[73] Professor (and sometime judge on the International Court) Mosler has reminded us[74] that there is a significant difference, in positive law terms, between the relation of the International Court to the U.N. Security Council and the General Assembly, on the one hand, and the relation of the constitutional judiciary to executive and legislative institutions under the main Municipal, national legal systems. The International Court has its own autonomous constitutional base, in its own Court Statute; and this is of course separate and distinct from the constitutional bases of the Security Council and General Assembly in the United Nations Charter. In contrast, in Municipal, national law, the courts and the other coordinate, executive and legislative institutions of government usually find their legal source of power in the one constitutional instrument or basic law. The contemporary trend with the International Court, in its relations to the other, coordinate international institutions, – the Security Council and General Assembly –, is in any case away from the older, national constitutional law models which used to see a competition or direct conflict of institutional authority, towards a new notion of complementarity and of positive cooperation in common World Community problem-solving.

A third main judicial policy, basing the "political questions" exception to jurisdiction in Comparative legal science, has more obviously subjective, usually highly pragmatic considerations, behind it: namely, that the particular issue involved before the Court may be simply too big in political terms (with incidental public passions running too high), for the judges to be able to handle it without themselves becoming embroiled in partisan political controversy.[75] Once again, the contemporary trends in the main Municipal, national law systems, as reflected in Comparative legal science, are all to cut down and reject any such judicial policy arguments and the "political questions" exception that would derive from them, on the score that, all too often, the particular issue will have become politically inflamed simply because the other, coordinate institutions of government have been unable or unwilling to venture into the fray. *Faute de mieux*, on this very contemporary approach, it is now argued that the judges, as a legally well-trained and detached and privileged legal *élite*, must step in and fill the gap as to community problem-solving created by the flight or deliberate inaction of coordinate executive and legislative power. Otherwise, a constitutionally intolerable, and politically dangerous, vacuum in application of community law-making power to resolve societal problems will result.

The then Professor Mosler, writing in the period between his first service as an *ad hoc* judge of the International Court, in *North Sea Continental Shelf* in 1969, and his subsequent election to a regular term on the Court, expressed the opinion that it was – "impossible to draw a logically satisfactory distinction between legal and political disputes",[76] which, for Court purposes, he viewed as the same as the justiciable/non-justiciable distinction. In this context, he understandably did not view the 1925 Locarno Arbitral and Conciliation Treaties' definition of *legal* disputes as "those in which the parties contest a right", as very helpful.[77] Accepting the principle that not all disputes which could be resolved under international law are necessarily appropriate for judicial settlement, how would one establish what is "non-justiciable" in terms somewhat more objectively meaningful than the purely circular definition that it is what is "not being considered by one party as appropriate for judicial settlement"? Dr. Mosler's answer:

> "it can only be partly defined by objective features: If a party aims at a change of the existing situation rather than at a clarification of the existing law, the judge cannot solve the problem. Today there is no better statement on this point than that made during the era of the League [of Nations], namely, that differences of opinion can be so strong, even in legal disputes, that they cannot be resolved by a simple legal decision."[78]

Much later, after service on and then retirement from the International Court, Mosler concluded that the many attempts, over many years, to establish a generally recognised definition of what is "political", as distinguished from what is "legal", had already been unproductive. In his view, the mere act of "find[ing] a case more or less predominantly political or legal would amount to a political choice".[79]

Deference may usefully be made, here, to early state practice regarding arbitration – a favoured form of Third Party settlement in the period immediately prior to World War I, before judicial settlement had emerged in its own right as an alternative mode of institutionalised Third Party settlement. The treaty arrangements established by states for purposes of international arbitration were dominated, in that time period, by the one clause which, following the pattern of the Franco-British Arbitration Treaty of 1903, would seek to refer to an arbitral tribunal "differences which may arise of a legal nature or relating to the interpretation of Treaties existing between the Contracting Parties", but only on condition that "they do not affect the vital interests, the independence or the honour of the two Contracting States and do not concern the interests of third parties". The interpretation of these particular limitations was left to the unilateral assessment of each party.[80]

An Imperial Russian draft presented to the First Hague Peace Conference of 1899 had proposed an enumerative list of issues which, because of a postulated *absence of vital interests and national honour*, were to be deemed suitable for compulsory arbitration: pecuniary claims for damages resulting from illegal acts or negligence where the principle of indemnity was recognised by both parties; interpretation and application of treaties relating to post and telegraph, railroads, submarines and telegraph cables, collisions on the high seas, international rivers and inter-oceanic canals, literary and artistic property, patents, health, currency, inheritance, exchange of prisoners, reciprocal assistance in the administration of justice, and frontiers.[81] This particular Imperial Russian approach to definition of what was, and what was not, suitable for Third Party settlement by the device of a listing, *in extenso*, of what should *not* be considered as touching vital interests, lapsed through failure to attract any general state support. No other, more precise or certainly more succinct, abstract, *a priori* definition was even ventured upon.

Another early attempt to separate "legal disputes" from "disputes involving conflicts of interests" and to treat the latter category as non-justiciable,[82] is redolent of the particular space-time dimension in which it emerged – Continental Western European legal theory of the mid-1920s. No one would be disposed to deny, today, that all legal disputes involve conflicts of interests. The attempt to supply a more concrete, empirical foundation for the proposed dichotomy by suggesting that disputes involving conflicts of interests are those which concern changes of existing legal situations, – with remission of debts, economic matters like access to commodities, preferential or national treatment, extradition without prior treaty basis, being offered as prime examples,[83] – is not much more satisfactory. The examples given reflect no more than the (transitory) opinions of earlier national legal *élites* as to what touched their own states' vital interests in their own particular time period, which were therefore considered too dangerous to be submitted to Third Party settlement. The general notion, implicit in all this, that it is no business of legal interpretation, as exercised by international tribunals, to change the law in the process of restating it, is no more than a tenet of the legal positivist credo, now in fairly general discard or disregard in the International Court's own jurisprudence since *Namibia*, 1971, and also in contemporary major Municipal, national systems of law.

If it be accepted, then, that there is no objective, *a priori* basis for separating "legal" from "political" disputes, and that "legal" disputes today are, if not also inherently "political" then at least mixed, "political"-and-"legal", then the criteria for separating the justiciable from the non-justiciable, and the exercise of Court jurisdiction from its non-exercise, become essentially pragmatic in character. Such criteria would involve judicial policy conclusions as to whether, and when, and in what degree, judicial interventionism on a particular tension-issue of contemporary international relations will help or hinder actual community problem-solving. The by now highly-developed (from Comparative Constitutional Law, and Municipal, national legal jurisprudence) canons or rules of prudence as to judicial policy-making and its practical possibilities and limits, as demonstrated and applied in the Judicial Self-Restraint/Judicial Activism continuum, seem more reliable guides to Court conduct today than the pursuit of an illusory "law"/"politics" dichotomy. In historical retrospect, *causes célèbres* of yesterday like the old Permanent Court's decision in

*Austro-German Customs Union* in 1931,[84] stand out not so much as examples of the un-wisdom of international judges' venturing upon high political-legal issues; for the problems exist, anyway, and are too dangerous to be left unresolved by relevant community institutions. Rather, such *causes célèbres* may indicate the dangers inherent in abstract, positivistic conceptions of the international judicial process and the approach to legal interpretation of a particular problem that is artificially divorced from its immediate socio-economic context. On this view, the eight-to-seven vote ruling of the old Permanent Court, in the *Austro-German Customs Union* Advisory Opinion in 1931, in its conscious and deliberate eschewing of policy considerations in law,[85] represented quite as much a great "self-inflicted wound" for the old Permanent Court and for International Law in general as that other, single-vote-majority, opinion rendered by the new International Court in *South West Africa. Second Phase* in 1966. In terms of practical consequences and also of the choice of a particular (positivist) approach to decision-making as conducing to them, each of the two decisions was as "political" as the alternative, policy-oriented approaches that they had eschewed would have been. The more consciously policy-oriented approaches espoused by the minority judges in each case could hardly have been as disastrous, in their actual end-results, as the professedly "neutral", abstract-logical decisions actually rendered turned out to be, in each case.

If the line of demarcation between justiciability and non-justiciability is to be determined pragmatically, according to the anticipated degree of success of any judicial ventures in community problem-solving, and the relevance of the judges' own special expertise in comparison to other, coordinate institutions with which the Court may or may not choose to act in concert and cooperation, then it is important to realise that the frontiers of justiciability/non-justiciability may be constantly shifting or changing; and that the Court's special competence and confidence in this domain is continually evolving and improving, experientially. The current U.S. judge on the International Court, Judge Schwebel, cited the Berlin blockade and the Suez Canal crisis of 1956 (among other issues) as examples of "major political issues of the day that have legal components: normally these cases do not come [to] the court."[86] Dr. Mosler also seems to have had reservations concerning justiciability for just such "sensitive political matters" as the status of Berlin and the Suez Canal: "The parties concerned ... will certainly not consider differences of opinion to be justiciable".[87] On the other hand, that prime exponent of the School of Sociological Jurisprudence in International Law, Julius Stone, expressly cited the Soviet-Western disputes over Berlin as perfectly capable of being –

"reduced to a series of legal questions eminently suitable for adjudication
by the International Court .... They would be legal questions beyond
doubt, no different in nature from many questions regularly decided by
the law courts of national societies".[88]

And Oscar Schachter[89], taking issue with the U.S. State Department's Legal
Adviser, Judge Sofaer,[90] in the aftermath of the *Nicaragua* Preliminary
rulings of 1984, noted that President Nixon had once proposed that the
Berlin issues be submitted to the International Court; and that the U.S.
Government had, in the past, sought to have the International Court pass
upon the lawfulness of armed acts in "aerial incidents", by bringing forward
cases against the Soviet Union, Czechoslovakia, and Hungary over the
shooting down of U.S. aircraft.

That was then, and this is now, of course! In the current, post-*Perestroika*
era in East-West relations, it is difficult to see how any of the main state
parties could or would regard its own vital interests as endangered, in any
way, by having the International Court rule on the status of, say, Berlin,
West and East, and its main legal elements. The problem of Berlin, on this
view, would be eminently justiciable today according to contemporary,
essentially pragmatic criteria that look to the ripeness of a particular issue
for judicial determination, and to the potential contribution of judicial
problem-solving in comparison to, or in cooperation with, other modes and
other arenas of international legal policy-making.[91]

## 7. THE RULES OF PROCEDURE, AND THE CREATIVE RôLE
## OF COURT PRACTICE IN THEIR DEVELOPMENT:
### *Aerial Incident of 3 July 1988 (Iran v. U.S.)* (1989)

The continuing intellectual conflict, within the International Court's ranks,
between the old-style, "logical", ultra-positivistic philosophy that reached
its apogée in the single-vote-majority decision in *South West Africa. Second
Phase* in 1966, and the newer, more flexible and pragmatic, policy-oriented
judicial approaches is reflected in the Court's ruling, in December, 1989, on
a highly technical, procedural, adjectival-law point: whether, following
Article 79 of the 1978 Revised Court Rules, a Respondent in a case had the
right to file Preliminary Objections to Jurisdiction and Justiciability even
before the Applicant in the case should have filed its Memorial, with the
further consequence, as it was argued, of automatically bringing about the
suspension of the proceedings on the Merits and preventing the Court from
examining any substantive issues. The matter had arisen in connection with
the Application filed by the Iranian Government with the Court in May,

1989, formally initiating proceedings against the United States in connection with the shooting down by a U.S. Navy warship, in July, 1988, of an Iranian civil passenger aircraft on a regularly-scheduled, internationally-registered flight, while in Iranian national airspace over Iranian national territorial waters, with the loss of 290 civil passengers and the air crew. In a Press conference on 14 August 1989, the Bush Administration had indicated that the U.S. had agreed to take part in the International Court case thus initiated by Iran, apparently in part because of a –

"recognition that Washington could not easily refuse to take part when it is working with the Soviet Union to increase the World Court's *rôle* in resolving international disputes. 'To have withdrawn would have hurt our credibility with the Russians', a senior official said."[92]

At the same time, however, it was indicated that, within the Bush Administration, there was some unhappiness with the State Department decision to take part in the case: the Defence Department reportedly opposed fighting the case because it –

"feared that the Court might contest America's right to protect neutral shipping. Administration officials said they will not accept any part of a judgment that goes beyond the facts of Iran's complaint."[93]

What ensued seemed a classic demonstration of the old (Leninist) adage, "two steps forward, one step back", reflecting the internal conflicts, within the Bush Administration, between the State Department and the Defence Department. By letter of 9 August 1989, the U.S. Administration named the State Department Legal Adviser, Judge Sofaer, as its official Agent in the case initiated by Iran. However, at the subsequent meeting between the President of the Court and the state parties, – which the President of the Court is required to convene under Article 31 of the Rules of Court, to discuss "questions of procedure", – the U.S. official Agent advised the Court President that the U.S. intended to file Preliminary Objections to Jurisdiction and Admissibility, and this prior to the filing of the Memorial by the Applicant state (Iran). The Iranian Government contested this U.S. position, arguing that, according to the Court Rules and Court practice, a Preliminary Objection should not be filed before the Memorial. The particular matter in contest was considered by the full Court, in its Order fixing time-limits for the filing of the Memorial by the Applicant, Iran, and for the filing of the Counter-Memorial by the Respondent, U.S., in accord with Articles 44, 45, and 48 of the Court Rules.[94] The Order was rendered, unanimously, by the full Court in an Opinion of Court, signed by the Court President, which consists of a series of Preambular recital clauses leading up to the single, very short, operative paragraph which is limited to fixing the time-limits for filing of the Memorial and Counter-Memorial and to "reserv[ing] the subsequent procedure for further decision". Perhaps the key to this, no doubt conscious, ellipsis is provided in the second last Preambular paragraph with its mention that the "Court is not at the present time seised of a preliminary objection by the United States": it is a principle of judicial self-restraint or economy, of which the late Mr. Justice Frankfurter of the U.S. Supreme court would certainly have approved, to avoid saying what is not strictly necessary to disposition of a matter. In the final Preambular paragraph the Court noted:

> "Whereas, in accordance with Article 79, paragraph 1, of the Rules of Court, while a respondent which wishes to submit a preliminary objection is entitled before doing so to be informed as to the nature of the claim by the submission of a Memorial by the Applicant, it may nevertheless file its objection earlier."

Judge Oda, in a Declaration annexed to the Court's Order, noted, (as the Court itself had noted), that the Court was not at that time seised of any Preliminary Objection by the U.S.; and he pointed out, from this, that the Court was not required, at that stage, to take any decision on whether a Preliminary Objection may be submitted before the filing of the Applicant's Memorial. Judge Oda concluded, – correctly, it may be suggested, – that –

> "if the Court is to make such an important interpretation of its Rules
> ... this should, in my view, be dealt with in the operative part, not in the preambular part of the Order."

The larger interest, in the present context, in *Aerial Incident of 3 July 1988. Order*, is, however, to be found in the two Separate Opinions filed, respectively, by the U.S. member of the Court, Judge Schwebel, and by the then recently-elected Guyanese member, Judge Shahabuddeen. Judge Schwebel, relying principally on an extra-judicial essay published by the then Judge Jiménez de Aréchega, in the *American Journal of International Law* in 1973,[95] concluded that a Respondent state would have the right to file a Preliminary Objection even before the Applicant state should have filed its Memorial. Judge Schwebel also essayed an historical survey of Court practice under the old Permanent Court and the present International Court, particularly the views of Judge Anzilotti who, from 1926 on, argued that the Court should only deal with Jurisdictional questions *after* it had before it the Merits of the case, and the counter-views of the then Court Registrar, Ake Hammarskjöld; and also the Court *jurisprudence*, involving cases in which the Respondent state did not choose to appear at all and also the more normal cases in which both Applicant and Respondent states appeared.

Judge Shahabuddeen, in his own Separate Opinion, covered the identical ground to Judge Schwebel, and also more. He relied strongly on the authoritative views of leading text-writers on Court practice,[96] to the effect that the Court's practice is only to take formal Preliminary Objections by the Respondent state *after* the Merits have been laid before it in the Memorial filed by the Applicant state. Judge Shahabuddeen also appears to join issue with Judge Schwebel as to the relative weight to be given to former Judge Jiménez de Aréchaga's extra-judicial views, (as revealed in his January, 1973, *American Journal* essay), on the meaning and import of the 1972 Revisions to the Court's Rules and the then Article 67 (now Article 79 of the 1978 Revised Rules). For, at the same time as his January, 1973, essay, Judge Jiménez de Aréchaga was, – as noted by Judge Shahabuddeen – offering, in a Joint Dissenting Opinion (with Judge Bengzon), in *Fisheries. Jurisdiction*[97]

"another uncontradicted and equally categorical statement (quoted more fully below): 'A preliminary objection must be filed within the time-limit assigned for the Counter-Memorial, that is to say, after the presentation of the Memorial, not before it .... Otherwise, a respondent might be able to block the proceedings before the Memorial is filed'".

Reviewing exactly the same cases as surveyed by Judge Schwebel, Judge Shahabuddeen concludes that the Court practice, over the years, as well as the *doctrines* (views of text-writers), clearly support the view that Preliminary Objections can only be offered by a Respondent state *after* the Applicant state has filed its Memorial.

This then leads on to the policy issue today, in terms of contemporary approaches to legal interpretation on the Court, as to the effect of developed Court practice on the language of the Court Rules. As Judge Shahabuddeen notes:

"... formal rules of procedure – at any rate where no conflict with an overriding constituent instrument is involved ... – develop through the way in which they are interpreted and applied by the court concerned as evidenced by its practice".

This, of course, is progressive, generic judicial interpretation as conceived and applied, in Common Law countries, even to constitutions and similar constituent instruments. The joinder of issue between Judge Schwebel and Judge Shahabuddeen is noteworthy, perhaps, in the sense that it occurs by way of two (concurring) Separate Opinions filed in support of a unanimous Court decision; but that is not unusual or unwelcome in the case of contemporary Municipal, national Constitutional Courts, where competing philosophical conceptions of the *rôle* of judicial decision-making emerge, dialectically, in the individual judicial opinions, concurring and dissenting. The real intellectual-legal differences between the two judicial approaches would appear to be clearly demonstrated in Judge Shahabuddeen's comments on the antinomy between abstract Rules, as written, and actual Court practice:

"... Under the strict terms of Article 79(1) of the Rules of Court a respondent would be entitled as of right to file a preliminary objection before the disclosure of the merits of the applicant's claim through its Memorial .... But that right has to be balanced against possibly substantial injustice which an applicant might suffer if its case were dismissed on a preliminary objection before it had the opportunity, through its Memorial, of developing and supplementing its application on points of possible deficiency pursuant to a right to do so which it not unreasonably thought it had under the rule as interpreted and applied by the Court in the course of its own practice .... In my opinion, the balance when struck speaks with persuasive fairness in favour of the continuance of that practice and of the corresponding interpretation of the Rules which it portrays. If there is to be a change – and there may be good reason why there should be – it should be made by way of a formal amendment of the Rules designed to take effect prospectively, and not by way of a decision of the Court retrospectively invalidating a practice of its own creation upon which reasonable expectations have been founded."

Judge Shahabuddeen's reservations with the Opinion of Court, which he nevertheless supported, were appropriately nuanced:

that it "approach[ed] the procedural situation as if it were designed solely to confer options on a respondent", whereas the "procedural *régime* actually in force (that is to say, the Rules of Court as well as the practice of the Court) is both more flexible and more balanced, and that, in particular, there are rights and expectations of an applicant which are also to be considered but which the recital [in the Opinion of Court] does not take into account."

## NOTES

1. Hughes, *The Supreme Court of the United States* (1928), pp. 50–1.
2. *Scott* v. *Sanford*, 19 Howard 393 (1857).
3. I.C.J. Reports 1966, p. 6.
4. *South West Africa, Preliminary Objections, Judgment*, I.C.J. Reports 1962, p. 319.
5. I.C.J. Reports 1966, p. 6.
6. Statute of the International Court of Justice, Article 24: ...
    "(2) If the President considers that for some special reason one of the members of the Court should not sit in a particular case, he shall give him notice accordingly.
    "(3) If in any such case the member of the Court and the President disagree, the matter shall be settled by the decision of the Court."
7. Court Statute, Article 55: ... "(2) In the event of an equality of votes, the President or

the judge who acts in his place shall have a casting vote."

8. *Nicaragua* v. *United States of America, Provisional Measures, Order of 10 May 1984*, I.C.J. Reports 1984, p. 169; *Jurisdiction and Admissibility, Judgment*, I.C.J. Reports 1984, p. 392; *Merits, Judgment*, I.C.J. Reports 1986, p. 14.

9. I.C.J. Reports 1966, p. 6, at p. 323.

10. *Lochner* v. *New York*, 198 U.S. 45, 74 (1905), (Holmes J., Dissenting Opinion).

11. Stone, *The Province and Function of Law* (1946); and see also Stone, *Precedent and Law. Dynamics of Common Law Growth* (1985).

12. See, generally, "Le problème dit du droit intertemporel dans l'ordre international", *Institut de Droit International. Report of Eleventh Commission* (Sorensen, *rapporteur*), *Annuaire*, (1973), p. 1; and see the present author's study, "The Time Dimension in International Law. Historical Relativism and Intertemporal Law," in *Essays in International Law in Honour of Judge Manfred Lachs*, (Makarczyk, ed.), (1984), p. 179; and see, also, Doehring, "Die Wirkung des Zeitablaufs auf den Bestand völkerrechtlicher Regeln",[1964] *Jahrbuch der Max-Planck-Gesellschaft* 70; Krause-Ablass, *Intertemporales Völkerrecht. Der zeitliche Anwendungsbereich von Völkerrechtsnormen* (1970), at p. 31.

13. I.C.J. Reports 1966, p. 6, at p. 441.

14. *Legal Consequences for States of the Continued Presence of South Africa in Namibia (South West Africa) notwithstanding Security Council Resolution 276 (1970), Advisory Opinion*, I.C.J. Reports 1971, p. 16.

15. *Ibid.*, pp. 31–2.

16. *Ibid.*, p. 303. And see also Merrills, "Sir Gerald Fitzmaurice's contribution to the jurisprudence of the International Court of Justice",[1975] *British Yearbook of International Law* 183.

17. Hudson, *The Permanent Court of International Justice, 1920–1942*, at p. 511.

18. As to the Judicial Activism/Judicial Self-Restraint continuum, see generally the present author's *The World Court and the Contemporary International Law-Making Process*, (1979), p. 17 *et seq.*; *The International Court of Justice and the Western Tradition of International Law* (1987). And see also Lauterpacht, *The Development of International Law by the International Court* (1958), p. 75 *et seq.*; De Visscher, *Problèmes d'interprétation judiciaire en Droit International Public* (1963), p. 14 *et seq.*; De Visscher, *Aspects récents du Droit procédural de la Cour internationale de justice* (1966).

19. Compare the comment by the then Professor Mosler:

"The question of impartiality, which at the time of the Permanent Court of International Justice was regarded as simply a problem of *personal integrity*, has become more complicated in recent years because of uncertainty over the law applicable. When there no longer exists common agreement on the substantive rules, ... the subjective attitudes of the individual judge assume increased importance."

Mosler, "Problems and Tasks of International Judicial and Arbitral Settlement of Disputes Fifty Years after the founding of the World Court",in *Judicial Settlement of International Disputes* (Mosler and Bernhardt, eds.) (1974), p. 3, at p. 10.

20. *Nuclear Tests (Australia* v. *France), Interim Protection, Order of 22 June 1973*, I.C.J. Reports 1973, p. 99; *Nuclear Tests (Australia* v. *France), Judgment of 20 December 1974*, I.C.J. Reports 1974, p. 253.

21. *Discussed in detail in the present author's The International Law of Détente. Arms Control, European Security, and East-West Cooperation* (1978); Nagendra Singh and

McWhinney, *Nuclear Weapons and Contemporary International Law* (1988).

22. See, generally, Politis, "Le problème des limitations de la souveraineté et la théorie de l'abus des droits dans les rapports internationaux", *Recueil des Cours de l'Académie de la Haye*, vol. 6, (1925), (I), p. 1; Leibholz, "Das Verbot der Willkür und des Ermessensmissbrauchs im völkerrechtlichen Verkehr der Staaten", *Zeitschrift für ausländisches öffentliches Recht und Völkerrecht*, vol. 1, (1929), p. 77; Schlochauer, "Die theorie des *abus de droit* im Völkerrecht", *Zeitschrift für Völkerrecht*, vol. 17, (1933), p. 373; Andrassy, "Les relations internationales de voisinage", *Recueil des Cours de l'Académie de la Haye*, vol. 79, (1951), (II), p. 77.

23. *North Sea Continental Shelf, Judgment*, I.C.J. Reports 1969, p. 3, at pp. 228–9 (Lachs J., Dissenting Opinion).

24. *Livre Blanc sur les expériences nucléaires* (*Comité interministériel pour l'information*, Paris), (June, 1973).

25. *Nuclear Tests (Australia v. France), Interim Protection, Order of 22 June 1973*, I.C.J. Reports 1973, p. 99.

26. *Nuclear Tests (Australia v. France), Judgment of 20 December 1974*, I.C.J. Reports 1974, p. 253.

27. *Ibid.*, pp. 264–6.

28. The Court here cited *Northern Cameroons. Judgment*, I.C.J. Reports 1963, p. 38.

29. I.C.J. Reports 1974, pp. 271–2.

30. *Ashwander v. Tennessee Valley Authority*, 297 U.S. 288, 346–8 (1936), (Brandeis J., Concurring Opinion).

31. I.C.J. Reports 1974, p. 267.

32. *Ibid.*, pp. 267–8.

33. Freund, "A Supreme Court in a Federation: some lessons from Legal History", *Columbia Law Review*, vol. 53 (1953), p. 597, pp. 617–8.

34. McWhinney, *Constitutionalism in Germany and the Federal Constitutional Court* (1962), pp. 34–40.

35. *Ibid.*, pp. 26–7.

36. *Western Sahara, Advisory Opinion*, I.C.J. Reports 1975, p. 12.

37. *Status of Eastern Carelia. Advisory Opinion of 23 July 1923*, P.C.I.J. Series B, No. 5, p. 7.

38. I.C.J. Reports 1975, p. 24.

39. I.C.J. Reports 1950, p. 65.

40. I.C.J. Reports 1950, p. 65, at p. 71; adopted by the Court in *Western Sahara*, I.C.J. Reports 1975, p. 12, at p. 24.

41. I.C.J. Reports 1975, p. 12, at p. 19.

42. I.C.J. Reports 1971, p. 16, at p. 27.

43. I.C.J. Reports 1975, p. 12, at p. 19.

44. I.C.J. Reports 1947–1948, p. 61.

45. I.C.J. Reports 1975, p. 12, at p. 19.

46. *Ibid.*, pp. 20–1.

47. *Ibid.*, p. 20.

48. *Ibid.*, p. 29.

49. *Ibid.*, p. 30.

50. *Ibid.*, p. 32.

51. *Ibid.*, p. 37.

52. *Aegean Sea Continental Shelf, Interim Protection, Order of 11 September 1976*, I.C.J. Reports 1976, p. 3.
53. Turkey, pursuant to its denial of Court jurisdiction, declined, unlike Greece, to exercise the right, under Article 31(3) of the Court Statute, to choose an *ad hoc* judge; and it also, on the model of France in the *Nuclear Tests* litigation, was not represented at the subsequent Court hearings, confining itself, again on the French model, to a written memorandum addressed to the Court by letter of 26 August 1976 under the title "Observations of the Turkish Government on the request of the Government of Greece for provisional measures, dated 10 August 1976." I.C.J. Reports 1976, p. 3, at p. 5.
54. *Ibid.*
55. I.C.J. Reports 1976, p. 3, at p. 15.
56. *Nuclear Tests (Australia v. France), Judgment*, I.C.J. Reports 1974, p. 253, pp. 259–60.
57. *Ibid.*, citing *Northern Cameroons, Judgment*, I.C.J. Reports 1963, at p. 29.
58. I.C.J. Reports 1988, p. 69, at p. 108.
59. *Ibid.*
60. *Military and Paramilitary Activities in and against Nicaragua (Nicaragua v. United States of America), Provisional Measures, Order of 10 May 1984*, I.C.J. Reports 1984, p. 169. And see, generally, Wengler, "Gerichtszuständigkeit und Klagezulässigkeit im Verfahren Nicaragua/Vereinigte Staaten vor dem Internationalen Gerichtshof", *Neue Juristische Wochenschrift*, (1985), p. 1266; Verhoeven, "Le droit, le juge, et la violence. Les arrêts Nicaragua c. Etats-Unis", *Revue Générale de Droit International Public*, vol. 91 (1987) p. 1159.
61. *Military and Paramilitary Activities in and against Nicaragua, Jurisdiction and Admissibility, Judgment*, I.C.J. Reports 1984, p. 392.
62. "Statement of Department of State on U.S. Withdrawal from Nicaragua Proceedings, 18 January 1985"; reprinted, in part, in "Contemporary Practice of the United States", *American Journal of International Law*, vol. 79, (1985), p. 438, p. 441; *International Legal Materials*, vol. 24 (1985), p. 246.
63. *International Legal Materials*, vol. 24 (1985), p. 1742.
64. *Military and Paramilitary Activities in and against Nicaragua, Merits, Judgment*, I.C.J. Reports 1986, p. 14.
65. "Statement of Department of State on U.S. Withdrawal from Nicaragua Proceedings, 18 January 1985", *American Journal of International Law*, vol. 79, (1985), p. 438, p. 441.
66. *Ibid.*
67. Rostow, "Disputes involving the Inherent Right of Self-Defence", *American Journal of International Law*, vol. 81, (1987), p. 264.
68. Acheson, *Proceedings of the American Society of International Law*, (1963), p. 13, at p. 14. And see, also, Chayes, "Law and the Quarantine of Cuba", *Foreign Affairs*, vol. 41, (1963), p. 550; Chayes, "A Common Lawyer looks at International Law", *Harvard Law Review*, vol. 78, (1965), p. 1396.
69. See, generally, the present author's *Supreme Courts and Judicial Law-Making. Constitutional Tribunals and Constitutional Review* (1986), p. 287 *et seq.*
70. *Ibid.*, p. 187 *et seq.*
71. I.C.J. Reports 1975, p. 29.
72. However, Judge Oda, in his Dissenting Opinion in *Merits, Judgment*, (I.C.J. Reports 1986, p. 14, at p. 212), though acknowledging, and citing, the Court judgment in *Merits* to the effect that – "the party which declines to appear cannot be permitted to profit from its absence, since this would amount to placing the party appearing at a disad-

vantage",(*ibid.*, p. 26), still expresses concern at the fact-finding difficulties created by the U.S. walk-out from the *Nicaragua* proceedings. *Ibid.*, p. 245.

73. *Supreme Courts and Judicial Law-Making* (1986), p. 151, pp. 287–8.

74. Mosler, "Political and Justiciable Legal Disputes: revival of an old controversy",in *Contemporary Problems of International Law: Essays in honour of Georg Schwarzenberger* (Bin Cheng and Brown, eds.) (1986), p. 216, at p. 228.

75. *Supreme Courts and Judicial Law-Making* (1986), pp. 288–90.

76. Mosler, "Problems and Tasks of International Judicial and Arbitral Settlement ...", in *Judicial Settlement of International Disputes* (Mosler and Bernhardt, eds.) (1974), p. 3, at p. 10.

77. *Ibid.*

78. *Ibid.*, p. 11, citing Bruns, "Völkerrecht als Rechtsordnung", *Zeitschrift für ausländisches öffentliches Recht und Völkerrecht*, vol. 3, (1933), p. 432.

79. Mosler, "Political and Justiciable Legal Disputes: revival of an old controversy",in *Contemporary Problems of International Law: Essays in Honour of Georg Schwarzenberger* (Bin Cheng and Brown, eds.) (1986), p. 216, at p. 229. As Mosler further remarked concerning the "legal"/"political" disputes dichotomy –

> "This distinction is more a pragmatic one than a logical one: legal disputes always have a greater or smaller political dimension".

(Mosler, "The Area of Justiciability",in *Essays in International Law in Honour of Judge Manfred Lachs* (Makarczyk, ed.) (1984), p. 409, p. 415). Mosler also invoked the late Professor Wolfgang Friedmann (in *Archiv des Völkerrechts*, vol. 14, pp. 305–9), in order to deny any theoretical distinction between legal and political disputes:

> "The reason why none of the politically critical issues of the post-World War II era – divided Berlin and divided Germany, the International Status of the Suez Canal, ... and the Vietnam War – were brought before the Court or can be expected in the future 'is not that they are inherently 'legal' or incapable of judicial settlement, but that, in the present condition of international society, the states are not willing, either directly, or through the intermediary of the United Nations, to submit politically critical issues to judicial settlement. This is a question not of any theoretical distinction between legal and political disputes but of approach'".

(Mosler, "Eine allgemeine, umfassende, obligatorische, internationale Schiedsgerichtsbarkeit",in *Staat und Völkerrechtsordnung. Festschrift für Karl Doehring* (Hailbronner, Ress, Stein, (eds.)) (1989), p. 607, p. 614.

80. von Mangoldt, "Arbitration and Conciliation",in *Judicial Settlement of International Disputes* (Mosler and Bernhardt, eds.) (1974), p. 431, at p. 501.

81. *Ibid.*, pp. 433–4. And see also Strupp, *Die wichtigsten Arten der völkerrechtlichen Schiedsverträge* (1917), p. 76.

82. Mosler, "Political and Justiciable Legal Disputes ...", *op. cit.*, (1986), p. 216, p. 223, citing Schindler, "Werdende Rechte",in *Festschrift für Fritz Fleiner* (1925), pp. 400–4.

83. *Ibid.*

84. *Customs Régime between Germany and Austria*, Series A./B., No. 41 (1931), p. 42.

85. Bloomfield, *Law, Politics and International Disputes* (1958), pp. 293–6.

86. Cited in Sturgess and Chubb, *Judging the World: Law and Politics in the World's Leading Courts* (1988), at p. 473.

87. Mosler, "Problems and Tasks of International Judicial and Political Settlement ...",in *Judicial Settlement of International Disputes* (Mosler and Bernhardt, eds.) (1974), p. 3, at p. 10.

88. Stone, *The International Court and World Crisis* (1962), pp. 7–9.
89. Schachter, [1986] *Proceedings of the American Society of International Law*, p. 210, at pp. 212–3.
90. Sofaer, "The United States and the World Court",[1986] *Proceedings of the American Society of International Law*, p. 204.
91. For analysis of this issue in the context of the Court's Advisory Opinion jurisdiction, see Judge Elias' study, "How the International Court of Justice deals with requests for Advisory Opinions",in *Essays in International Law in Honour of Judge Manfred Lachs*, (Makarczyk, (ed.)) (1984), pp. 355, 362, 373. A final legal regulation of the Berlin question was achieved, belatedly – but painlessly and easily, with the Treaty of 31 August 1990 between the two Germanies, West and East (*Vertrag über die Herstellung der Einheit Deutschlands*), and the complementary "Two-plus-Four" Treaty of 12 September 1990 (involving the two Germanies and the Four Former victor-states from World War II) (*Vertrag über die abschliessende Regelung in bezug auf Deutschland*).
92. New York Times, 15 August 1989.
93. *Ibid.*
94. *Case concerning the Aerial Incident of 3 July 1988 (Islamic Republic of Iran v. United States of America), Order of 13 December 1989*, I.C.J. Reports 1989, p. 132.
95. vol. 67, p.1, at p. 19.
96. Rosenne, *Procedure in the International Court. A Commentary on the 1978 Rules of the International Court of Justice* (1983), p. 161; Guyomar, *Commentaires du Règlement de la Cour internationale de justice* (1983), p. 508; and also Paul Guggenheim, as counsel in *Interhandel, I.C.J. Pleadings 1959*, p. 449).
97. I.C.J. Reports 1972, p. 181, at p. 185.

# The Jurisdiction of the Full Court of the International Court, and the Special Chambers Gloss to Jurisdiction

## 1. COMPULSORY JURISDICTION UNDER ARTICLE 36(2) OF THE COURT STATUTE

The Court Statute, Article 36(1), defines the jurisdiction of the International Court, comprehensively, as comprising – "all cases which the parties refer to it and all matters specially provided for in the Charter of the United Nations or in treaties and conventions in force." We have already looked at the Court's Advisory Opinion jurisdiction, specially authorised in Article 96 of the United Nations Charter and affirmed in Article 65 of the Court Statute. The Advisory Opinion jurisdiction is initiated by request to the Court by the U.N. General Assembly or the Security Council and, beyond that, by any other U.N. organ or specialised agency that might at any time be so authorised by the General Assembly.

The jurisdiction of the Court is also established in a considerable number of contemporary international treaties, in respect to the adjudication of disputes arising under those treaties. It was in this particular context that President Gorbachev, in his address to the United Nations on 7 December 1988, advanced the proposal that all States recognise the binding jurisdiction of the International Court with respect to the interpretation and application of human rights agreements. In February, 1989, by Decree of the Presidium of the Supreme Soviet, the Soviet Government followed up that proposal by formally accepting the Court's jurisdiction as to six specific multilateral Conventions on various aspects of protection of Human Rights.[1]

The key aspect of Court jurisdiction, for purposes of the conflict of the mid- and late-1980s, between the United States Government and the International Court, is the Compulsory Jurisdiction. On the eve of the *Nicaragua* litigation, the U.S. Government attempted, on 6 April 1984 (through the so-called Shultz Letter) to modify its own prior, general acceptance of the Compulsory Jurisdiction of the International Court by excluding, for a two-year period, all disputes relating to Central America.[2] When this U. S. Government venture failed and the Court went ahead nevertheless and exerted Preliminary Jurisdiction,[3] having already decreed Provisional Measures pending any final decision,[4] the U.S. Administration had reacted angrily by withdrawing in January, 1985, from any further participation in the *Nicaragua* case;[5] and then, in October, 1985, by formally notifying the U.N. Secretary-General of the termination of its original acceptance of the Compulsory Jurisdiction of the Court, as made in 1946 and modified (as noted) in 1984, the termination to take effect on six months' notice.[6]

The Compulsory Jurisdiction is specified, in detail, in Article 36 of the Court Statute:

(2) "The state parties to the present Statute may at any time declare that they recognise as compulsory *ipso facto* and without special agreement, in relation to any other state accepting the same obligation, the jurisdiction of the Court in all legal disputes ...

(3) "The declarations referred to above may be made unconditionally or on condition of reciprocity on the part of several or certain states, or for a certain time."

Article 36 also stipulates that —

"Declarations made under Article 36 of the Statute of the ["old", pre-War,] Permanent Court of International Justice and which are still in force shall be deemed, as between the parties to the present Statute, to be acceptances of the compulsory jurisdiction of the International Court of Justice for the period which they still have to run and in accordance with their terms". (Article 36(5)).

Any dispute over whether the Court has, indeed, jurisdiction is to be settled by decision of the Court. (Article 36 (6)).

The Legal Adviser to the U.S. State Department, Judge Sofaer, in defending, after the event, the U.S. Government decision of October, 1985, to withdraw from the Compulsory Jurisdiction of the Court, cited some comparative statistics on state practice as to acceptance of such jurisdiction.[7] Only 47 of the 162 states entitled to accept the Court's Compulsory Jurisdiction had, at the time of the U.S. decision to withdraw, actually done so, this number representing a proportion of states substantially lower than in the late 1940s. Among the Permanent Members of the U.N. Security Council, apart from the U.S. only the United Kingdom had adopted Compulsory Jurisdiction in any form. Neither the Soviet Union nor any other Socialist bloc state had ever done so. Judge Sofaer stressed that many of the

U.S.' closest friends and allies – and here he identified France, Italy, and West Germany – did not accept Compulsory Jurisdiction; and those states that did often attached Reservations depriving such acceptance of much of its meaning. Judge Sofaer here quoted the United Kingdom's Reservation which expressly retained the power to decline to accept the Court's jurisdiction, in any dispute, at any time before a case was actually filed.[8]

Judge Sofaer also cited the U.S.' own unhappy experience with Compulsory Jurisdiction, in never having been able, in seven different attempts, to the bring a state before the Court successfully.[9] Paradoxically, the reasons for this were not only the failure of other states to accept Compulsory Jurisdiction, but also the principle of Reciprocity as applied to the U.S.' own Declaration of 1946 accepting such Compulsory Jurisdiction. By attaching the so-called Connally Reservation to that 1946 U.S. Declaration (to the effect that the U.S. would not accept the Compulsory Jurisdiction over any dispute involving matters essentially within the Domestic Jurisdiction of the U.S., as determined by the U.S. itself), the U.S. Government necessarily conceded that any state sued by the U.S. might avail itself of just such a power, on a reciprocal basis, to deny jurisdiction.[10] He cited, here, Bulgaria's reciprocal invocation of the Connally Reservation, against the U.S., when the U.S. tried to sue Bulgaria in 1957 on claims arising from the loss of lives of U.S. citizens in an Aerial Incident of that time involving Bulgaria's shooting down of a civilian airliner that had entered Bulgarian air space. The Bulgarian reciprocal invocation of the Connally Reservation had forced the U. S. Government to discontinue the case before the International Court.[11] Judge Sofaer conceded that the Connally Reservation, with its "self-judging" nature that had in fact been criticised, at the time it was made, by the Executive branch of the U.S. Government, had severely undercut the example the U.S. Government had attempted to set to other states, in the immediate post-War era, with its own, U.S. 1946 acceptance of the Compulsory Jurisdiction of the Court.

In the immediate context of his defence of the U.S. Government's October, 1985, announcement of withdrawal from the Compulsory Jurisdiction of the Court, Judge Sofaer had some sharp criticisms to make of what he called the Court's "composition", which he labelled as a "source of institutional weakness".[12] Specifically, he noted that, at that time, nine of the Court's fifteen judges came from states that did not accept the Court's Compulsory Jurisdiction, and that most of these states had never used the Court at all. We shall return to these particular criticisms, which take us back to our earlier examination of the Court's character as "independent", but also as "representative" tribunal, a little later. Judge Sofaer's criticisms can be examined at the same time as other, much less temperate attacks on the Court, in the same vein, advanced by other Reagan Administration spokesmen.

Judge Sofaer does concede, – though the concession is hardly surprising, – that it was the U.S. Government's unhappiness with the International Court's Preliminary rulings in *Nicaragua*, in 1984, that "provided the chief motivation for the administration's review of our acceptance of the Court's Compulsory Jurisdiction".[13] The U.S. had contended, unsuccessfully, that Nicaragua had itself never accepted the Court's Compulsory Jurisdiction in a valid or effective way: that argument, if sustained, would, on the reciprocity principle, have prevented the U.S. from being held to its original, general acceptance of Compulsory Jurisdiction. The U.S. had also contended, again unsuccessfully, that Nicaragua was seeking to bring before the Court "political and security disputes that were never previously considered within the Court's mandate".[14] On the basis of the contemporary marked evolution and broadening of the Court's approach to justiciability, already discussed, this particular objection might seem rather less persuasive than the first (jurisdictional) one and, in any case, to come rather strangely from the U.S. as the home of Legal Realism and of the modern, creative, policy-making approaches to the Judicial Process.

On the strict jurisdictional point, however, the U.S. would seem to have a much stronger argument. Article 36(2) of the Court Statute, establishing the base for the Court's Compulsory Jurisdiction, is generally referred to as the *Optional Clause*, indicating the premise on which such jurisdiction is established, – namely, the consent of a state to be so bound. The consensual element is indispensable in the origin, and continuance, of Compulsory Jurisdiction for any state. One of the obvious, public contradictions in the International Court's assertion of jurisdiction against unwilling state respondents in recent years – against France, in *Nuclear Tests* ;[15] and against the U.S. in *Nicaragua*;[16] or even against Honduras, in *Case concerning Border and Transborder Armed Actions* in 1988,[17] – is that by the time the complaint had been deposited with the Court or, even more, by the time the Court had begun hearing the complaint, the respondent's state's consent to Court jurisdiction had disappeared or had become notional at best. It would require a form of exercise in legal fiction – that the respondent state must still be presumed *objectively* to consent to the Court's Compulsory Jurisdiction under the Optional Clause, – even though, subjectively, that state clearly no longer wishes to maintain that earlier or original consent to jurisdiction. This continuing, objective state consent to Court jurisdiction will, following the Court's *jurisprudence*, be presumed in at least several different instances. First, it will be presumed where what is involved is a state's own error or oversight as to withdrawing an earlier or original unqualified general acceptance of the Compulsory Jurisdiction under the General Act of 1928,[18] at the time of its most recent declaration of adherence to Court jurisdiction. This was the situation, of course, with the French Government in *Nuclear Tests*.[19] The extent of the French Government's apparent error, in this regard, is noted by Judge de Castro in his Dissenting Opinion in *Nuclear Tests. Judgment*, in 1974:

> "There still remains a teasing mystery; why did the French Government not denounce the General Act at the appropriate time and in accordance with the required forms, in exercise of Article 45, paragraph 3, of the Act, at the time in 1966 when it filed its declaration recognising the jurisdiction of the Court subject to new reservations? It seems obvious that the French Government was in 1966 not willing that questions concerning national defence should be capable of being brought before the Court, and we simply do not know why the French Government preserved the Court's jurisdiction herein vis-à-vis the signatories to the Act. [Though various hypotheses have been put forward to explain this apparently contradictory conduct]. But this anomalous situation cannot be regarded as sufficient to give rise to a presumption of tacit denunciation of the General Act by the French Government, and to confer on such denunciation legal effectiveness in violation of the provisions of the Act itself. To admit this would be contrary to legal security and even to the requirements of the law as to presumptions."[20]

The presumption of a continuing, objective state consent to Court jurisdiction will also, following the Court's *jurisprudence*, be applied in the case where a state is guilty of *laches* (delay) as to excluding from an earlier, general acceptance of Compulsory Jurisdiction, some new category or categories of matters. This was the situation with the U.S. Government's too belated attempt, in *Nicaragua* in 1984, to "correct" its earlier, 1946, general acceptance of Compulsory Jurisdiction by excluding any cases involving Central America for the next two years. In the latter case, the U.S. Government did, literally, beat the gun in relation to a rumoured, impending *Nicaragua* process, by filing its own exclusion and limitation of its earlier, general acceptance of Compulsory Jurisdiction in 1946, – on 6 April 1984, three days before the Government of Nicaragua filed its complaint in the International Court. Unfortunately for the U.S. Government, the terms of the U.S. Declaration of acceptance of Compulsory Jurisdiction in 1946 specified that that Declaration would remain in force – "until the expiration of six months after notice may be given to terminate this declaration";[21] and the Court had no particular intellectual problems in holding the U.S. Government as bound by this.[22]

In *Border and Transborder Armed Actions*,[23] where the Nicaraguan complaint was that Honduras had aided and abetted the operations of bands of the so-called "Contra" rebels carrying out armed attacks on Nicaraguan territory, the International Court, properly enough since it was a more limited, "regional" dispute between two Central American states, preferred to locate its jurisdiction in the relevant "regional", agreed Treaty dispositions on Peaceful Settlement of Disputes – in this case, on the 1948 Pact of Bogotá (American Treaty of Pacific Settlement) – rather than in the larger and more general jurisdiction provided by the Declarations by both parties accepting the Compulsory Jurisdiction of the Court under Article 36(2) of the Court Statute. The Opinion of Court, signed by President Ruda,[24] was not disputed, in the special Declaration and the three other Separate (Concurring) Opinions accompanying it,[25] as to the Court's assertion of jurisdiction in the case. However, Judge Oda, in his Separate Opinion,[26] felt it worthwhile to record his doubts as to whether the states party to the Pact of Bogotá really intended, in that Pact's system of peaceful settlement, to accept the Compulsory Jurisdiction of the International Court. This provided the occasion for Judge Oda to review the jurisprudence of the old Permanent Court and of the present International Court, in order to stress the *consent* of the parties, and their *intention* to confer jurisdiction on the Court, as the necessary basis of any Court exercise of jurisdiction:

"… One cannot lay too much stress upon the paramount importance of the expression of the acceptance of the Court's jurisdiction, which is invariably required for the Court to entertain a case, as the first and critical task of the Court is always to ascertain the intention of the Parties. I doubt whether this particular point has been given all the weight due to it."[27]

The judicial emphasis, here, upon the subjective will of the parties, amply demonstrated in the facts, closely resembles the late 19th century German Civil Law theories of Contract, developed at the *apogée* of *laissez-faire* liberalism, which insisted on finding any contractual foundation in the union of the individual wills, putting aside the earlier, historically-based emphasis on forms. The International Court as a whole, in moving, in accord with all the dominant trends of Municipal, national law seen in Comparative Law perspective, away from purely subjective intent to a form of objective intent, in which the consent of a state, and also continuance of such consent, will now be presumed from state conduct or even state non-conduct, is clearly favouring a new, more expansive or beneficial, conception of its own jurisdiction. The extra opportunity thereby provided for a Court contribution to the "progressive development of International Law", has to be balanced against the evident political and legal anguish of states, (and sometimes superpowers), enjoined against their latter-day, present will to answer for the conformity or non-conformity to International Law of their conduct in political-legal *causes célèbres* like *Nuclear Tests* and *Nicaragua*. The calculated self-restraint of the Court majority's final legal message in *Nuclear Tests*,[28] after its politically and legally strongly contested exercise of jurisdiction in the first place,[29] perhaps reflects a tacit judicial acknowledgment of the frequent practical dilemmas involved in the Court's new, more facultative approach to a finding of existence of Compulsory Jurisdiction under the Optional Clause, and a corresponding Court attempt to balance the conflicting policies accordingly.

## 2. ON "REGIONALISM", AND ON AN ALLEGED "REGIONAL" BIAS IN THE COURT'S DECISIONS

Beyond the postulated Law/Politics dichotomy and the insistence that the Court majority had crossed over into an impermissible "No-Man's-Land" involving a claimed "inherent sovereign right that cannot be compromised," of a superpower, "to defend itself or to participate in collective self-defence against aggression",[30] there was a further and more pervasive objection offered by the U.S. State Department to the International Court's *Nicaragua* rulings. The Legal Adviser to the State Department, Judge Sofaer, voiced this particular criticism in more conventionally periphrastic diplomatic terms by referring to the "Court's composition" as a "source of institutional weakness".[31] Harking back to the halcyon, immediate post-War era of Western dominance in the United Nations, Judge Sofaer commented:

"Whereas in 1945 the United Nations had 51 members, most of which were aligned with the United States and shared its views regarding world order, there are now 160 members. A great many of these cannot be counted on to share our view of the original constitutional conception of the U.N. Charter, particularly with regard to the special position of the permanent members of the Security Council in the maintenance of international peace and security. This same majority often opposes the United States on important international questions."[32]

The U.S. State Department formal statement accompanying the announcement in January, 1985, after the *Nicaragua* Preliminary rulings, that the U.S. would not participate, henceforward, in any further proceedings before the International Court on the Nicaraguan complaint against the U.S., was much less circumspect:

"We have seen in the United Nations, in the last decade or more, how international organisations have become more and more politicised against the interests of the Western democracies. It would be a tragedy if

these trends were to infect the International Court of Justice. We hope
this will not happen, because a politicised Court would mean the end of
the Court as a serious, respected institution. Such a result would do
grievous harm to the goal of the rule of law."[33]

There are echoes of this U.S. State Department complaint in the subsequent,
Dissenting Opinion to the International Court's decision on *Merits. Judgment* in June, 1986, rendered by the U.S. judge on the Court,[34] which
singles out certain portions of the Court's judgment as relating to the −
"process of decolonisation ... colonial domination", and which the U.S.
judge sees as −

"inferentially endorsing an exception to the prohibition against intervention, in favour of the legality of intervention in the promotion of so-
called 'wars of liberation', or, at any rate, some such wars, while con-
demning intervention of another political character."[35]

This particular ground of complaint against the Court majority's approach
to the *Nicaragua* rulings is noteworthy as coming from the U.S. judge on
the Court. It is not adverted to by any one of the three judges on the Court
representing former European Imperial, "colonial" states: neither the French
judge nor the Italian judge, who joined with the Court majority in ruling
against the U.S. on the substantive International Law issues involved in
*Nicaragua*, nor even the British judge who, though one of the three dissenters in the 12-to-3 *Merits* ruling against the U.S., dissented on other, limited
and technical, non-substantive grounds, quite distinct and different from the
issues now raised by the U.S.[36]

The unkindest cut of all, in the U.S. State Department's January, 1985,
statement, however, was the attack, by implication, on the personal integrity
of individual judges of the Court, the more so because the charge failed to
offer any specifications or supporting evidence:

"Much of the evidence that would establish Nicaragua's aggression
against its neighbours is of a highly sensitive intelligence character. We
will not risk U.S. national security by presenting such sensitive material
in public or before a Court that includes two judges from Warsaw Pact
Nations."[37]

The only two judges from states belonging to the Warsaw Pact on the Court
at the time of the *Nicaragua* rulings were Judge Lachs (Poland), and Judge
Morozov (Soviet Union). Judge Morozov participated in the two Prelimi-
nary judgments, rendered by the Court in 1984 on the *Nicaragua* complaint,
but retired because of ill-health in 1985, and so took no part in the final
*Merits* decision of the Court in 1986. His successor, Judge Tarassov, (also
Soviet Union), elected in December, 1985, for the balance of Judge
Morozov's regular term, also took no part in the *Merits* decision of the

Court. That left only Judge Lachs who might meet the State Department's characterisation of "judges from Warsaw Pact Nations". In a quietly dignified reply to these innuendoes, which were repeated in somewhat ameliorated form in the U.S. media as involving – "the presence of Communist judges, and those of other incompatible ideologies [on the Court]",[38] Judge Lachs pointed out that when he had first been elected to the Court in 1966, he had received co-nominations from thirty-one states, including the U.S. and other major Western states. Judge Lachs might have added that, for his re-elections to the Court in 1975 and in 1984, he had had an equally impressive number and range of Western states as co-nominators. Instead, he limited himself to pointing out that Article 2 of the Court's Statute stipulates that – "The Court shall be composed of a body of independent judges, elected regardless of their nationality"; and that the empirical record of the Court's judgments over the years, and also of the coalitions of judges that have made up the Court majorities for those judgments, – "provide few pointers to whether their authors may be termed as capitalist, Communist, feudal or whatever."[39] Judge Lachs' response amounted, in fact, to a reasoned statement of the principle, amply vindicated in the Court's practice over the years, of the "universality of the Court's vocation."[40] In *Border and Transborder Armed Actions*, *(Nicaragua* v. *Honduras)*, in 1988, Judge Lachs supplemented this earlier response by way of general principle by citing, laconically and without further comment, (for any elaboration would surely have been superfluous), that of the nineteen cases in which he had personally taken part during his years on the Court, he had been with the Court majority in eighteen of those cases.[41] What does this do to *a priori* theories based on the supposed *rôle* of "Warsaw Pact judges" in shaping decisions *against* the U.S. Government? In *Nicaragua*, *Merits*, *Judgment* in 1986,[42] the 12-to-3 Court majority that upheld the Nicaraguan Government's substantive-legal complaints against the U.S. Government was constituted as follows: three Western European judges (from France, Italy, Norway): two Asian judges (India, China); two Latin American judges (Argentina, Brazil); two African judges (Nigeria, Sénégal); one Arab judge (Algeria); one Eastern European judge (Poland); and one *ad hoc* judge, (nominated by Nicaragua), from France.

The theory of a "conspiracy" *rôle* of the Socialist (Soviet and Eastern European) judges on the Court, sometimes advanced in the U.S. in the revived Cold War era of the late 1970s and the early and mid-1980s, has always lacked a scientifically demonstrated, empirically verifiable, foundation. Indeed, it might be suggested that like other, uni-dimensional portraits of judicial behaviouralism on the Court, that seek to explain judicial votes on the Court and the judicial opinions filed in support of them by reference solely to the state of nationality of the judges concerned or at least to their political-ideological "regional" grouping, it is an essentially simplistic and technically unsophisticated approach to a complex social phenomenon. One needs to employ a multiple-causation enquiry with analysis in depth of the number of different variables which will be mutually interacting and sometimes conflicting in the particular case, in order to explain, and ultimately to predict, actual patterns of judicial decision-making on the Court. Among the significant key variables operating within the International Court and its decision-making are certainly not merely the state of political affiliation of the judge and that state's own national interest as conventionally perceived. But key elements, also, must be distinctive national legal education and professional-legal training; prior practical legal experience (whether in national Universities and scientific academies, national Supreme Courts, national diplomatic service); any direct openings to public life on the part of individual judges (whether in national Parliament or national Cabinet (Council of Ministers)); and, finally, the individual judges' own general philosophical orientation, and their varying degrees of personal commitment to change in Law and Society and also to the direction of such change. It should be remembered that International Court judges, being elected for a term of nine years, and, for all practical purposes, being irremovable from office during that time, may occasionally outlive their own state's administration that had originally sponsored them for election to the Court or even the dominant "regional" coalition of states whose lobbying and voting support was crucial to their election to the Court in the first place.

The complexity of the social-scientific analysis required in order to offer rational explanations of even single judicial votes within a Court, and the multi-causal character of what is, necessarily, a collegial decision-making process on a multi-member tribunal like the International Court, are amply demonstrated in the record of the successive U.S. judges on the International Court since the Court's re-constitution after World War II. The party-political and also cultural diversity of those U.S. judges, not merely in terms of individual intellectual formation and general and also professional-legal education and experience, but, even more, in their differing degrees of comprehension of, and response to, societal conditions underlying the positive law and in their differing commitments, in consequence, to legal change, amply reflect the plural character of U.S. political life, and the changing political-ideological platforms of the different U.S. Presidents who actually sponsored the jurists concerned for election to the Court. We might, for these purposes, readily set up a form of judicial-personality continuum, with allegiance to legal positivism and to strict and literal interpretation, as the sign-post for judicial construction, at the one end, and represented by the first post-World War II U.S. judge on the Court, G.H. Hackworth; with sociological jurisprudence and a dynamic, evolutionary, policy-oriented approach to past Court precedents and past legal *doctrines* generally, at the other end, and represented, most eloquently, by Philip Jessup; and with judges like Hardy Dillard and Richard Baxter more or less in the middle of the intellectual-legal continuum.

In sharp contrast, the Soviet judges on the International Court over the same general time period since War's end in 1945, now extending for more than forty years, have been uniformly consistent in their approach to decision-making and in their general judicial "style"; and, hence, they have been eminently predictable as to their actual judicial vote, and their reasoning in support thereof, in this in advance of actual problem-situations. The explanation for this lies not merely in the continuing bureaucratic momentum in the Soviet Foreign Ministry over the same time period, surviving through the frequent changes in Soviet personnel on the Court. It is certainly influenced, in part, by received Soviet historical experience with the old Permanent Court between the two World Wars, and by the bitter Soviet reaction, then, to the attempt in *Eastern Carelia*, in 1923,[43] to compel the Soviet Union, a non-party to the Court Statute and a non-member, at the time, of the League of Nations, to answer before the Court through the stratagem of the Advisory Opinion route to jurisdiction. But it clearly has a good deal to do, also, with the dominant trends and emphasis in Soviet legal education over that same time period, including herein especially the denial of any independent law-making, policy-making *rôle* for the courts in Soviet Municipal, national law. Vyshinsky's text on Soviet constitutional law,[44] used as a basic text-book in the Soviet Law Schools from the time of its appearance in the late 1930s onwards, delved into the unhappy U.S. constitutional experience with the ultra-conservative, "Old Court" majority on the U.S. Supreme Court up to the time of the Roosevelt-inspired "Court Revolution" of 1937, in order to raise to the status of constitutional dogma Vyshinsky's denial of any independent, discretionary *rôle* for the judiciary in the approach to the interpretation of statutes or executive decrees. It is hardly surprising that such intellectual-legal attitudes, formed in an internal, Municipal law context, should carry over into the international domain, particularly since these attitudes were reinforced in international arenas by the obvious political fact-of-life of the post-War United Nations and related international institutions like the Court, that the Soviet Union, even with support from its political allies and associated states in Eastern Europe and elsewhere, was bound to be decisively out-voted on any matter raising East-West ideological issues. The numbers simply were not there, either in the

U.N. General Assembly or on the Court itself, to carry through special Soviet positions.

Detailed, case-by-case analysis of Soviet and Soviet bloc judges' votes on the International Court in the early post-War years, made by Western researchers whose detachment from the Soviet Union and Socialist bloc's political positions could hardly be questioned, indicated, quite conclusively, the absence of any significant or sustained "Soviet" or "Soviet bloc" factor in the final outcome of the various Court decisions or rulings given in that period, or in the way the individual judicial votes were actually cast in those Court decisions and rulings. Perhaps this is not so surprising for that early era of the International Court, *before* the marked expansion in United Nations membership under the impact of Decolonisation and Self-Determination of Peoples on a World-wide scale had begun to transform the International Court's *clientèle*, from the pre-War, Western and Western European, restricted "family compact", political category. One would have to wait, then, until the 1960s before the shift from a predominant judicial emphasis on legal technique (the values of the rival parties being so often essentially the same), to difficult issues of judicial value-choice and judicial value-preference, would become apparent in Court decision-making. And here, again, it would be not so much a question of East-West, inter-systemic, Communist-Capitalist political-ideological conflicts, that might replicate before the Court the Cold War confrontations that one still found, at the time, in other, non-judicial arenas like the U.N. General Assembly and Security Council. Rather, as the angry public debate after the decision in *South West Africa. Second Phase*, in 1966,[45] shewed, it would involve the interactions of different visions of World public order and of the movement and direction of World history, to which old East-West, Communist-Capitalist stereotypes would hardly be particularly relevant or helpful as a guide to Court decision-making.

The U.S. scholar, Professor Zile,[46] in reviewing the contribution to the International Court's jurisprudence of its first Soviet member, Judge Krylov, who served on the Court from 1946 to 1952, makes a signal discovery of relevance to our appraisal of latter-day critiques of the *rôle* of the Soviet judges on the International Court, that it was never, in the early post-War period, a dominant or even a major *rôle*. There is, of course, no occasion for a direct vote either for or against the Soviet national interest, for the obvious enough reason that the Soviet Union, not having accepted the Compulsory Jurisdiction of the Court under the Optional Clause in Article 36(2) of the Court Statute, could not be made a defendant before the Court and was never, itself, a plaintiff state before the Court. Judge Krylov in fact participated in only eleven cases, and was absent, apparently for reasons of illness, from four other cases.[47] Krylov's successor as Soviet judge, Golunsky, (1952-3), never took up his seat on the Court; while Golunsky's successor, Kozhevnikov (1953–1961), was "noticeably silent" throughout his term on the International Court, except for the occasional curt (invariably no more than a page) Declaration annexed to the Court's judgment in what was, during his own tenure, a relatively dull and uncontroversial period in the Court's business and work-load.[48]

In the *Corfu Channel Case (Preliminary Objection)*, in 1948,[49] Judge Krylov had an early opportunity of sitting in judgment upon the then fraternal, Socialist bloc country, Albania, in the complaint from Great Britain arising from damage to British warships and loss of life and injury to their crews, caused by mines located in Albanian territorial waters in what was accepted as an international strait with consequent right-of-passage attaching under International Law. Krylov joined with the Polish judge, Winiarski, and the Yugoslav judge, Zoriac, in that case, in rallying to the Court majority's holding that Albania had accepted the International Court's jurisdiction, by consent expressed in a letter to the Court. Only the *ad hoc* Albanian judge (as it happens, a Czechoslovak jurist) dissented in this 15-to-1 majority ruling by the Court in favour of exercise of jurisdiction. Krylov, however, dissented from the Court's 11-to-5 majority decision, in *Corfu Channel Case (Merits)*,[50] holding Albania liable to make compensation to Great Britain for the damage resulting from the explosion of the mines, Krylov basing his dissent upon the absence of clear and indisputable proof that Albania was responsible, and being joined in opposition to the Court majority on this point by Judges Winiarski (Poland), Badawi (Egypt), and Azevedo (Brazil), and by the *ad hoc* Albanian judge (the Czech jurist). Krylov also dissented from the Court majority's further, 14-to-2, conclusion that Great Britain had committed no breach of Albanian Sovereignty by the original act of passing through the Corfu Channel, Krylov being joined in this particular view, once again, by the Brazilian judge. Krylov, understandably, was in accord with the unanimous further conclusion of the Court that Great Britain, by a second, later, operation in the Corfu Channel, – the so-called Operation Retail, designed ostensibly to gather evidentiary proof of Albania's complicity in the laying of the mines – had thereby infringed Albania's Sovereignty. Consequent on his denial of the Court's jurisdiction to judge the case, Krylov also dissented from that part of the Court's decision in which the Court, by a 12-to-2 majority, fixed the amount of money damages payable by Albania to the United Kingdom.

The legal issues in the several *Corfu Channel* judgments were sufficiently complex, and Judge Krylov's individual legal positions sufficiently well-reasoned and nuanced in their conclusions, and the collegial support he had from judicial colleagues sufficiently varied or plural in inter-systemic terms, for professional analysts to eschew any simplistic, black-and-white characterisations of Krylov's individual votes as hewing to a "party line".

In *Conditions of Admission of a State to Membership in the United Nations*, in 1948,[51] the first of the International Court's two Advisory Opinions on the issue of the legal criteria for admission of new States to U.N. membership, which had politically deadlocked the U.N. Security Council and General Assembly over their first decade, Krylov took issue with the Court majority in their interpretation of Article 65 of the Court Statute. Krylov's position seemed to reduce to a separation-of-powers argument, involving judicial self-restraint and deference to the other, coordinate, political organs of the U.N., – the Security Council and General Assembly:

"Whereas the Permanent Court, in interpreting the Covenant of the League of Nations, sought to consider concrete situations or existing disputes, the Court, in the present case, is about to make a pronouncement, with quasi-legislative effect, concerning decisions to be taken by the political organs of the United Nations."[52]

The approach is technical, and in accord with long-range Soviet technical positions, which we will see developed, with appropriate theoretical foundation, in the later (1960s) opinions of the then Soviet judge, Koretsky, that the U.N. Charter, as a Treaty and not a Constitution, is to be interpreted strictly, and in accord with its literal dispositions as to law-making competence and functions among the different U.N. institutions that it created. Krylov voted with the Court majority in the second, Advisory Opinion on the same general issue, *Competence of the General Assembly for the Admission of a State to the United Nations*, in 1950,[53] though without filing any Separate Opinion. The Soviet Union had, however, at the written stages of the Court proceedings, filed documents reasserting the earlier Soviet position against Court jurisdiction.

The conclusion by the West German jurist, Günther, in surveying, a quarter of a century ago, the contributions of the early Soviet judges on the International Court over the first two decades of the post-World War II-period, Judges Krylov, Golunsky, and Kozhevnikov – seems essentially correct on the empirical record of the Court's *jurisprudence*:

"No eye-catching quality of originality marks the special votes of the Soviet judges. They occupy themselves continually with the conceptual world of the traditional International Law. Even if the Court majority should once take a strong step forward ... then the Soviet judges will be found among the zealous defenders of the old, the already in place, the usual, the accustomed, – with which a collision is to be avoided at all costs."[54]

Not without cause, the invidious comparison, in this regard, might be made of those early Soviet judges with the great Chilean jurist, Judge Alvarez, who served on the International Court from 1946 to 1955, and who sought, in his Special Opinions, to break out of the constraints of what he viewed as an essentially static, conservative, "old" or "classical" International Law, in favour of a "droit international nouveau".[55] Professor Suzanne Bastid would devote a full teaching semester seminar, at the Sorbonne, to Judge Alvarez' innovatory approach, as developed in his Court Opinions and his scientific writings.

An intellectually larger, more comprehensive and self-consistent, Soviet approach to the International Court and its jurisdiction and the limits of justiciability, that built on the earlier foundation laid by Judge Krylov, was able to be provided, in the 1960s, by Judge Koretsky, who was elected to the Court in the regular, triennial elections of 1961. The first major opportunity came in *Certain Expenses of the United Nations*[56] with the Advisory Opinion rendered by the International Court, in 1962, by 9-to-5 vote. This precipitated the U.S.-sponsored, politically controversial and ultimately unsuccessful attempt to deprive the Soviet Union and France of their votes in the U.N. General Assembly, in terms of Article 19 of the U.N. Charter,[57] because of those two states' failure to pay their special assessments in contribution to the, by-now, politically much contested, United Nations operation in the post-Decolonisation, former Belgian Congo. It was, in fact, the Polish President of the International Court, Winiarski, who there formulated principles of judicial interpretation that revealed, very dramatically, basic doctrinal differences between Soviet bloc and Western jurists as to the nature and character of the Charter. In President Winiarski's words, in his Dissenting Opinion:

"The Charter, a multilateral treaty which was the result of prolonged and laborious negotiations, carefully created organs and determined their competence and means of action.

"The intention of those who drafted it was clearly to abandon the possibility of useful action rather than to sacrifice the balance of carefully established fields of competence, as can be seen, for example, in the case of voting in the Security Council. It is only by such procedures, which were clearly defined, that the United Nations can seek to achieve its purposes. It may be that the United Nations is sometimes not in a position to undertake action which would be useful for the maintenance of international peace and security or for one or another of the purposes indicated in Article 1 of the Charter, but that is the way in which the

Organisation was conceived and brought into being ..."[58]

Judge Koretsky, for his part, made the same point, but even more succinctly and directly, in his Dissenting Opinion:

"I am prepared to stress the necessity of the strict observation and proper interpretation of the provisions of the Charter, its rules, without limiting itself by reference to the purposes of the Organisation: otherwise one would have to come to the long ago condemned formula: 'The ends justify the means'."[59]

Since the majority of the Court upheld the validity of the expenditures for the U.N. Congo operation authorised by the General Assembly as being legitimate "expenses of the Organisation" within the meaning of Article 17(2) of the Charter, the temptation might be there to write off the two, Soviet and Socialist bloc, Dissenting Opinions as *ad hoc* special legal pleading in defence of their parent states' presumed political interests. That would, it is clear, have been an overly simplistic reading of the minority judicial positions in *Certain Expenses of the United Nations*. For the two, Soviet and Socialist bloc, judges were joined by three other dissenters, – the distinguished French jurist and sometime (1949–52) Court President, Judge Basdevant, who, perhaps least of all the members of the Court, could be accused of making a particular ruling because it favoured his own parent state, (France); and also two Latin American judges, Moreno Quintana (Argentina) and Bustamante y Rivero (Peru).

The more substantial explanation of Judge Koretsky and Judge Winiarski's intellectual positions in *Certain Expenses of the United Nations* would seem to reside elsewhere than in the particular nationality of the judges concerned. As a U.S. jurist remarked:

"Nationality is not to be confused with a method of legal thought which a judge acquires through his legal training and which is closely associated with each legal system."[60]

The Civil Law/Common Law disciplinary division within the Court's ranks sometimes appears much more pervasive than the philosophical division between Continental Western Europe and Continental Eastern Europe. The U.S. judge, Philip Jessup's brilliant Dissenting Opinion in *South West Africa. Second Phase* in 1966,[61] with its strong dose of Anglo-Saxon Legal Realism and of Pragmatism, North American-style, stands out from the rest of the judicial opinions in that case as radical, even revolutionary, in legal-doctrinal terms. The positions of President Winiarski and Judge Koretsky, in *Certain Expenses of the United Nations*,[62] have a strong Civil Law element in them, which is not surprising in view of the continuing Civil Law foundation to both Polish and Soviet law, in each case originally "received" from Continental Western Europe and continued, in the Soviet case, as an Imperial Russian inheritance adapted, with certain substantive law modifications, to the post-Revolution Soviet society and continued to the present day.

The concept of the U.N. Charter as a limited treaty and certainly not as a Constitution for World Government; and, in its capacity as treaty, to be construed strictly and, in any case, against those arguing for a cutting down of state sovereignty, had distinctively Soviet elements that corresponded to Soviet conceptions, at that particular time, of the political reality of the Soviet political minority status in a then Western-dominated United Nations and other main international institutions like the Court. It is certainly an intellectual-legal approach with which that arch legal positivist and strict constructionist, the British judge, Sir Gerald Fitzmaurice, should have felt completely at home. What is even more interesting, however, is that it is an approach that would be applied, consistently and without any backward glances, by the Soviet judges on the Court, thereafter, even though the political reality which was supposed to be one of its supports and justifications, – the claimed Western political domination of the United Nations and its main organs – had probably ceased to be true even by 1962, the time of the *Certain Expenses of the United Nations* ruling,[63] and had certainly disappeared by the end of the same decade. In *South West Africa. Second Phase*, in 1966,[64] Judge Winiarski had no particular intellectual problems in rallying, without any Separate Opinion on his part, to the ultra-positivist, strict-and-literal construction views of the then Court President, Sir Percy Spender, and the British judge, Sir Gerald Fitzmaurice, which became the politically much-contested, 8-to-7 majority, Opinion of Court, in that case. Judge Koretsky broke with the Court majority in *South West Africa. Second Phase* in 1966, but singularly refrained from any temptation to file a triumphantly "anti-Colonialist" Dissenting Opinion in that case.[65] To have done so would have been completely out of character and style for Koretsky, as judge, and would have offended against his well-known regard for the concept of "collegiality" within the Court and the consequent limits on the manner and mode of permissible judicial dissents. It would also have involved a clear repudiation of long-range and consistent Soviet doctrinal-legal approaches to the judicial process and the rules of legal interpretation. Koretsky's Dissenting Opinion was written on the same deliberately restrained basis of technical, procedural, adjectival law argumentation as the Court majority's Opinion of Court, and is refreshingly free from political-legal name-calling or partisan political-legal rhetoric.

### 3. THE CONTEMPORARY SPECIAL CHAMBERS GLOSS TO COURT JURISDICTION

The U.S. State Department's January, 1985, statement announcing that the U.S. would not participate further in the International Court's hearing of the Nicaraguan Government's complaint against the U.S., and that the U.S. would reconsider its U.S. acceptance of the Compulsory Jurisdiction of the Court, ended with the Parthian shot that the State Department would henceforth construe the "competence" of the Court as being limited to "specific disputes ... brought before it by special agreement of the parties".[66] The State Department text, here, was at pains to commend the particular *modus operandi* adopted for the then recent Canada-U.S. dispute over the *Gulf of Maine*.[67] By special agreement of the two state parties – Canada and the U.S. – neither of which had experience, in its own Municipal, national Court system, with Special Chambers or *bancs* or Senates, the Canadian and U.S. national Supreme Courts both operating always in *plenum* or Full Court, the matter had been submitted to a five-judge Special Chamber of the International Court, in terms of Article 26(2) of the Court Statute.

The promised follow-up action by Secretary of State Shultz in "clarification" of the U.S. acceptance of the Court's Compulsory Jurisdiction had come in October, 1985, with the U.S. Government depositing formal notice of the termination of the original U.S. Declaration of 1946 made under Article 36(2) of the Court's Statute.[68] The State Department took the occasion to repeat the charges already made in its January, 1985, text, of a "blatant misuse of the Court for political and propaganda purposes."[69] The State Department Press Statement complained, now, of the Court's process "being abused for political ends".[70] The U.S. Administration simultaneously announced a Special Agreement with the Italian Government to submit to a Special Chamber of the Court a commercial law dispute involving a U.S. company and its Italian subsidiary.[71] Though clearly a relatively minor, politically non-controversial issue as between the U.S. and Italian Governments, the U.S. Administration's *rôle* in sponsoring the matter's reference to a Special Chamber of the International Court was apparently intended to highlight the U.S. avowal, made in connection with the earlier U.S. retreat from the Compulsory Jurisdiction of the Court, that the U.S. was not abandoning international judicial settlement, as such, but simply giving up on the *plenum* or Full, fifteen-judge International Court which it stigmatised, for the purpose, as too "political". Continued U.S. championing of the institution of the five-judge Special Chamber within the Court would, however, presumably be predicated upon the U.S. Administration's being able to continue to maintain its own special interpretation of the Court Statute and Court Rules as to constitution and composition of such Special Chambers. This would imply having the parties to a case make their own choices of the judges for such Special Chamber, and, if necessary, impose those choices upon the Full Court. In the practical result, this would tend to ensure Special Chamber panels that would be limited in their membership to what, in United Nations' special parlance, is termed "like-minded states" – for U.S. purposes, North American and Western European-stocked Special Chambers, rather than panels modelled on the representative, plural-systemic type of tribunal that the *plenum* or Full Court of fifteen judges has effectively become over the years.

Examination of the Court Statute and application thereto of the ordinary, "golden" rules of legal interpretation, leave very little room for doubt or equivocation as to whether it is the parties (as the U.S. Administration has contended), or the Full Court, that should determine and decide upon the composition and make-up of a Special Chamber of the International Court. The Court Statute also envisages, apart from that Chamber of five judges, allowed under Article 29, to "hear and determine cases by summary procedure" – the creation of Chambers "composed of three or more judges as the Court may determine, for dealing with particular categories of cases; for example, labour cases and cases relating to transit and communications". (Article 26(1)). Judge Lachs, in reviewing the historical origins of the institution of Special Chamber on the Court, going back to the old Permanent Court and to the Treaty of Versailles of 1919, and particularly that Treaty's Articles 336 and 376 and the provisions of the Peace Treaties dealing with navigation, transit and communications, has made the case for a *functional* specialisation within the Court through a Special Chamber system, as a means of mobilising the varied specialist expertise to be found within the Full Court's fifteen-judge membership.[72] One such functionally-specialised panel suggested by Judge Lachs would have been devoted to the protection of the Environment, particularly as to pollution of rivers and lakes on borders between States; and another such specialised panel would have been devoted to the Law of the Sea. One is reminded, here, of the lesson of the Sibylline books and of the merits of introducing reforms when they are still timely. If the statutory provision for the creation of functionally-specialised chambers of the International Court had been picked up earlier by the Court, and acted upon in its original intent as suggested by Judge Lachs, it might have headed off the latter-day historical tendency, in the recourse to the judicial process as a means of Third Party international disputes-settlement, to create parallel international tribunals to the International Court, specialised by subject matter, of the nature of the one provided by the Third United Nations Conference on the Law of the Sea in its Final Act. Judge Lachs would seem correct in signalling the problems for the organic unity of International Law posed by any such separate and autonomous, potentially competing or rival, international tribunals.[73]

The public controversy surrounding Special Chambers, however, relates not to the inchoate provision in the Court Statute for functionally-specialised panels of the Full Court, (Article 26(1)), but to the accompanying provision allowing for creation of panels of a general jurisdictional character, unqualified by subject matter:

Article 26.(2). "The Court may at any time form a chamber for dealing with a particular case. The number of judges to constitute such a chamber shall be determined by the Court with the approval of the parties."

As the Court Statute concludes on the point:

Article 26.(3). "Cases shall be heard and determined by the chambers provided for in this Article if the parties so request."

At issue in the debate surrounding the first Special Chamber created by the International Court for the Gulf of Maine case[74] was the degree of deference to be accorded by the Full Court to the particular preferences of the particular state parties to a case as to the choice of the judges from among the regular, fifteen-member Full Court, to make up the panel for the Special Chamber in the case. The Court Statute, as already noted, would appear conclusive, in its language, of the question. According to the Court Statute, Article 26(2). it is the "number of judges to constitute such a chamber" that the International Court in its Full bench of fifteen judges is to determine "with the approval of the parties". The Rules of Court which are dependent upon the Court Statute for their legal efficacy, and which are also legally subordinate to the Court Statute, and incapable, ex hypothesi, of overcoming or controlling the Statute's language, might nevertheless have contributed, in their 1972 version, and again in their 1978 revised version, to an element of ambiguity or doubt taken up and used by the U.S. State Department in behalf of the State Department's own special interpretation. Article 26(1) of the 1972 Rules of Court required the President of the International Court to consult with the parties regarding the "composition of the Chamber", – this in addition to the requirement in Article 26(2) of the same Rules which repeated the provision of the Court Statute, Article 26(2), as to the Court's determining the "number" of judges for any Chamber with the approval of the parties. Article 17(2) of the current, 1978 revised Rules of Court states the requirement under Article 26(2) of the old, 1972 Rules a little more strongly, perhaps, with its stipulation that: "when the parties have agreed, the President shall ascertain their views regarding the composi-

tion of the Chamber, and shall report to the Court accordingly."[75] Article
18(1) of the 1978 revised Rules of Court, repeating exactly the provisions
of Article 27(1) of the 1972 Rules, stipulates that – "Elections to all
Chambers shall take place by secret ballot", a provision that would hardly
seem necessry if, as the U.S. Administration contends, the fifteen-member
Full Court's *rôle* is to be reduced to a wholly formal one of ratifying the
state-parties' choice of the judges for a Special Chamber.

In the lead-up events to constitution of the Special Chamber for *Gulf of
Maine*, the then Court President, the British judge, Sir Humphrey Waldock,
– since it was the first such Special Chamber of the International Court, –
seems to have been determined to play an active *rôle*. In the event, President Waldock clearly envisaged his own *rôle* and that of the Full Court of
fifteen judges, in the selection of the judges for the panel, as a very positive
one and, in any case, as being conclusive upon the parties. It is understood –
from discussions at the *Institut de Droit International* reunion in Dijon in
August, 1981, that the five-judge panel for the Special Chamber that Sir
Humphrey had prepared to propose to the Full Court would not have been
limited in its membership to North America and Western Europe, but would
have been broadly representative of the principal legal systems of the World
and also the main political-geographical regions; and that the five-judge
panel would also have had some functional (Law of the Sea) specialisation
within its membership. It would also *not* have included judges of the same
nationality as the two parties. The principle of excluding, as judges on the
panel, nationals of the two state parties is especially persuasive if we
remember that the Special Chamber was to be limited to five judges only.
Sir Humphrey's disposition to exclude nationals of the two state parties is,
in any case, hardly explained, in the specific, *Gulf of Maine* context, by the
then U.S. judge, Richard Baxter's, overly polite willingness to recuse
himself on the basis of some notional prior "interest" (some earlier participation, as consultant, in work on the dossier of the case for one of the states
within the United States federal system). After President Sir Humphrey
Waldock's sudden death in the late summer of 1981, it was left to his
successor, the interim, Acting President, Judge Elias (Nigeria), to finalise
the arrangements for the panel for *Gulf of Maine*, for presentation for
approval by the Full Court. The Acting President's burden was complicated
not merely by the fact that the late President Waldock had himself intended
to preside over the Special Chamber in *Gulf of Maine*, but also by the
sudden death of the distinguished Danish jurist, Professor Sorensen (not a
member of the International Court) who had already been approached by
President Waldock and had agreed to serve in the *Gulf of Maine* Special
Chamber. Judge Baxter, the U.S. judge, had also died at this time; and

though he would not, by virtue of his own full accord with President Waldock, have been a member of the Special Chamber, the particular, seemingly somewhat precious or artificial, ground that Judge Baxter had advanced for voluntarily recusing himself from the panel membership, disappeared with him and would not be available in respect of his successor as U.S. judge on the Court.

In the result, the U.S. now pressed for the representation, in the five-judge panel for the Special Chamber in *Gulf of Maine*, of the new U.S. national judge on the Court, and this compelled, in accordance with the Court Statute's ordinary stipulations, the choice also of an *ad hoc* judge for Canada, leaving only three places remaining in the panel. These were filled by the then French, Italian, and West German judges on the International Court, with the extra complication, in the case of the choice of the French judge, that his legal term, as judge on the Court, had only two weeks remaining at the time of his appointment to the Special Chamber. This extra complication arose because, although the Court had already been renewed as to a third of its fifteen-judge membership in the October, 1981, regular, triennial elections to the Court, it was the "lame duck" Court that was convened on 20 January 1982 for purposes of deciding on the Full Court's Order legally constituting the Special Chamber. The renewed Full Bench of the International Court, with its new French national judge, Judge de Lacharrière, would not come into legal being until two weeks later. The appointment to the Special Chamber, in this way, of the about-to-retire French national judge, Judge Gros, was the subject of criticism, on general principle, in the Dissenting Opinions accompanying the Full Court's Order of 20 January 1982, formally constituting the Special Chamber.[76] Such criticism does not seem fully disposed of by the rather novel suggestion, advanced much later by the current U.S. national judge on the Court, that what was involved at the time may have been *ad hominem* objection by the then Soviet national judge on the Court to the particular French judge so named to the Special Chamber.[77]

The division, within the Full Court of the International Court, over constitution of the Special Chamber in *Gulf of Maine* is reflected in the Special Declaration by Judge Oda (Japan) and the Dissenting Opinions by Judge Morozov (Soviet Union) and Judge El-Khani (Syria) accompanying the Court Order. Judge Oda, in his Declaration, contented himself with the tart comment:

"While I voted in favour of the Order, it should in my view have been made known that the Court, for reasons best known to itself, has approved the composition of the Chamber entirely in accordance with the latest wishes of the parties as ascertained pursuant to Article 26,

paragraph 2, of the Statute and Article 17, paragraph 2, of the Rules of
Court."[78]

Judge Morozov, in his Dissenting Opinion, was more caustic. He, first of
all, considered that the *old* Bench of the Full Court's approval of the
members of the Special Chamber should have been postponed for the mere
two weeks necessary to enable the *new* Bench of the Full Court, as
reconstituted after the Autumn, 1981, regular elections to the Court, to
make the choices of judges involved. And Judge Morozov also castigated
the Court majority Order constituting the Special Chamber for taking as a –

> "point of departure the erroneous presumption that, contrary to Article
> 26, paragraph 2, of the Statute, the Parties ... may not merely choose
> what should be the number of the members of the Chamber, but also
> formally decide and propose the names of the judges who should be
> elected by secret ballot, and even present these proposals to the Court in
> the form of some kind of ultimatum."[79]

In categorically rejecting what he characterised as the "incorrect presumption of the Parties that they may dictate to the Court who should be
elected", Judge Morozov insisted on the "sovereign right of the Court to
carry out the election independently of the wishes of the Parties, by secret
ballot in accordance with the provisions of the Statute and Rules of
Court."[80]

Judge El-Khani, in his Dissenting Opinion, was equally scornful of the
Court majority's acceptance of the parties' dictate as to the composition and
membership of the Special Chamber:

> "I find that the imposition of an unduly close time limit for the Cham-
> ber's formation and of a particular composition renders the Court no
> longer master of its own acts, deprives it of its freedom of choice and is
> an obstacle to the proper administration of justice. Furthermore it
> diminishes the prestige of the Court and is harmful to its dignity as the
> principal judicial organ of the United Nations. It results in its regionalisa-
> tion by depriving it of its basic and essential characteristic of univer-
> sality .... On these grounds I find that this ought not to constitute a
> precedent, as it would be a dangerous course to follow in the future."[81]

In retrospect, the Special Chamber system within the International Court, as
actually interpreted and applied by the Court majority in *Gulf of Maine*,
begins to look like a reform *manqué*, with too little consideration by the
judicial majority of the effects on the Court *qua* judicial and not arbitral
tribunal, and on the integrity of the judicial process, of ceding to the parties'
dictates as to the actual membership of the Chamber. Such a particularised
interpretation, as already noted, was not merely not required by the language of the Court Statute but ran counter to the words used and also, it

may be suggested, to their spirit. The reform by way of the Special Chamber institution, in any case, seems to have been ventured upon too late and only after the pressures for creation of autonomous tribunals, functionally-specialised by subject matter (as with the Law of the Sea), and jurisdictionally separate and distinct from the International Court, had gathered political strength within the United Nations and its specialised negotiating conferences. It might also be suggested that, in their actual choice of judges for the Special Chamber, as accepted and ratified by the Full Court in its Order creating the Chamber, the two state parties in *Gulf of Maine* took a rather narrowly parochial view of a substantive (Law of the Sea) problem with a genuinely transcultural, legal dimension, and with multi-systemic legal implications in the "progressive development of International Law" as enjoined by the United Nations Charter.

The U.S. judge on the International Court, Judge Schwebel, has suggested that in its actual, substantive-legal ruling, the Special Chamber in Gulf of Maine, notwithstanding its wholly Western, (North American and West European), composition, did not manifest "a peculiarly 'Western' or 'Atlantic' outlook".[82] Yet it is, of course, a decision couched in carefully chosen, analytical-positivist terms, without openings to that "new" International Law of the Sea that was at the core of the debate in the marathon sessions of the Third United Nations Conference on the Law of the Sea throughout the decade of the 1970s and on to the Final Act of 1982. The analytical-positivist approach may well, in the view of the judges composing the Special Chamber in *Gulf of Maine*, have been enjoined by the particular subject matter of the dispute involved, and by the plethora of technical, historical source materials, on which counsel for the two parties chose to base their respective legal arguments. The two parties were of course also, in United Nations' parlance, "like-minded states", and they shewed no evident public interest or concern for having their case used as a vehicle for re-making International Law so as better to conform to new societal imperatives of the contemporary World Community. The analytical-positivist approach, at this particular time in international relations and in International Law, tends to correspond very well to the rather more defensive attitudes to legal change to be found in some key Western Foreign Ministries; and it may, in this sense, rightly be considered as "Western" rather than universal.

That alternative, and different, intellectual-legal approaches were still possible, however, in the particular fact-context of *Gulf of Maine* seems amply confirmed by the Dissenting Opinion filed by Judge Oda to a subsequent judgment rendered by the fifteen-judge Full Court in *Continental Shelf (Libyan Arab Jamahiriya/Malta).*[83] Judge Oda and Judge

Nagendra Singh were the two most widely-recognised experts on the Law of the Sea in the Court's ranks at the time the *Gulf of Maine* panel was formed, and they had been excluded from the joint list of judges for the five-judge Chamber submitted by the two parties to the Full Court and accepted by the Full Court in its Order constituting the Chamber. In his Dissenting Opinion in *Continental Shelf (Libyan Arab Jamahiriya/Malta)*, Judge Oda took the opportunity of making a detailed critique of the holding by the Special Chamber in *Gulf of Maine* and its stated legal rationale, writing what amounted, in the relevant parts of his Opinion, to an *ex post facto* Dissent to the Special Chamber judgement in *Gulf of Maine*.[84]

This raises the question of the claims to general legal authority, as International Court *jurisprudence*, of judgments rendered by five-judge Special Chambers, as distinct from judgments of the Full Court. The Court Statute itself affirms, in its Article 27, that judgments rendered by the Chambers provided for in its Article 26 – "shall be considered as rendered by the Court."[85] Of course the International Court, as a plural-systemic tribunal, is not in any way constrained by Anglo-Saxon Common Law-style notions of *Stare Decisis*. Article 59 of the Court Statute declares that any decision of the Court – "has no binding force except between the parties and in respect of that particular case." The conclusion seems clear that the legal authority, for the future, of any Special Chamber decision must rest on the intellectual persuasiveness and power of its own internal reasoning and its response to rapidly changing societal conditions in the World Community; and that the legal-cultural balance, or representativeness, of a Special Chamber's judicial composition for any case must be a major factor in any claims for legal authority advanced in behalf of its final ruling.

The strong intellectual reservations voiced by the three judges who chose to file either Declaration or Dissenting Opinions to the Court's Order of 1982 constituting the Special Chamber in *Gulf of Maine*, seem to have made their mark on those judges' colleagues on the Court. Perhaps it has also been relevant that the successive Court Presidents, (whose *rôle* in communicating to the Full Court the views of the states parties to a dispute as to composition of a Special Chamber, is the key one under Article 17(2) of the present, 1978, Rules of Court), have, in the immediate aftermath of *Gulf of Maine* and up to the present, come from non-Western or at least non-aligned states (Judge Elias (Nigeria), and then Judge Nagendra Singh (India)) and then Judge Ruda (Argentina)). It is to be noted that Judge Elias, though he was the Acting President of the Court at the time the first Special Chamber was formally constituted by the Full Court, in *Gulf of Maine*, and then was President of the Court in his own right for the succeeding normal three-year term, has pointedly avoided himself serving as a member of a

Special Chamber, then or thereafter. As Judge Elias has commented, in relation to the extended political manoeuvring by the state parties preceding the Full Court vote on formal constitution of the panel for *Gulf of Maine*:

"President Waldock having begun his consultation with the parties earlier in the year 1981 before his untimely death which had included the discussions as to the number to form the Chamber and also the names of the judges to compose the Chamber, Acting President Elias had no choice but to resume the negotiations at that point when the Chamber procedure was received in the *Gulf of Maine* case. The question of forming a Chamber on the procedure of consultation between the President and the parties was pointed out as a *fait accompli*, to re-open which the parties regarded as taking a dangerous step."[86]

Judge Elias, on the general issue of the political and legal merits of Special Chambers of the Court as an alternative to, or substitute for, the normal, fifteen-member, Full Court jurisdiction, leaves no doubt as to his own considered opinion:

"There is common sense in the view that the opinion of the majority of a high calibre of judges such as those of the International Court of Justice is more likely to arrive at a modicum of acceptable justice than is a verdict arrived at by a small body of judges of about five chosen as friends of both parties, however knowledgeable these friendly judges might be....

"This seems to point out another but analogous criticism of the Chamber procedure; the principle that it smacked too much of a parochial application of the judicial process, involving a feeling that, after all, the judgment of the Chamber had been arrived at as a compromise solution to the problem raised therein, and not as what is absolutely the best in the circumstances. This stems from one's feeling of unease that what in an arbitration is arrived at in the end is not necessarily the right one, but what is acceptable in the circumstances to the parties whose friends the arbitrators were; those who paid the piper could call the tune, and what is insidious about it all is that the whole Chamber procedure smacks too much of an arbitration procedure covered up under the garb of the International Court by the provision of Article 27 of the Statute of the Court, saying that the judgment of the Chamber is to be considered as the judgment of the Court."[87]

The first Special Chamber constituted after *Gulf of Maine* involved, once again, a strictly "regional" dispute, this time between two recently Decolonised, francophonic African states. Nevertheless, for *Frontier Dispute (Burkina Faso/Mali)*,[88] the Special Chamber, as constituted by the Full Court in 1985, was now determinedly representative in inter-cultural, inter-systemic terms: Judge Lachs (Poland), Judge Ruda (Argentina), and Judge Bedjaoui (Algeria), with two *ad hoc* judges (neither of the state parties to the dispute having a national on the Full Court), Judge Luchaire (France) and Judge Abi-Saab (Egypt).

The next Special Chamber was formed in 1987 for a commercial case involving the U.S. and Italy. The Special Chamber's establishment had been presaged in the U.S. State Department public announcements of the U.S. withdrawal from the Compulsory Jurisdiction of the International Court, following on the Court's Preliminary rulings in *Nicaragua* in 1984.[89] It was seemingly offered by the U.S. State Department, then, as a token of the U.S.' continued commitment to the principle of international judicial settlement, albeit with the nuance of a distinguishing between rejection of the jurisdiction of the Full Court (which the U.S. Administration now characterised as too "political"), and the acceptance of the jurisdiction of a limited, five-judge panel of the Court in whose selection, according to the U.S. Administration's own interpretation of the Court Statute and Court Rules, the state parties' choice (and, if desired, their veto) would be controlling upon the Full Court.

For *Elettronica Sicula S.p.A (Elsi)* (*United States of America* v. *Italy*),[90] the membership of the Special Chamber, as announced by the Full Court, comprised President Nagendra Singh (India), Judge Oda (Japan), Judge Jennings (United Kingdom); plus Judge Ago (Italy) and Judge Schwebel (U.S.A.). For *Land, Island and Maritime Frontier Dispute* (*El Salvador/Honduras*),[91] – once again a strictly "regional" (Central American) dispute – the Special Chamber, as constituted by the Full Court, later in 1987, comprised Judge Oda (Japan), Judge Sette-Camara (Brazil), Judge Jennings (United Kingdom); plus two *ad hoc* judges (neither of the state parties to the dispute having a national on the Full Court) Judge Valticos (Greece) and Judge Virally (France).

What seems to have emerged, in the developed Full Court practice, after the obvious mis-steps in the process of constitution of the first Special Chamber, in *Gulf of Maine*, is a continuing, civilised dialogue between the fifteen-member Full Court (through its President) and the parties to a dispute desiring to proceed by the Special Chamber route. In such new, post-*Gulf of Maine* practice, the Court President is able to take full account of the state parties' views; but the President will maintain the integrity of the International Court, *qua* judicial tribunal, by having the Full Court, and not the parties, determine the final choice of judges for the panel for the Special Chamber.[92] In the result, in the aftermath of *Gulf of Maine*, such Special Chambers as have been formed have all revealed, in their actual membership, a sensitiveness to the needs, in the plural World Community of today, to have panels that are as plural and representative as possible, in inter-cultural, inter-systemic terms. If the state parties to a particular dispute do not like that, then they can always exercise their right to go to some other mode of settlement than judicial settlement – arbitration, for example, in which the state parties would, *ex hypothesi*, have full control of the choice of the arbitrators. The state parties would, of course, thereby eschew the extra prestige attaching to any final decision to their dispute deriving from its having been rendered by the International Court.

The advantages of having an International Court decision, as opposed to an International Arbitral award, under a system where the Full Court determines the composition of the Special Chamber in consultation with the parties, must evidently be considerable, judging by the current disposition of states – and especially "new", ex-Colonial states – to utilise the Court, in its Special Chamber jurisdiction, for settlement of their disputes. As Judge Oda has reminded us, it is a not unimportant additional consideration that the Special Chambers, – apart from their presumed extra speed in disposing of cases because of their extra flexibility in comparison to the numerically much larger, Full Court – are also, as part of the International Court, able to use the Court's premises and all its other facilities.[93] This means, in the case of very many of the "new", ex-Colonial states, avoiding the heavy financial burden, involved in Arbitrations, of having themselves to pay the Arbitrators' salaries and allowances, and also having to mcct costs of special court rooms and administrative and support services.

In retrospect, it may be noted that one of the strong political arguments advanced by the proponents of the Special Chamber system, at the time of the *Gulf of Maine* at the opening of the decade of the 1980s – namely, that the fifteen-member Full Court could attract no cases, and that it was necessary to concede to state parties the right to pick and choose their own judges for the limited, five-member panels, if the Court were to remain viable – is amply refuted in the empirical record of the Court's agenda and case load at the close of the decade. The list of cases prepared then by the International Court's Registrar shews that since *Nicaragua v. U.S.A. Merits* was decided on 27 June 1986, the fifteen-member Full Court had decided three cases, with a fourth removed from the general list, and with seven further cases pending before the Full Court. By comparison, only two cases had been decided by five-member Special Chambers, with one further such case pending.[94] Of these two cases decided by Special Chambers, *Elsi (U.S. v. Italy)* has a certain element of the contrived and precious, as a relatively trivial or anodine commercial case involving a U.S. Company and its foreign affiliate. The respondent State, Italy, could reasonably have chosen to contest more strongly the U.S. *jus standi*; the Court might properly have concluded that the case was not receivable after all. As it was, all parties seemed disposed to be cooperative in facilitating an apparent small gesture of reconciliation by the U.S. to the jurisdiction of the Court, after the earlier U.S. Administration attacks on the *Nicaragua* rulings (1984–1986), and after the U.S. withdrawal in 1985 from the Compulsory Jurisdiction of the Court.[95]

## NOTES

1. *Official Documents*: "Soviet Union accepts Compulsory Jurisdiction of ICJ for Six Human Rights Conventions", *American Journal of International Law*, vol. 83 (1989), p. 457.
2. *I.C.J. Yearbook 1984–1985*, p. 99.
3. *Nicaragua v. United States of America, Jurisdiction and Admissibility, Judgment*, I.C.J. Reports 1984, p. 392.
4. *Nicaragua v. United States of America, Provisional Measures, Order of 10 May 1984*, I.C.J. Reports 1984, p. 169.
5. "Statement by Department of State on U.S. Withdrawal from Nicaragua Proceedings, 18 January 1985", in "Contemporary Practice of the United States", *American Journal of International Law*, vol. 79 (1985), pp. 438, 441; *International Legal Materials*, vol. 24 (1985), p. 246.
6. "United States: Department of State Letter and Statement concerning termination of Acceptance of I.C.J. Compulsory Jurisdiction, 7 October 1985", *International Legal Materials*, vol. 24 (1985), p. 1742.
7. Sofaer, "The United States and the World Court", *Proceedings of the American Society of International Law*, (1986), p. 204, p. 206.
8. See, in this regard, Judge Oda's comprehensive survey, "Reservations in the Declarations of Acceptance of the Optional Clause and the Period of Validity of those Declarations: the effect of the Shultz Letter, " *British Year Book of International Law* (1988), p. 1.
9. Sofaer, *Proceedings of the American Society of International Law*, (1986), p. 204, at p. 207.
10. *Ibid.*, pp. 206–7. And see Oda, *op. cit.*, *British Year Book of International Law* (1988), p. 1.
11. *Ibid.*, p. 207.
12. *Ibid.*
13. *Ibid.*, p. 205.
14. *Ibid.*, p. 206.
15. *Nuclear Tests (Australia v. France), Interim Protection, Order of 22 June 1973*, I.C.J. Reports 1973, p. 99. And see, generally, *The World Court and the Contemporary International Law-Making Process* (1979), p. 40 *et seq.*
16. *Nicaragua v. United States of America, Jurisdiction and Admissibility, Judgment*, I.C.J. Reports 1984, p. 392.
17. *Border and Transborder Armed Actions (Nicaragua v. Honduras), Jurisdiction and Admissibility, Judgment*, I.C.J. Reports 1988, p. 69.
18. Court Statute, Art. 37: "Whenever a treaty or convention in force provides for reference

of a matter to a tribunal to have been instituted by the League of Nations, or to the Permanent Court of International Justice, the matter shall, as between the parties to the present Statute, be referred to the International Court of Justice."

19. See *Nuclear Tests. (Australia v. France), Judgment of 20 December 1974*, I.C.J. Reports 1974, p. 253.
20. *Ibid.*, p. 372, at p. 384.
21. *I.C.J. Yearbook 1984–1985*, p. 99.
22. *Nicaragua v. United States of America. Jurisdiction and Admissibility. Judgment*, I.C.J. Reports 1984, p. 392, at pp. 416–419 (Opinion of Court).
23. I.C.J. Reports 1988, p. 69.
24. *Ibid.*, p. 71.
25. Declaration (Judge Lachs), *ibid.*, p. 108; Separate Opinion (Judge Oda), *ibid.*, p. 109; Separate Opinion (Judge Schwebel), *ibid.*, p. 126; Separate Opinion (Judge Shahabuddeen), *ibid.*, p. 133.
26. *Ibid.*, p. 109.
27. *Ibid.*, pp. 124–5 (Oda J., Separate Opinion). This emphasis upon consent of the parties as the basic premise on which present jurisdiction must be founded – and, seemingly, a continuing subjective consent and not merely a presumed consent, – is at the basis, also, of Judge Oda's detailed survey of state practice as to acceptance of the Optional Clause: Oda, *op. cit., British Year Book of International Law* (1988), p. 1. And see also Mosler, "Jurisdiktion und Konsens der Parteien, " *Festschrift für Karl Josef Partsch zum 75 Geburtstag*, (1989), p. 253; Oellers-Frahm, "Probleme und Grenzen der obligatorischen Gerichtsbarkeit," *Archiv des Völkerrechts*, vol. 27 (1989), p. 442.
28. *Nuclear Tests (Australia v. France) Judgment of 20 December 1974*, I.C.J. Reports 1974, p. 253.
29. *Nuclear Tests (Australia v. France), Interim Protection, Order of 22 June 1973*, I.C.J. Reports 1973, p. 99.
30. "Statement by Department of State on U.S. Withdrawal from Nicaragua Proceedings, 18 January 1985", *American Journal of International Law*, vol. 79 (1985), pp. 438, 441; *International Legal Materials*, vol. 24 (1985), p. 246, p. 248.
31. Sofaer, "The United States and the World Court", *Proceedings of the American Society of International Law* (1986), p. 204, p. 207.
32. *Ibid.*
33. *International Legal Materials*, vol. 24 (1985), p. 246, p. 248.
34. I.C.J. Reports 1986, p. 14, at 259 (Schwebel J., Dissenting Opinion).
35. *Ibid.*, p. 351.
36. I.C.J. Reports 1986, p. 14, at p. 528 (Jennings J., Dissenting Opinion).
37. "Statement by Department of State on U.S. Withdrawal from Nicaragua Proceedings, 18 January 1985", *American Journal of International Law*, vol. 79 (1985), p. 438; *International Legal Materials*, vol. 24 (1985), p. 246, p. 248.
38. Judge Manfred Lachs, Letter-to-the-Editor, "Inconsistency in Judging Judges", *The New York Times*, New York, 26 July 1986.
39. *Ibid.* And see also Lachs, "A few thoughts on the Independence of Judges on the International Court of Justice", *Columbia Journal of Transnational Law*, vol. 25 (1987), p. 593.
40. Lachs, Letter-to-the-Editor, *The New York Times*. 26 July 1986. In a somewhat unusual step, the British judge, Sir Robert Jennings, who had been one of the three Dissenters in the Court's 12-to-3 majority holding against the U.S. in *Merits, Judgment* in 1986, took

the step of publicly dissociating himself, in his Dissenting Opinion, from the U.S. State Department's public attack on the integrity of the Soviet and Socialist bloc judges on the Court:

"I also wish to express my regret that, in a Court which by its Statute is elected in such a way as to assure 'the representation of the main forms of civilisation and of the principal legal systems of the World', the United States in its statement accompanying the announcement of the non-participation in the present phase of the case should have chosen to refer to the national origins of two of the Judges who took part in the earlier phases of the case". I.C.J. Reports 1986, p. 14, p. 528 (Jennings J., Dissenting Opinion).

41. I.C.J. Reports 1988, p. 69, p. 108 (Lachs J., Declaration). In addition to the nineteen Judgments in which he had participated while a member of the International Court, Judge Lachs had also participated in five Advisory Opinions and in four of these he had been with the Court majority. In the one Advisory Opinion in which Judge Lachs had been in the minority on the Court, the U.S. judge had also been in the minority. Lachs, *Columbia Journal of Transnational Law*, vol. 25 (1987), p. 593, p. 596. And see also Lachs, Letter-to-the-Editor, *American Journal of International Law*, vol. 84 (1990), p. 231.

42. I.C.J. Reports 1986, p. 14.

43. *Status of Eastern Carelia, Advisory Opinion of 23 July 1923*, P.C.I.J. Series B, No. 5, p. 7.

44. Vyshinsky, *The Law of the Soviet State* (1938) (English transl., Babb), (1954)), p. 241.

45. *South West Africa, Second Phase, Judgment*, I.C.J. Reports 1966, p. 6.

46. Zile, "A Soviet contribution to International Adjudication: Professor Krylov's jurisprudential legacy", *American Journal of International Law*, vol. 58 (1964), p. 359.

47. *Ibid.*, p. 384.

48. *Ibid.*

49. I.C.J. Reports 1948, p. 15.

50. I.C.J. Reports 1949, p. 4.

51. I.C.J. Reports 1948, p. 57.

52. *Ibid.*, pp. 108–9 (Krylov J., Dissenting Opinion).

53. I.C.J. Reports 1950, p. 4.

54. Günther, *Sondervoten sowjetischer Richter am Internationalen Gerichtshof* (1966), p. 126.

55. *Ibid.*, pp. 125–6. And see, generally, Alvarez, *Le droit international nouveau dans ses rapports avec la vie actuelle des peuples* (1959).

56. I.C.J. Reports 1962, p. 151.

57. U.N. Charter, Art. 19:

"A Member of the United Nations which is in arrears in the payment of its financial contributions to the Organisation shall have no vote in the General Assembly if the amount of its arrears equals or exceeds the amount due from it for the preceding two full years ..."

58. I.C.J. Reports 1962, p. 151, p. 230.

59. I.C.J. Reports 1962, p. 151, p. 268.

60. Samore, "The World Court Statute and Impartiality of Judges", *Nebraska Law Review*, vol. 34 (1955), p. 618, p. 628.

61. I.C.J. Reports 1966, p. 6, p. 323 (Jessup J., Dissenting Opinion).

62. I.C.J. Reports 1962, p. 151.

63. I.C.J. Reports 1962, p. 151.
64. I.C.J. Reports 1966, p. 6.
65. I.C.J. Reports 1966, p. 6, p. 237 (Koretsky J., Dissenting Opinion).
66. "Statement on the U.S. Withdrawal from the Proceedings initiated by Nicaragua in the International Court of Justice, 18 January 1985", *International Legal Materials*, vol. 24 (1985), p. 246, p. 249.
67. *Delimitation of the Maritime Boundary in the Gulf of Maine Area, Constitution of Chamber, Order of 20 January 1982*, I.C.J. Reports 1982, p. 3; *Judgment*, I.C.J. Reports 1984, p. 246.
68. "Department of State Letter and Statement concerning Termination of Acceptance of I.C.J. Compulsory Jurisdiction, 7 October 1985", *International Legal Materials*, vol. 24 (1985), p. 1742.
69. *International Legal Materials*, vol. 24 (1985), p. 246, p. 247.
70. *International Legal Materials*, vol. 24 (1985), p. 1742, p. 1744.
71. *Ibid.*, p. 1745.
72. Lachs, "The Revised Procedure of the International Court of Justice", in *Essays on the Development of the International Legal Order* (Kalshoven, Kuyper, and Lammers, eds.) (1980), p. 21, p. 42.
73. *Ibid.*, p. 44.
74. I.C.J. Reports 1982, p. 3; I.C.J. Reports 1984, p. 246.
75. The public controversy, since the announcement of the Court's Preliminary ruling in *Gulf of Maine, Constitution of Chamber, Order of 20 January 1982*, I.C.J. Reports 1982, p. 3, has undoubtedly been stimulated by the special Declaration and also the two Dissenting Opinions annexed to that ruling (see, *infra*). The Court has not yet published its official records on the committee discussion leading up to the 1978 revisions to the Rules of Court. Judge Lachs and Judge Jiménez de Aréchaga, as members of the Court committee, could no doubt provide authoritative and conclusive guidance as to the intentions of the Court drafters as to the 1978 revised Rules, but neither has yet chosen to make public comment. Judge Jiménez de Aréchaga did comment, in 1973, on the earlier, 1972, Rules of Court: "The Amendment to the Rules of Procedure of the International Court of Justice", *American Journal of International Law*, vol. 67 (1973), p. 1. The current U.S. member of the Court, Judge Schwebel, who was not, however, a member of the Court at the time either of the 1972 or the 1978 revisions to the Rules of Court, has offered his own views: "*Ad Hoc* Chambers of the International Court of Justice", *American Journal of International Law*, vol. 81 (1987), p. 831. And see the response thereto by the present writer, *ibid.*, vol. 82 (1988), p. 797; and also the thoughtful, highly nuanced comments by Judge Oda (who had appended a special Declaration to the Court's 1982 ruling in *Gulf of Maine. Constitution of Chamber*), "Further thoughts on the Chambers Procedure of the International Court of Justice", *ibid.*, vol. 82 (1988), p. 556. More generally, see the present writer's "Special Chambers within the International Court of Justice: the Preliminary, Procedural Aspect of the *Gulf of Maine* case", *Syracuse Journal of International Law and Commerce*, vol. 12 (1985), p. 1; Guyomar, "La constitution au sein de la Cour Internationale de Justice d'une Chambre chargée de régler le différend de frontières maritimes entre les Etats-unis et le Canada", *Annuaire Français de Droit International*, vol. 27 (1981), p. 213; Stern, "Chronique de jurisprudence de la Cour internationale de Justice", *Journal de Droit International*, vol. 111 (1984), p. 652; Zoller, "La première constitution d'une Chambre spéciale par la Cour internationale de Justice. Observations sur l'Ordonnance du 20

janvier 1982", *Revue Générale de Droit International Public*, vol. 86 (1982), p. 305.
And see also Mosler, "Aktuelle Aspekte des Verfahrensrechts des Internationalen
Gerichtshofes", in *Völkerrecht und Rechtsphilosophie (Internationale Festschrift für
Stephan Verosta zum 70 Geburtstag* (Fischer, Kock, and Verdross, eds.) (1980), p. 249;
Oellers-Frahm, "Internal Subdivisions of International Judicial Institutions", in *Reports
on German Public Law* (XIII International Congress of Comparative Law) (Bernhardt
and Beyerlin (eds.) (1990), p. 29; Meyer, *Archiv des Völkerrechts*, vol. 27 (1989),
p. 414.

76. *Gulf of Maine, Constitution of Chamber, Order of 20 January 1982*, I.C.J. Reports
    1982, p. 3, p. 11 (Morozov J., Dissenting Opinion); p. 12, p. 13 (El-Khani J., Dissenting
    Opinion).

77. Schwebel, *op. cit.*, *American Journal of International Law*, vol. 81 (1987), p. 831, p.
    845. Judge Schwebel's objection on this particular point is directed to Judge Morozov:
    he does not offer any explanation for Judge El-Khani's similar criticism.

78. *Gulf of Maine, Constitution of Chamber, Order of 20 January 1982*, I.C.J. Reports
    1982, p. 3, p. 10 (Oda J., Declaration).

79. *Ibid.*, p. 11.

80. *Ibid.*

81. *Ibid.*, p. 12.

82. Schwebel, *op. cit.*, p. 846.

83. I.C.J. Reports 1985, p. 13.

84. I.C.J. Reports 1985, p. 13, pp. 165–9.

85. The claims to legal authority for a decision by a Special Chamber, which Article 27 of
    the Court Statute would establish by legislative fiat, may be somewhat deflated by
    Ambassador Rosenne's historical explanation of the rather banal circumstances under
    which the present Article 27 was conceived and drafted in the first place, as a mere
    cosmetic provision, conveniently designed to retain the enumeration of the Court
    Statute as originally drafted: "Article 27 of the Statute creates the legal fiction that a
    decision of a Chamber is 'considered as rendered by the Court'. This is a purely formal
    statement which was inserted into the Statute in 1945 primarily to preserve the
    numbering of the subsequent provisions, Article 27 of Statute of the Permanent Court of
    International Justice having been dropped, and to remove any doubt over the applica-
    tion of Article 94 of the Charter to decisions of Chambers. A judgment of the Court
    does not 'bind' Members of the Court who did not take part in the decision, and by the
    same token decisions of Chambers cannot 'bind' any Member of the Court who was not
    a member of the Chamber. This increases the difficulty of pinpointing the position of
    the Court on these matters."
    Rosenne, "Equity", in *Forty Years International Court of Justice: Jurisdiction, Equity
    and Equality* (Bloed and van Dijk, eds.) (1988), 87, 93.

86. Elias, *The United Nations Charter and the World Court* (1989), p. 212.

87. *Ibid.*, pp. 217–8.

88. *Frontier Dispute (Burkina Faso/Mali), Constitution of Chamber, Order of 3 April 1985*,
    I.C.J. Reports 1985, p. 6.

89. *International Legal Materials*, vol. 24 (1985), p. 1742, p. 1745.

90. *Elettronica Sicula S.p.A (Elsi), (U.S.A. v. Italy), Constitution of Chamber, Order of 2
    March 1987*, I.C.J. Reports 1987, p. 3.

91. *Land, Island and Maritime Frontier Dispute (El Salvador/Honduras), Constitution of
    Chamber, Order of 8 May 1987*, I.C.J. Reports 1987, p. 10; and see Zimmermann, "Die

Entscheidung im Streitfall vor dem IGH zwischen El Salvador und Honduras", *Zeitschrift für ausländisches öffentliches Recht und Völkerrecht*, vol. 50 (1990), p. 646.

92. Judge Oda, in his Declaration attached to *Land, Island and Maritime Frontier Dispute (El Salvador/Honduras), Constitution of Chamber, Order of 8 May 1987*, (I.C.J. Reports 1987, p. 10, at p. 13), sums up the presently developed practice of the Court as to Special Chambers, in the light of the stipulations in Article 26(2) of the Court Statute and Article 17(2) of the Rules of Court: "The Court, being sovereign in judicial proceedings, is free to choose any composition it likes; yet the possibility must also be borne in mind that sovereign States have the legal right to withdraw a case if they prefer a composition different from that determined by the Court. In practical terms, therefore, it is inevitable, if a chamber is to be viable, that its composition must result from a consensus between the parties and the Court. To ensure that viability, it accordingly behoves the Court to take account of the views of the parties when proceeding to the election. Nevertheless, the Chamber is a component of the Court, bound by its Statute and Rules; and the process of election whereby it comes into being should be as judicially impartial as its subsequent functioning."

93. Oda, "Further Thoughts on the Chambers Procedure of the International Court of Justice", *American Journal of International Law*, vol. 82 (1988), p. 556, p. 562.

94. List of cases before Court since *Nicaragua v. U.S.A. (Merits)*, decided on 27 June 1986: [as supplied by the Registrar, International Court of Justice].

*Before Full Court*
*Decided*:
> *Application for Review of Judgement No. 333 of the United Nations Administrative Tribunal* (Advisory Opinion of 27 May 1987)
>
> *Applicability of the Obligation to Arbitrate under Section 21 of the United Nations Headquarters Agreement of 26 June 1947* (Advisory Opinion of 26 April 1988)
>
> *Border and Transborder Armed Actions (Nicaragua v. Honduras): Jurisdiction of the Court and Admissibility of the Application* (Judgment of 20 December 1988)

*Removed from General List*:
> *Border and Transborder Armed Actions (Nicaragua v. Costa Rica)* (Order of 19 August 1987)

*Pending*:
> *Military and Paramilitary Activities in and against Nicaragua (Nicaragua v. United States of America)* (Compensation)
>
> *Border and Transborder Armed Actions (Nicaragua v. Honduras)* (Merits) [likelihood of discontinuance]
>
> *Maritime Delimitation in the Area between Greenland and Jan Mayen* (Denmark v. Norway)
>
> *Aerial Incident of 3 July 1988 (Islamic Republic of Iran v. United States of America)*
>
> *Certain Phosphate Lands in Nauru (Nauru v. Australia)*
>
> *Applicability of Article VI, Section 22, of the Convention on the Privileges and*

*Immunities of the United Nations* (ECOSOC request for advisory opinion)

*Arbitral Award of 31 July 1989* (Guinea-Bissau v. Sénégal)

———

*Before Chambers*
*Decided*:
*Frontier Dispute (Burkina Faso/Republic of Mali)*: Judgment of 22 December 1986

*Elettronica Sicula S.p.A (ELSI)*: Judgment of 20 July 1989

*Pending*:
*Land, Island and Maritime Frontier Dispute (El Salvador/Honduras)*

95. See, in this regard, Wengler, "Die Entscheidung des IGH im '*Elsi*'-Fall," *Neue Juristische Wochenschrift*, (1990), (no. 10), p. 619, (7 March 1990); Jeancolas, "L'Arrêt Elettronica Sicula S.p.A (*ELSI*) du 20 juillet 1989", *Revue Générale de Droit International Public*, vol. 94 (1990), p. 701, at p. 703, p. 708, pp. 709–13.

CHAPTER IV


# The Contemporary International Court as Independent, and as Representative Tribunal


## 1. JUDICIAL INDEPENDENCE, AND JUDICIAL "INTEREST"

The International Court of Justice, as successor to the old, Permanent Court of International Justice of the between-the-two-World-Wars era, is constituted, under the United Nations Charter, as "the principal judicial organ of the United Nations".[1] The provisions as to selection of the Court's judges are established in the Court's Statute. The Court is to consist of "fifteen members, no two of whom may be nationals of the same state";[2] and these are to be elected by the U.N. General Assembly and Security Council,[3] from a list of persons "nominated by the national groups in the Permanent Court of Arbitration" or by *ad hoc* national groups specially appointed by their governments for that purpose.[4] As to the qualifications of the judges, the Court Statute stipulates that the Court shall be: –

"composed of a body of independent judges, elected regardless of their nationality from among persons of high moral character, who possess the qualifications required in their respective countries for appointment to the highest judicial offices, or are jurisconsults of recognised competence in international law."[5]

As the Nigerian jurist, Taslim Elias, – sometime distinguished academic scholar in his own right, and thereafter national civil servant and national Supreme Court justice, and, most recently, Judge (and also President) of the International Court –, has noted, these provisions as to judicial independence and moral character correspond to the "requirement ... commonly acknowledged, at least in theory, in nearly all legal systems in the world today."[6]

The particular requirement of judicial independence, interpreted as it has tended to be in Municipal, national law, as excluding judges who have a personal "interest" in the outcome of a case from participating in the hearings or deliberations or final decision, has presented only occasional controversies. The Court Statute provides for a member of the Court's voluntarily recusing himself, and it also allows of the Court President's notifying any member – "if the President considers that for some special reason [that member] should not sit in a particular case", with the matter to be settled by decision of the Court as a whole in the event of disagreement between the President and the member concerned.[7] In the *South West Africa. Second Phase* in 1966,[8] a personally strong Court President, Sir Percy Spender (Australia), successfully (and without Court vote) had insisted that a Court member, Sir Mohammed Zafrullah Khan (Pakistan), recuse himself on the ground of his earlier participation in U.N. General Assembly discussions on the general issues involved in the case. The final Court decision in *South West Africa. Second Phase* was rendered only by an 8-to-7 vote, on the second, tie-breaking vote exercised by Judge Spender in his capacity as President. Since Judge Zafrullah Khan would almost certainly have voted with the seven (as it turned out) minority judges in favour of the Court's exercising jurisdiction to decide on the non-applicability of the *Apartheid régime* of racial separation to the former League of Nations Mandate, (now U.N. Trust Territory) of Namibia (South West Africa), the denial of his participation and vote in the case effectively determined the final outcome of the Court's decision. It then, inevitably, became part of the subsequent political back-lash against the Court in the storm over the *South West Africa. Second Phase* decision and its practical consequences.[9] In a subsequent Court *volte face*, in the *Namibia* Advisory Opinion in 1971,[10] the Court, in apparent reaction to the bitter political and legal criticisms levelled against it, in the U.N. General Assembly and elsewhere in the intervening five years, in effect "corrected" the 1966 decision (by lop-sided, 13-to-2 and 11-to-4, votes, on the main substantive-legal issues).

The *Namibia* Advisory Opinion of 1971 was preceded by its own skirmishes over preliminary, procedural issues going to the question of judicial disqualification for alleged "interest". The (white minority) Government of South Africa, in the Court hearings on *Namibia*, mounted objections against three members of the Court, – Judge-President Zafrullah Khan, and Judges Padilla Nervo and Morozov, – based upon their past involvement in various activities, within the United Nations. In terms of the official Opinion of Court, the white minority Government of South Africa's complaints against the three judges focussed upon allegations as to: –

"statements made or other participation by the Members concerned, in their former capacity as representatives of their Governments, in United Nations Organs which were dealing with matters concerning South West

Africa ...; activities in United Nations organs of the Members concerned, prior to their election to the Court ...; participation of the Member concerned, prior to his election to the Court, in the formulation of Security Council resolution 246 (1968), which concerned the trial at Pretoria of thirty-seven South West Africans and which in its preamble took into account General Assembly resolution 2145 (XXI)."[11]

The Full Court in *Namibia* rejected, by unanimous vote, the Government of South Africa's objections to Judge-President Zafrullah Khan[12] and to Judge Padilla Nervo;[13] and the Court also rejected, by a 10-to-4 vote, the objection to Judge Morozov.[14] Judge Fitzmaurice, in an Annex to his Dissenting Opinion to the official Opinion of Court in *Namibia*, remarked, caustically:

"In the light of the explanations as to this, given in the Opinion of the Court, it has now to be concluded that, outside the literal terms of Article 17, paragraph 2, of the Statute, no previous connection with the subject-matter of a case, however close, can prevent a judge from sitting, unless he himself elects as a matter of conscience not to do so".[15]

Judge Gros, in his own Dissenting Opinion, was even more bitter:

"The Court's decision contradicts the principle, to which Article 17 of the Statute lends formal expression, that a Member must not participate in the decision in any case in which he has previously taken part in some other capacity. This Article, moreover, is an application of a generally accepted principle of judicial organisation deriving from an obvious concern for justice".[16]

As a practical matter, of course, the strict and literal application of the terms of the Court Statute here in question – Article 17(2)[17] and particularly the grab-all, "or-in-any-other-capacity" concluding phrase, would decimate the ranks of the Court, granted that service in a national Foreign Ministry or in a national Delegation to the United Nations General Assembly is considered as a highly desirable, if not indispensable qualification and experience for purposes of candidacy for election to the contemporary Court. Some rather more flexible and pragmatic interpretation would obviously be needed today, as the Court majority had no difficulty in concluding, in *Namibia*, when it rejected the objections there advanced which involved a more general, national, professional-legal "interest" at best and not a strictly private, personal interest.[18]

Objections based on any such more general, national, professional-legal "interest" would also seem contradicted by the Court Statute's own express affirmation that – "judges of the nationality of each of the parties [to a case] shall retain their right to sit in the case before the Court",[19] with its further provision for a State-party that is not already represented by one of its own nationals to choose an *ad hoc* judge to sit on the Court for purposes of its case.[20] Judge Fitzmaurice, in his Dissenting Opinion in *Namibia* already referred to, objected[21] to the Court majority's rejecting (by 12-to-3, and 10-to-5 votes)[22] the Government of South Africa's request to be permitted to appoint an *ad hoc* judge for purposes of the *Namibia* process. But the Court majority's rulings on the point are referable to other considerations than the present ones (no "legal question actually pending between two or more States").[23] The *ad hoc* judges, as a special institutional element of the International Court, are often the objects of the conventional wit and wisdom that they never, never vote against their own state's cause; but their general relevance and importance in the development of the grand lines of the Court's jurisprudence have always been marginal at best, since *ad hoc* judges are necessarily extra-collegial and outside the special Court family even though legally participating in all of the Court's functions for the particular case for which they are designated by their own State.

The institution of the *ad hoc* judge is connected, logically, to that other principal statement, in the Court Statute, of the qualifications for election to the Court. In some respects, this statement may be antinomic to the insistence on judicial "independence", so far as the latter goes beyond that rather narrow private, personal interest or bias as to the outcome of a particular case in which one is participating as a judge, enjoined under most Municipal, national legal systems. Under Article 9 of the Court Statute, –

> "At every election [of judges], the electors shall bear in mind not only that the persons to be elected should individually possess the qualifications required, but also that in the body as a whole the representation of the main forms of civilisation and of the principal legal systems of the world should be assured".

This takes us directly into consideration of the larger conception of the International Court as "representative" institution. It is a conception that assumes a particular importance today as the World Community itself has evolved, through the historical processes of Decolonisation, Self-Determination, and Independence, away from its earlier, restrictive, narrowly Western European, or Western "family compact" status, to a genuinely plural international society that now includes all main political-ideological and ethno-cultural systems. These fundamental changes in the international society are reflected, in the contemporary era, in corresponding changes in the composition and character of the main international institutions like the U.N. General Assembly, the Security Council and U.N. Specialised Agencies. It should be rather surprising if the International Court, as international institution, were not also affected in its turn.

Judge Elias has pointed out, as to the stipulations in Article 9 of the Court

Statute, that the two expressions "civilisation" and "legal system" are not coterminous. He views them, in a more contemporary legal interpretation, as properly intended to "represent the divergent ways of political thought and social action as well as the diverse juridical ideas of the world today", rather than as merely replicating the old, pre-Decolonisation, Western European, Imperial, mode of dividing and separating International Law and its domain into – the "two previously dominant Anglo-American [Common Law] and Civil Law political and legal hegemonies".[24]

Judge Elias notes that the language of Article 9 of the Court Statute was repeated, in terms, in Article 8 of the Statute of the International Law Commission. U.N. General Assembly Resolution 36/39 codified and concretised the principles of representation to be applied in elections to the International Law Commission, for the current thirty-four State membership on the Commission, into the five separate categories:[25]

> *eight* nationals from African states;
> *seven* nationals from Asian states;
> *four* nationals from Eastern European states;
> *seven* nationals from Latin American states;
> *eight* nationals from Western European and Other states.

Neither the U.N. Charter nor the Court Statute contains any stipulation as to "equitable geographical distribution" in relation to elections to the International Court. This is the phrase used in Article 23 of the U.N. Charter in regard to the filling of the ten seats provided, on the Security Council, for non-permanent Members; and around that phrase a highly nuanced system of constitutional Customs or Conventions establishing appropriate "regional" balances on the Security Council has emerged in concrete State voting practice over the years. We will examine the extent to which similar "regionally"-weighted Customs or Conventions may be said to have grown up in the State practice as to voting in elections to the International Court, yesterday and now today. The enquiry is relevant to the examination and appraisal of the charges – advanced, formerly, by Third World states against the dominant Court majorities of the early post-War period up to the time, certainly, of the *South West Africa, Second Phase* decision of 1966,[26] and advanced again by the U.S. State Department in the special context of the *Nicaragua* rulings of 1984–1986[27] – which alleged a particularistic, "regional" bias on the part of certain, at least, of the judges of the Court.

## 2. JUDICIAL REPRESENTATION: THE NOMINATION SYSTEM FOR THE INTERNATIONAL COURT

The Court Statute creates an elaborately structured system for the nomination of candidates for election to the Court, based upon notionally independent, expert committees constituted by the different national groups within the Permanent Court of Arbitration in The Hague.[28] For purposes of the screening and nomination of their own nationals and other States' nationals for election to the International Court, these national groups are formally autonomous, and are supposed to communicate their nominations directly to the Secretary-General of the United Nations without passing through the intermediary of their own national Foreign Ministries. The Permanent Court of Arbitration is, today, an honorific, decorative survival from other, earlier eras – immediately before the first World War, and thereafter between the two World Wars – when Third Party international arbitrament of disputes between states was both considered legally progressive, and also resorted to frequently, within the Western European and general Western legal family.[29]

The Permanent Court of Arbitration itself, as has been remarked often enough, is neither permanent, nor a court *stricto sensu*. It is, in fact, a panel of jurists from which states may draw if they should decide to constitute a special arbitral tribunal for purposes of the Convention of The Hague of 1907 for the Pacific Settlement of International Disputes.[30] In fact, today, when states do choose (and infrequently, at that) to opt for an arbitral form of settlement of their disputes, they invariably prefer to go outside the Permanent Court of Arbitration jurisdiction and to set up their own special, *ad hoc* arbitral machinery for the particular problem-situation involved. The Convention of The Hague of 1899 requires each state party to that Convention to "select four persons at the most of known competency in questions of international law, of the highest moral reputation and disposed to accept the duties of arbitrators".[31] The members of the National Groups so constituted hold office for a term of six years, which term can be (and frequently is) renewed indefinitely; and the members draw no salary or expenses unless they should actually serve on an arbitral panel, in which case any honorarium or expenses would be paid by the States party to the particular arbitration involved. As at the time of the 1984 regular, triennial elections to the International Court, there were seventy-five states formally listed as participating in the Arbitration Court's activities.[32] These states covered all principal legal systems and most major states, and among these latter four of the five permanent members of the Security Council. The People's Republic of China reportedly was still studying a request made to it, in June, 1972, after it was finally seated in the "China" seat in the U.N. General Assembly, to rally to the Arbitration Court. Nevertheless, those seventy-five states officially participating in the Arbitration Court in 1984 were still less than half the then membership of the United Nations. Further, among these seventy-five states, only sixty-one had bothered to constitute a National Group for purposes of the Arbitration Court,[33] all remaining states being presumably content, for purposes of the regular, triennial and also any casual elections, to the International Court, to appoint an *ad hoc* National Group limited to the making of nominations for the one particular election involved. By the time of the 1987 regular, triennial elections to the International Court, the number of states formally listed as participating in the Arbitration Court's activities had risen to seventy-six,[34] with no more than sixty-three of these having actually constituted a National Group.

The political reality with the National Groups that nominate candidates for election to the International Court of Justice – whether the regular National Groups formally constituted for purposes of the Arbitration Court or else any purely *ad hoc* groups – is that their members are all appointed by the national government concerned; and while, according to the formal theory, they communicate directly with the U.N. Secretary-General, there is the ultimate political sanction to any undue display of independence on the part of their members that their own state is under no legal obligation to vote for all or any of the candidates whom the National Group may choose to nominate. This suggests the merits of a high degree of pragmatism and also attention to their own state's policy exigencies, by the members of the National Groups, when they actually propose candidates. It is clearly indispensable, for these purposes, that there be a close exchange and liaison between the National Group and the national Foreign Ministry, and this is no doubt best achieved by having the Foreign Ministry Legal Adviser serve as a member of the National Group. Some states do indeed accord deference to the Court Statute's insistence, in several of its articles, on looking for jurists of high professional-legal or scientific-legal attainments,[35] and also on consulting the national high courts and national academic-legal institutions for purposes of obtaining advice on appropriate candidates.[36] However, since that process remains secret and is necessarily selective, the results may often hardly accord with the high ideals of the Court Statute's original drafters. The impression emerges, from consultation of the empirical record of state practice, that in the case of very many states the National Groups have been essentially moribund. At the time of the 1984 regular, triennial elections to the Court, for example, there were no less than four National Groups with members first appointed in the 1940s and still serving four decades later,[37] while appointments to National Groups, dating back to the 1950s, were common-place, and these involved major powers too.[38]

What this suggests, of course, is a certain administrative inertia in national Foreign Ministries as to appointments to, and renewals of, a post that is essentially dignified but largely inactive except at the regular three year intervals when a third of the International Court's membership will be up for vote in the Security Council and General Assembly. On the positive side, of course, there are certain obvious advantages in familiarity with the individual dossiers of the (relatively small) group of *Papabili* (or generally accepted, politically credible candidates for election to the International Court). For not merely do many of these names recur, from one regular, triennial election to the International Court to another, but there seems also to be a body of accumulated, practical wisdom – particularly in some of the older national Foreign Ministries – as to which national candidacies are politically viable and which, in contrast, are no more than impossible dreams, granted the long-range trends both as to representation of different "regions" within the International Court's ranks, and also as to designation of the preferred "regional" candidate within a particular "regional" grouping of states. The influence of national Foreign Ministries in the actual composition of the National Groups is particularly apparent in the case of the permanent members of the Security Council – the Soviet Union, the U.S., France, and Great Britain;[39] for the Foreign Ministry Legal Advisers and former Legal Advisers are always present and are usually accompanied by representatives of other professional-legal and academic-legal skill-groups who have themselves served also as salaried consultants or advisers or special counsel to the Foreign Ministry concerned.

Yet one of the interesting long-range trends in the process of election to the International Court of Justice is an evident latter-day diminution in the relevance or importance, to the final voting result, of the number or quality of supporting nominations from other National Groups than that of the state of nationality of a particular candidate for election to the Court. Past practice, paralleling Municipal, national elections for public office, had suggested the psychological merits of creating a band-wagon effect or impetus, leading to final victory in the balloting through mobilising as many and as "regionally" varied a group of co-nominating states as possible in support of a supposedly favoured candidate, prior to the actual vote at the United Nations. Recent examples now suggest that this band-wagon strategy has either been much exaggerated as to its past practical effects; or else that it has now become out-dated because of the supervening development of Parliamentary-style lobbying in the corridors of the U.N. General Assembly and Security Council at the actual time of the elections to the Court, or else because of other, far subtler but more direct, forms of behind-the-scenes diplomatic pressures exercised in the national capitals themselves.

In the case of the 1987 regular, triennial elections to the International Court, with five seats open for election and the incumbent five judges having all decided to present themselves for re-election, there were nine candidates.[40] In terms of nominations by National Groups, Judge Bedjaoui (Algeria) easily headed the list, and in fact in the subsequent electoral balloting at the United Nations he received much the largest number of votes of any candidate. In terms of actual number of nominations, Judge Bedjaoui was followed, at some distance, by Judge Ago (Italy) and by Judge Sette-Camara (Brazil), in that order; with Judge Schwebel (U.S.A.) and Judge Tarassov (Soviet Union) following at a still greater distance. The other four, non-incumbent candidates each received only a handful of nominations; yet one of these, Mohammed Shahabuddeen (Guyana), though having secured only three nominations by National Groups, was nevertheless elected as a Judge, defeating one of the incumbents (Judge Sette-Camara). The absence of correlation between number of nominations, and number of final votes, in the 1987 Court elections, stands out.[41]

Perhaps even more striking, in this regard, is the record of the election to fill the casual vacancy on the International Court created by the death of Judge (and sometime President) Nagendra Singh (India) in December, 1988. The election, held in April, 1989, saw six candidates, subsequently reduced to four when two of the six withdrew before the United Nations balloting.[42] Perhaps because of an unusual delay on the part of the Indian National Group in nominating an Indian candidate to succeed Judge Singh, other states felt encouraged to disregard a long-standing courtesy (not yet perhaps hardened into any firm constitutional Convention) that casual vacancies on the Court would normally be filled by electing someone of the same nationality as the preceding Judge. Entering first, and also very early, into the race, a candidate from Sri Lanka quickly put together thirteen nominations, – far more than any other candidate, including the late-nominated Indian candidate; and among these thirteen nominations for the Sri Lankan candidate were five from member-states of the Security Council.[43] When the votes were finally cast, in the United Nations, the Indian candidate, Chief Justice Pathak of the Supreme Court of India, won very easily, on the first ballot. The unfortunate Sri Lankan candidate finished a distant third, with no more than sixteen votes in the General Assembly and only two votes in the Security Council. Since the National Groups of no less than five member-states of the Security Council had, as already noted, nominated the Sri Lankan candidate, three of those member-states of the Security Council evidently chose to ignore their own National Groups' choice in actually casting their votes in the secret ballot in the Security Council, opting instead to support the ultimately successful Indian candidate. This raises the question whether the legal fiction of National Groups operating and nominating independently of their respective national governments should not yield today, in any future revision of the Court Statute, to the contemporary reality that the choice of judges for the International Court is now deemed by member-states of the United Nations as politically too important to be left to legal "laymen", outside the professional-legal divisions of the national Foreign Ministries.

The changing *rôle* of the International Court over the last several decades and, more importantly, changing state perceptions (and, sometimes, state dismay or fears) as to that *rôle*, certainly help to explain the withering away of the intellectual-scientific screening function stipulated for the National Groups under the Court Statute[44] which seems to have envisaged such National Groups, ideally, as a form of nominating college composed of intellectually detached jurisconsults. The evident *dédoublement fonctionel* of the present day between National Groups on the Arbitration Court and national Foreign Ministries is confirmed in certain, no doubt also politically frank and realistic, aspects of state practice in regard to the National Group membership. There is no legal bar, and today no apparent political bar either, to individual members of National Groups themselves being candidates for election to the International Court, and this without having to recuse themselves from participation in the National Group or in its continuing activities (including the screening of their own personal candidacies). Various suggestions to the contrary stem from some strict, and perhaps exaggerated in contemporary terms, Municipal, national legal Customs or Conventions as to disqualification for interest. These are not, however, universal in Comparative Law experience, and are not necessarily automatically transferable to an international legal environment. Again, there is absolutely no legal bar, and today no apparent political bar either, to incumbent judges of the International Court continuing to serve, at the same time, as members of their own National Groups within the Permanent Court of Arbitration. After the 1987 regular elections to the International Court, among the International Court's fifteen judges no less than eight were also members of their respective National Groups (from Argentina, France, India, Italy, Nigeria, Norway, Poland, United Kingdom). Four of the other states then represented on the International Court, (Algeria, Guyana, the People's Republic of China, and Sénégal) had no formally-constituted National Groups within the Arbitration Court. Only three states then represented on the International Court, having formally-constituted National Groups, (Japan, the Soviet Union, and the United States) seemed to consider it necessary or desirable to separate the functions of official nominator (and member of the National Group within the Arbitration Court) from those of candidate for election to the Court or of judge on the Court.

## 3. ELECTIONS TO THE INTERNATIONAL COURT: CHANGING TRENDS IN "REGIONAL" REPRESENTATION ON THE COURT

The judges of the International Court are, in accord with the Court Statute, elected by a double majority – in the U.N. General Assembly and also in the Security Council, which function, in effect, as twin electoral colleges and vote separately,[45] with no power of veto, in the case of the Security Council vote, on the part of Permanent Members of the Security Council.[46]

In the early post-War period it was often claimed that the *new* International Court of Justice, like its predecessor the *old* Permanent Court of International Justice, was loaded with Western, or Western-influenced and Western-leaning, judges. More recently, the same charge of ethno-cultural or "regional" weighting has again been levelled against the Court; but this time the attacks, coming from Western states and predominantly from the U.S., have gone to an alleged anti-Western bias on the Court and to an alleged dominance of the Court by Third World states. Both these criticisms, with their different substantive content and philosophy, can easily be checked, and verified or rejected, against the detailed, empirical record of elections of judges to the *new* Court, over the whole post-War period to the present.

It is readily understandable that the *old* Permanent Court of the between-the-two-World-Wars era should have had a general Western, and more specifically Western European, public image. That public image reflected, almost exactly, its actual membership. The World Community of that particular era in international relations was characterised by the institutions of Western European Imperialism and Colonial authority in Asia, Africa, and the Caribbean; and it was still limited, essentially, in the membership of its World organisation, the old League of Nations, to Western Europe and the Latin American states. Among the Original Members of the League of Nations (from which the defeated "enemy" states of the First World War were, *ex hypothesi*, excluded), the only states not falling into that "Western" category were China, Japan, Siam, and Liberia. Two other states that had signed the Peace Treaty of Versailles, setting up the League of Nations – the U.S. and the Hedjaz – did not ratify the Treaty. The Covenant of the League of Nations provided for the establishment of a Permanent Court of International Justice, – "competent to hear and determine any dispute of an international character which the parties thereto submit to it", and also having jurisdiction to "give an advisory opinion upon any dispute or question referred to it by the Council or by the Assembly" [of the League of Nations].[47] All members of the League of Nations were qualified to become parties to the Court Statute, but so also were other states provided certain conditions were fulfilled. It is not surprising, however, granted the Western European "family compact" character of the League of Nations, that the Court's agenda was also essentially Western European in character, with a great deal of it concerned with the interpretation (and enforcement) of the Treaty of Versailles, with the vindication of which the League of Nations was inevitably, and in political terms unfortunately, linked. The membership of the Permanent Court of International Justice, over its life period from 1922 to 1945, reflecting the political composition of the League of Nations, was limited, for practical purposes, to Western European states and their political-military allies in the Balkans and in Latin America. The only judges not fitting this general description were from Japan and China and the United States (the successive U.S. judges having to be elected in their personal capacity, in so far as the U.S. Government never chose to become a party to the Court Statute).

With the new International Court of Justice established in 1946, it is hardly surprising that, for the first six years and through two successive regular elections of judges, the Court closely resembled, in its state-membership composition, the old Permanent Court. Thirteen of the fifteen judges chosen in the first comprehensive elections to the Court in 1946 (for three-year, six-year, or nine-year terms, as the case might be), were from Europe, North America, and Latin America, leaving only two others – from China and Egypt respectively. In the new political-ideological terms reflecting the post-World War II reality of Bipolarity and the division of the World Community into the rival, U.S.-dominated and Soviet-dominated, political-military blocs, as well as in more conventional, political-geographical terms, the membership of the International Court in the early period, 1946 to 1952, broke down as follows: 4 from Western Europe (Belgium, France, Norway, Great Britain); 2 from North America (Canada, U.S.A.); 4 from Latin America (Brazil, Chile, El Salvador, Mexico); 3 from Eastern Europe (Soviet Union, Poland, Yugoslavia); 1 from Asia (Nationalist China), and 1 from Africa (Egypt). It was not until the third regular elections to the International Court, in 1951, that the first impact of Decolonisation was seen, with the election of an Indian judge (Sir Benegal Rau), in displacement of one of the Western Europeans (Charles De Visscher, Belgium).

The Court Statute itself enjoins the members of the Security Council and the General Assembly, in casting their votes for candidates, to ensure that – "in the [Court] as a whole the representation of the main forms of civilisation and of the principal legal systems of the world should be assured".[48] There is a latent contradiction, or at least an ambiguity, inherent in this twin formulation. As Judge Elias has remarked, –
"the two expressions 'civilisation' and 'legal system' are not coter-

minous, but are intended to represent the divergent ways of political thought and social action as well as the diverse juridical ideas in the world of today. The United Nations has by its hitherto vigorous policy of decolonisation, especially in Asia and Africa, succeeded in replacing the two previously dominant Anglo-American and Civil Law political and legal hegemonies with a plethora of independent and increasingly separate ones of the newly independent States ..."[49]

Judge Elias also notes that neither the United Nations Charter nor the Court Statute contains any stipulation that, in respect of membership of the Court, due regard be paid to "equitable geographical distribution", such as exists under Article 23 of the U.N. Charter in regard to the election of the non-permanent members of the Security Council.[50] The enlargement of the Afro-Asian representation on the Court is attributed by Judge Elias to the marked expansion of U.N. General Assembly membership, which itself created the general pattern of according increased membership in the main U.N. organs and Specialised Agencies to the "new" states.[51]

It is clear that the concept of "representation" on the International Court has evolved, beyond any Common Law/Civil Law dichotomy or even a "Cold War" era, East/West (Communist/Capitalist) mode of classification. It is not until the 1960s, however, that significant changes in the Court's membership, involving what we might call (for want of a better, more inclusive term) its "regional" balance, begin to occur; and then it is as a result of the historical waves of Decolonisation and the consequent admission of a plethora of "new" states from Asia, Africa, and the Caribbean to the United Nations.[52] The United Nations had 55 member-states in 1946, and the number remained as low as 60 until late 1955, when the famous East-West compromise, "package deal" saw 16 states admitted together and thereby broke a decade-long log-jam as to admission of new member-states to the U.N. By 1960, with rapidly succeeding Western European abandonments of Imperial hegemony in Asia and Africa, the U.N. membership had climbed to 100 and it was to continue to move, in leaps and bounds, to its current 160-odd total by the 1980s. The new political facts-of-life so created within the U.N. were reflected in the rare amendment to the U.N. Charter, effected in 1963 and entering into force in 1965, whereby Article 23 was changed so as to increase U.N. Security Council membership from 11 to 15 (though without at the same time increasing the votes of the five permanent members of the Security Council).

In the 1963 regular, triennial elections to the International Court, Latin American seats were reduced from 4 to 2, with the two seats concerned going to Africa (Sénégal) and to Asia (Pakistan). The Court had, by that stage, 4 Western European seats (France, Great Britain, Greece, Italy), 2

Eastern European seats (Soviet Union, Poland), 1 North African/Arab seat (Egypt), 3 Asian seats (Nationalist China, Japan, Pakistan), 1 African seat (Sénégal), 2 Latin American seats (Peru, Mexico), 1 British Commonwealth seat (Australia), and the U.S.A. The changes, thereafter, have been largely marginal, apart from the addition of a second African seat (anglophone, Common Law-influenced Nigeria, to balance francophone, Civil Law-influenced Sénégal), in the 1966 regular elections. The Nigerian candidate in 1966 defeated an Australian candidate for what had been loosely considered, since 1946, as an "old" British Commonwealth seat, (first held by Canada and then by Australia). The defeat of a new Australian candidate in 1966 was undoubtedly helped by the angry political back-lash, in the U.N. General Assembly, against the one-vote-majority, *South West Africa. Second Phase*[53] decision rendered by the Court only two months earlier. The majority opinion (which seemingly sanctioned the extension of the *régime* of *Apartheid* to the old League of Nations Mandate and present U.N. Trust Territory of Namibia) had been signed by the Court President, Sir Percy Spender, himself an Australian. On the other hand, replacing an Australian judge by a Nigerian judge meant continuing a tradition of having yet another anglophone, Common Law jurist from the Commonwealth, though this time not from the "old" (white, European) Commonwealth but from the "new" (the recently Decolonised Asian and African countries of the erstwhile British Empire). Historical continuity with the past was maintained with that particular "succession" in 1966; but henceforth the emphasis would be much less legal-systemic in nature, and much more upon particular geographical-civilisation area. The "old" Commonwealth seat would now become "regionalised" as a "reserved", sub-Sahara, anglophone African one.

These basic "regional" patterns – the 4 Western European seats, the 2 Soviet and Eastern European seats, 2 Latin American seats, 3 Asian seats, 2 sub-Sahara African seats (one francophone Civil Law, one anglophone Common Law), 1 Arab seat (which may often be a North African seat) and one U.S. seat – have persisted to the present day with only modest incremental changes and adjustments to accord to new political or demographic realities. The "Chinese" seat on the International Court, generally accepted as a vested right in 1946 in succession to the "reserved" Chinese place on the old Permanent Court before the War, continued as a Nationalist (Taiwan) Chinese seat long after the successful establishment of the People's Republic (Communist) Government of China. This was because of the then Western-dominated United Nations' refusal to face the new political reality in mainland China of the downfall of the old Nationalist *régime*, and the United Nations' further refusal, in consequence, to seat the

People's Republic delegation in the Chinese seats in the U.N. Security Council (as permanent member) and in the General Assembly, in displacement of the existing Nationalist (Taiwan) delegation. There is a certain point, however, when a legal fiction (here, that the Government of Taiwan continued to be the Government of mainland China) becomes patently absurd and politically impossible to maintain any longer. After two decades, the Nationalist (Taiwan)-held, reserved Chinese seat on the Court was allowed to lapse in the 1966 regular elections. In 1971, the U.N. Security Council and General Assembly finally "corrected" the matter of Chinese representation in both bodies by new votes of their Credentials committees in much-belated recognition of the political reality created in China in 1948 with the downfall of the Nationalist Government and the victory of the People's Republic Government. With a still further and regrettable time-lag, the People's Republic of China was finally able, in the 1984 regular, triennial elections to the Court, to reclaim the Chinese seat. However, doing so meant squeezing out, in the electoral processes, a retiring Arab judge (Judge El-Khani, Syria) who was a candidate for re-election; and this reduced Arab representation on the Court to a bedrock, single-seat, status.

Another incremental adjustment occurred in the 1987 regular elections to the Court when a retiring Brazilian judge (Judge Sette-Camara), who was a candidate for re-election, was beaten out for one of the, by now reduced to two, Latin American seats on the Court by a candidate from the Caribbean area – the former British Empire colonial enclave in South America, and now independent state, of Guyana. There were some special, casual or local, factors that may partly explain this particular result. Although the retiring Brazilian judge was generally considered to have performed very well in his first judicial term, his state, Brazil, was perhaps considered too ambitious politically since it also presented, at the very same U.N. Session, a candidate for election to the Security Council, who was, in fact, elected. There may also be, – in comparison to other accepted "regions" represented in the Court membership –, a more developed custom, with the Latin American seats on the Court, of rotating them regularly among the different states of the region, and this normally tends to imply a single term, only, on the Court for any state from the region. The election of Judge Shahabuddeen of Guyana was also viewed as correcting a hitherto existing anomaly and "regional" injustice: the recently Decolonised Caribbean states were not numerically sufficient, in their own right, to be accepted as a special "region" for purposes of elections to the fifteen-judge Court, and they also did not fit easily into existing, recognised "regions" other perhaps than Latin America. Geographical propinquity, here, would prevail over basic legal-systemic differences, the Caribbean countries being more generally anglophone Common Law than hispanic Civil Law in terms of national legal culture. In fact, Caribbean countries had, in recent years, applied and been admitted to the Organisation of American States, giving an extra political-cultural and legal-cultural dimension or balance to that Latin American specialised regional organisation in the process. All of the member-states of the presently expanded O.A.S., in fact, in spite of their linguistic and legal-systemic differences, share the one common historical experience of exposure to Western European Imperialism in its varied manifestations, the differences between British, French, Dutch, Portuguese, and Spanish colonial administrations adding to the richness of the contemporary collective, "regional" jurisculture. Since the successful Guyanese candidate in the 1987 regular elections to the Court not merely narrowly defeated the Brazilian candidate in a difficult, five-ballot vote, but also easily out-distanced a second Caribbean candidate (from Jamaica), it is worth noting two other, casual factors which attest to the many cross-currents militating against too mechanical and rigid a deference to established "regional" blocs in the battles for seats on the Court. It was noted that the Guyanese candidate bore a Muslim name, which may have helped attract votes from the many Islamic states in the U.N. General Assembly in comparison, for example, to the unsuccessful Jamaican candidate who did not. Again, and much more importantly perhaps in view of Judge Elias' comments on the increasing political awareness or sophistication operating on the casting of states' votes in the Security Council and the General Assembly in the elections to the Court, there is a noticeably increased attention to the candidates' differing degrees of commitment – preferably evidenced publicly, and *prior* to their actual candidacies for the Court – to the U.N. Charter's injunction in favour of "encouraging the progressive development of international law".[54] The successful Guyanese candidate in the 1987 elections in fact had an impressive record of research and scholarship on legal history and social development in the particular "region" for which he was now seeking a seat on the Court.[55]

## 4. "REGIONAL" IDIOSYNCRASIES OR GAPS IN THE REPRESENTATIVE CHARACTER OF THE INTERNATIONAL COURT TODAY

It seems generally agreed that the International Court of Justice should remain at its present number of fifteen judges. The Court, as Judge Bedjaoui has recently reminded us, has its own autonomous traditions and acquired experience, in continuous line of historical development, from the beginning of the 1920s, in the old Permanent Court of International Justice.[56] Analogies sought to be drawn from Comparative Law and from multi-Senate tribunals in other legal systems, national or even supra-national "regional", have no automatic relevance or carry-over to the international legal system, quite apart from the obvious difference between culturally particularistic, national or limited "regional", systems on the one hand and the multi-cultural, inclusive World Community of today.[57] The pre-condition for a viable "reception" or transfer, from one legal system to another, of positive law institutions or processes or substantive ideas developed in the first system, is a demonstrated minimum congruence of basic societal conditions from which that positive law developed, as between the two systems.[58] If the International Court is to continue to function collegially, it can hardly afford any increase in numbers: the general consensus, from Comparative Law, is that eight or nine judges constitute an ideal number for a tribunal functioning as a *plenum* or Full Court,[59] and that even fifteen is pushing this to the working limit. The International Court's tentative experimentation, in recent years, with the Special Chamber system (or panel of five judges, whose selection from the Full Court membership is heavily influenced, if not indeed dictated as some claim, by the parties to a case), is hardly persuasive in any argument to increase judicial numbers as a means of fostering a multi-Senate system within the Court, – even if the number of cases on the Court's docket warranted such a step, which, arguably, has not been the case in modern times. The convenient political expedient, followed in the case of the U.N. Security Council with the 1963 Amendment to the U.N. Charter increasing the Security Council from eleven to fifteen members so as to allow of more frequent representation of the "new", Third World countries, hardly seems relevant to the International Court, for these reasons. There is also the disappointing experience with the U.N.'s International Law Commission, where successive increases in Commission membership, – from an original fifteen states in 1947, to twenty-five in 1961, and then to thirty-four in 1981,[60] ostensibly to ensure a fairer or more equitable distribution of "regional" representation within the Commission – have manifestly not been accompanied by any corresponding change in the Commission's performance record or a speeding up of its agenda; or by any increase in the Commission's public image and reputation after the high hopes of its earlier years.[61] In the case of the International Law Commission, and the 1981 increases in its membership, the United Nations at least tried to codify the system of "regional" representation within Commission ranks: eight seats to be reserved for African states; seven for Asian states; three for Eastern Europe; six for Latin America; eight for "Western European or Other" states; and two further seats which would alternate, as to the one seat between Africa and Eastern Europe, and as to the other seat between Asia and Latin America.[62] Even with the comparative luxury of thirty-four seats to dispose of, however, the regular elections for the International Law Commission have not been without their occasional anguish and dismay. In the 1986 regular elections to the Commission, for example, two of the most richly experienced, retiring candidates (Sir Ian Sinclair, United Kingdom; W. Riphagen, The Netherlands) were defeated for re-election.[63] While other political factors certainly played a part, there was the evident, readily understandable desire to rotate the office of Commission member so as to allow representation also for small states within the eight, reserved "Western European or Other", seats, – in the instant case, to allow representation for Greece, Iceland, and Ireland.

Surveying the ranks of the International Court in this optic, some important "regional" (legal-systemic, ethno-cultural, or political-ideological) groups are, clearly, under-represented on the current Court in comparison to other "regions". Two seats in fifteen hardly seems enough for Latin America today, particularly if Latin America be expanded, as notional "region", to include also the "new", Caribbean states. One seat is clearly inadequate for the Arab states, particularly if Africa, as "region", be considered as limited to two, sub-Sahara states; to say nothing of the Middle Eastern or West Asian Arab states. Asia, with three seats only, creates pressing problems of representation for smaller states if, as at the present time, there seems to be a developing Custom (not yet, however, become a constitutional Convention) to endow the emergent "new" World powers like Japan and India, and of course (once more, since the 1984 regular elections) China, with quasi-permanent status as members of the Court. The evident marked political deference, by latter-day voting majorities in the Security Council and in the General Assembly, to the claims to representation on the Court advanced by these particular "new" World powers from Asia, has been greatly helped by the evident rich intellectual quality and experience of the individual candidates whom they have successfully sponsored in each case for election to the Court. An at best inchoate claim to a reserved place on the Court becomes legitimated more easily with quality candidates. It may be argued, in any case, in behalf of the "new" Asian World powers, that their claims to quasi-permanent representation on the Court are at least as persuasive, objectively, as those of the "old" or traditional World powers (and permanent members of the Security Council, at that) like the United Kingdom and France. It is sometimes mistakenly assumed that each of the permanent members of the Security Council has a legally reserved seat on the Court. Not only is this not so, but even their legal power of veto in the Security Council is expressly denied to the permanent members of the Security Council in the case of elections to the International Court.[64] In the case of the United Kingdom and France, their well-established legal-systemic traditions, plus accumulated diplomatic skills in the political lobbying in the Security Council and in the General Assembly at the actual time of the Court elections, and not least an unbroken tradition of excellent candidates, have combined to maintain a sort of continuing easement over a seat on the International Court. But the French, and particularly the British, vote totals have declined markedly in recent times,[65] and this would seem to be one of the "soft" areas within the Court if extra representation is somehow to be accorded to any one of several other, seemingly under-represented, competing "regions". Even within the "Western European and Other" states, the plight of the smaller states, in terms of ever securing election to the Court in the future, is clear enough. Perhaps the European Community, as a supra-national, "regional bloc" in its own legal right, will resolve that particular dilemma by working out rational rules for rotation of the four, presently "reserved" Western European seats on the Court among its member-states; and *a fortiori* if these four presently "reserved" should ever be reduced to three seats.

One, perhaps not unexpected, consequence of the much heightened interest in the Court elections in recent years has been to place a premium on incumbency, and for states to increase the pressures on their own nationals who are already serving as judges on the Court to present themselves for re-election. At the 1987 regular elections to the Court, all five retiring judges (from Algeria, Brazil, Italy, the Soviet Union, and the United States) were thus candidates for re-election, and all of these but the Brazilian were re-elected. The new political factor of states' pushing for the re-election of their own incumbent judges on the Court creates its own incidental problems within the Court; for the tactic, if successful, inevitably increases the median age of the judges on the Court. It thus presents a heightened possibility of mid-term vacancies through death or disablement, and a consequent partial election in between the regular, triennial elections. There are, indeed, suggestions that some otherwise highly qualified judges who might have wanted to present themselves for re-election but who were in uncertain health, were persuaded by their own national Foreign Ministries to desist in favour of another candidate from their own state, in order to avoid in the future a potentially strongly contested partial election and resulting possible loss of the national seat on the Court. Just how intense and fiercely partisan these partial elections now seem to be becoming – in consequence, no doubt, of states' new awareness of the policy-making potential inherent in judicial settlement – was clearly demonstrated in the fight for the succession to the seat left vacant on the Court in December, 1988, by the sudden death of Judge (and sometime Court President) Nagendra Singh of India. The Indian Government, for reasons, one understands, of disagreements within its own National Group as to the best choice of a national candidate to succeed to Judge Singh, was rather slow, – dangerously slow, – in getting off the mark and in announcing the choice of its national candidate, or even whether it intended to contest the seat at all. On the latter point, perhaps, the Indian Government should not be criticised, since there is a long-standing tradition (not perhaps so firm as to be a constitutional Convention, but dating back to the old Permanent Court nevertheless) that the state of nationality of an incumbent judge who has died or retired in mid-term, should be accorded the courtesy of being allowed to finish off the balance of the judicial term involved by putting forward another of its own nationals in what would become, by Gentleman's Agreement, an uncontested election. The practice as to such partial elections, going back, as noted, to the old Permanent Court, indicates that in the overwhelming majority of cases a jurist of the same nationality as the previous incumbent has been elected; and that in all but two of the remaining cases an intra-"regional" succession was made with the consent and blessings of the state of nationality of the previous incumbent. A survey of the record of the old Permanent Court and of the new International Court, up to the time of the partial election, held in April, 1989, to replace Judge Singh, is strongly supportive of the principle of continuity of original state representation, in the case of elections to fill a partial vacancy on the Court.

With the old Permanent Court, there were thirteen cases of partial elections held from 1923 onwards. In eleven of these cases a jurist of the same nationality as the previous incumbent was elected as replacement. In the remaining two cases, a consensual, intra-"regional" succession occurred – in 1935 from Germany to Sweden; and in 1937 from Sweden to Finland.

With the new International Court, there were ten cases of partial elections, held from 1951 to 1987. In six of these cases a jurist of the same nationality as the previous incumbent was elected as replacement. Of the remaining four cases, two were examples of a consensual, intra-"regional" succession – from El Salvador (Guerrero) to Panama (Alfaro), in a 1959 election in which there were eleven nominated candidates; and from Egypt (U.A.R.) (Badawi) to Lebanon (Ammoun), in a 1965 election in which there were five nominated candidates, of whom three withdrew before the actual vote. That leaves the two cases where there were, indeed, genuinely adversarial contests with important ethno-cultural or political-ideological differences at stake.

When the Indian judge on the Court, Sir Benegal Rau, died in 1953, there was a fierce contest over the succession in the subsequent, 1954, partial election, between India and Pakistan. In a field of twelve candidates, the Pakistan candidate (Sir M. Zafrullah Khan) finally beat out the Indian candidate (Mr. Justice Pal) after the Indian candidate had secured a majority, but not an absolute majority, in the General Assembly, and after some at least questionable procedural rulings by the General Assembly President that seem to have worked against the Indian candidate.[66]

When the Egyptian judge on the Court, El-Erian, died in 1981, there was again a fierce contest over the succession in the 1982 partial election – between an Egyptian candidate and an Algerian candidate. At the time, there were sharp differences of opinion between Egypt and the other members of the relevant Arab "regional" group, over Egypt's position on the so-called Camp David Accords and the U.S.-sponsored plan for Middle Eastern peace. In the result, Algeria, with an excellent candidate who had a distinguished record of service, as a diplomat, in UNESCO and then in the U.N. General Assembly, and before that as an academic-legal scholar, was elected.

Against this background of developed Court practice, and aided by the delay in the Indian Government's announcement of any intention to enter the partial election and to designate a national candidate, six candidates entered the lists for the succession to Judge Singh in the April, 1989, special election, with two of these (from Syria and the Philippines) withdrawing before the actual vote.[67] Once the Indian Government had finally named its choice – the then serving Chief Justice of the Supreme Court of India and a distinguished internationalist in his own right, R.S. Pathak, it became apparent that there would be a repeat of the contest of 1953 between India and Pakistan, with Pakistan nominating a former Justice of its own national Supreme Court. What was unusual in the April, 1989, partial election was that in a contest over what was, without question, a "reserved" Asian "regional" seat on the Court, ten Western states opted very quickly to enter the political fray and, disregarding the claimed principle of continuity which was strongly advanced by India, to co-nominate a candidate (in the event, from Sri Lanka).[68] The Sri Lankan candidate also received three other, non-Western, nominations (from Peru and from Sénégal, but from only one Asian state, his own home state). This tally of thirteen nominations for the Sri Lankan candidate was by far the largest number of nominations received by any of the ultimate four candidates. By comparison, the Indian candidate received eight nominations (importantly, among these, from the United Kingdom, Brazil, and Yugoslavia); the Pakistan candidate three nominations; and a Thailand candidate two nominations (from his own state, and, Yes!, also from Liechtenstein). In the political show-down between India and Pakistan now approaching, several states opted to be politically prudent by nominating two candidates for the one vacancy. The politically most realistic of these prudent states, perhaps, was Argentina which chose to nominate both the Indian and the Pakistan candidates. Two other states, Peru and the United States, having rushed in very early and nominated the Sri Lankan candidate, evidently sought to abandon, with as much dignity as still possible, a by now evidently lost cause, by making second, late nominations – in the case of Peru, of the Pakistan candidate; and in the case of the United States, of the Indian candidate. In the result, as noted earlier, the Indian candidate won, on the first ballot, in the Security Council and in the General Assembly, beating the Pakistan candidate by a three-to-one majority in the Security Council and a two-to-one majority in the General Assembly, and leaving the Sri Lankan and the Thailand candidates trailing far behind.

The result of the April, 1989, partial election must be taken, first of all, as a fairly clear, latter-day confirmation of the claimed rule of continuity and the principle (rule of courtesy, if you wish) of allowing, under normal circumstances, a candidate of the same nationality as the previous incumbent to fill a partial vacancy on the Court for the balance remaining in the regular nine-year judicial term. Beyond that, the impressive margin of electoral victory for the Indian candidate strengthened the claim of India, as a "new" Asian World power together with Japan, to be accorded the same courtesy at least as France and the United Kingdom (these latter as permanent members of the Security Council), if not the Soviet Union, the People's Republic of China, and the U.S., of a more or less assured, "reserved" seat on the International Court. As against that, however, the fierceness of the contest for the April, 1989, casual election, and the quite unprecedented nature of the national Foreign Ministry lobbying and counter-lobbying that preceded it, point to the frustrations of smaller and even "middle" states that now see their access to membership of the International Court blocked by the rigidities of the "regional" representation rules that are now accepted or applied, *de facto*, for purposes of elections to the Court. The strains seem particularly great in the case of "regions" such as Asia which, with only three seats on the Court, must, on ordinary population numbers alone, be considered as grossly under-represented on the Court today in comparison to other, more traditional but less populated "regions". The political pressures to capture an extra seat for Asia, in future regular elections to the Court, will undoubtedly be there.

So far, the emphasis has been on the interaction and interplay of states, and state authority, in the elections to the Court. What is the relevance, in all this, of the intrinsic intellectual capacities and professional-legal or academic-scientific qualifications of the actual candidates concerned? Certainly, one element in the hitherto unbroken representation on the International Court of those erstwhile, World powers and acknowledged members of the "Big Five" at War's end in 1945 and at the founding of the United Nations, France and Great Britain, has been the sustained professional and intellectual legal quality of their successive national candidates for election to the Court. In politically marginal situations, or where a break-through is sought by way of establishing a new principle as to representation or else breaking an old, outdated one, it helps to have an outstanding candidate. Japan and West Germany, in the delicate transition from that "enemy state" status that is referred to, in terms, in the United Nations Charter,[69] understandably sought extra political and legal legitimacy by securing election of their own nationals to the Court; and both countries met the challenge of candidacy for the Court by offering attractive, "electable" candidates as the opportunities first arose.[70] It clearly was influential, in the partial election of 1982 already discussed, that the ultimately successful candidate, Judge Bedjaoui, had such exceptional academic-scientific as well as diplomatic-legal attainments. And in the April, 1989, partial election, the sheer size of the successful Indian candidate's majorities in the Security Council and in the General Assembly was undoubtedly aided by the fact that he was, by all counts, the intellectually most distinguished and professionally experienced jurist among the various candidates.

On the International Court, not less than on the International Law Commission which used to be regarded as a prime recruiting ground for potential judges, there has been a noticeable change in the character and the training and experience of the elected members – away from the scholar-jurists of an earlier time to the functionalists or technocrats of the Foreign Ministry Legal Divisions. The analysis here is complicated by the fact that candidates, – at least in their official *curricula vitae* as supplied for purposes of seeking nominations to the Court as well as for the actual elections – often seem to wear a number of hats at the same time, as professor, professional diplomat, and specialised civil service lawyer. Yet the trend is clear, and it is fair to say that, today, those judges of the Court who are nationals of World powers tend to have been Foreign Ministry Legal Advisers or, less than that, to come from academic or similar legal skill-groups with heavy continuing ties to their own national governments as consultants or special advisers. There are some long-range consequences in all this, – in view of all the openings to what Professor Georges Scelle identified as the *dédoublement fonctionnel*, – for the classical notions of judicial independence and judicial neutrality. But these classical International Law notions, as we have already remarked, have been under attack as unrealistic and out-dated in contemporary *Realpolitik* terms. A casual element in the trend to elect Foreign Ministry Legal Advisers, of course, is the fact that the twin electoral colleges – the U.N. Security Council and the General Assembly – tend to be populated by delegates who are either themselves Foreign Ministry Legal Advisers or who are, at least in constant touch with their national Foreign Ministry Legal Divisions. The U.N. General Assembly's Sixth (Legal) Committee, in this respect, is the most readily accessible arena, either for building one's own candidacy for ultimate election to the Court or else for lobbying in behalf of another national candidacy, in a continuing, year-to-year, collegial environment. Balancing this, however, is Judge Elias' wise reminder[71] that states today, with increasing electoral sophistication, now tend to look beyond surface qualifications and to weigh, according to their own particular values, the various candidates' degree of commitment to the "progressive development of international law." It is this new type of enquiry, directed to substantive-legal values, that no doubt accounts for the current evident down-grading of past or present membership in the International Law Commission as a factor in the choice of judges for the Court. For the opposite reasons, the academic-scientifically prestigeful *Institut de Droit International*, once (no doubt, with exaggeration) considered as a club for ex-judges, present judges, and would-be judges, would become far less relevant, with the mounting emphasis on the Court's new *rôle* as another, additional key arena for international legal policy-making. Considerations of legal science in the pure sense would sensibly yield, in this new optic, to considerations of states' own vital interests, in the nomination and election of International Court judges.

## 5. ON "POLITICS" IN THE COURT ELECTIONS, AND CURRENT, ALLEGED "REGIONAL" BIASES IN COURT REPRESENTATION

The alleged "politicisation" of the International Court has been one of the main reasons advanced by U.S. State Department spokesmen for the U.S. retreat from the Compulsory Jurisdiction of the Court in the aftermath of the *Nicaragua* judgments of 1984 and 1986. The charge of "politics" in relation to the International Court has two different aspects – the first aspect, (which we have already examined), of the claimed operation of "political" and not "legal" factors in the actual decision-making of the Court and in the contributions of particular judges, or groups of judges, to the Court's decisions; and a second aspect of the claimed entry of non-technical, "political" factors in the processes of nomination of candidates for the Court and in the actual elections thereto, as conducted in the U.N. Security Council and General Assembly. As to this second aspect, the conclusion is clear that the nominating phase, officially exercised by the expert, independent jurisconsult committees that the National Groups in the Permanent court of Arbitration are supposed to be, is now, and probably always has been, substantially determined by the relevant national Foreign Ministries in accord with their conceptions of their own national policy interests. There is no reason why that should not be so, however; and the nomination process, since involving one hundred and sixty odd states, each of which is entitled to nominate up to four candidates (no more than two of whom can be of the nominating state's own nationality)[72] is sufficiently diverse and plural in its potential operation to ensure a broadly-based access to candidacies to the Court through a plethora of candidates of different legal and general cultures and different political-ideological systems. States do, in fact, exercise their power to make co-nominations to the full, and seem consciously to try for "regional" balance in so doing. The action of the ten Western states, already referred to, in entering the battle for an Asian "regional" seat in the April, 1989, partial election by endorsing *en bloc* a single Asian candidate who ultimately placed only a distant third in the final balloting, at least illustrated the openness of the nominating process. It is beside the point, for present purposes, that it may have been a political error for those Western states, in so far as it involved their doing what Western states themselves sometimes accuse non-Western, and especially Third World states, of doing – namely trying, by their very early co-nominations, to influence the political outcome of an election of prime concern to another, distinct and different "region" to their own.

As for the Court elections themselves and the alleged anti-Western bias manifest in the actual voting records in the U.N. Security Council and General Assembly, only two cases, – both of these in the earlier years of the International Court, – evidence well-qualified Western candidates' going down to defeat before Third World candidates. In each of the two cases the successful Third World candidate concerned also had impressive legal qualifications. In the 1951 regular elections to the Court, the distinguished Belgian incumbent judge, Charles De Visscher, was defeated for re-election,[73] under the special political circumstances of the time of the need, in view of then recent expansion of United Nations membership to include recently Decolonised, non-Western countries, of finding a second Asian seat on the Court (in addition to the existing Asian seat held by Nationalist China). The second Asian seat was opened up, then, for newly Decolonised

India, and the successful candidate was the distinguished jurist, Sir Benegal Rau. In the 1966 regular elections, the distinguished Australian scholar-diplomat, Sir Kenneth Bailey, who had been an unsuccessful candidate, in 1946, in the first post-War regular elections, against the Canadian candidate, J.E. Read, for the then accepted, "old" British Commonwealth seat, was a candidate to succeed his co-national, the retiring Court President, Sir Percy Spender. President Spender had cast the second, tie-breaking vote in the Court's eight-to-seven decision in *South West Africa. Second Phase*[74] rendered only two months before the 1966 Court elections; and there was undoubtedly an element of political back-lash against the Court majority in the ensuing General Assembly vote on the judicial candidates, since the Court decision had been widely assailed, in the intervening several months, as being politically charged in favour of the white minority government of South Africa and its *Apartheid régime*.[75] However, at the time of 1966 regular elections to the Court, there was also a certain appropriateness in passing on the "old" British Commonwealth seat, first held by Canada and then by Australia, to another (as it happened, anglophone Common Law-influenced) Commonwealth country, – in this case, the recently Decolonised state of Nigeria. This rotation within the Commonwealth had the incidental, important asset of allowing for a second, sub-Sahara African seat on the Court, the anglophone Common Law character of Nigeria balancing the francophone Civil Law character of the one such sub-Sahara African state already represented on the Court, – Sénégal – whose candidate had first been elected in the 1963 regular, triennial elections.

All the other shifts and changes within the Court, affecting Western representation, have tended to be of a marginal character only. The International Court has, in fact, maintained a steady, consistent quality in its patterns of "regional" representation since the 1966 regular elections. Where political influences have operated, they have tended to be within the "regional" constituencies themselves, and to be determined by the members of those "regional" groupings as an internal, "regional" political matter, using their own intra-"regional" rules of the game to decide which particular state's national, in the end, is to be nominated and elected. In a very real sense, today, the International Court has become a representative tribunal, fully reflecting the legal-systemic, ethno-cultural, political-ideological, and geographical diversity of contemporary United Nations membership.[76]

## NOTES

1. United Nations Charter, article 92.
2. Statute of the International Court of Justice, article 3 (1).
3. *Ibid.*, arts. 4 (1), 10 (1) and (2).
4. *Ibid.*, art. 4 (1) and (2).
5. *Ibid.*, art. 2.
6. Elias, Report, in *Judicial Settlement of International Disputes* (Mosler and Bernhardt, eds.), (1974), p. 19.
7. Court Statute, art. 24 (1), (2), and (3).
8. *South West Africa, Second Phase, Judgment,* I.C.J. Reports 1966, p. 6.
9. A second judicial vote that would almost certainly also have been with the seven judges favouring the Court's exercising jurisdiction, was temporarily lost with the death of Judge Badawi during the course of the hearings: his successor in the resulting partial election, Judge Ammoun, was elected after the conditional closing of the Court's hearings in *South West Africa. Second Phase*, but would have been eligible, nevertheless, to participate in the written and judgment phase. Judge Ammoun, (whether or not under pressure is not clear), chose not to do so. See, generally, Torres Bernárdez, "Resignations at the World Court", in *International Law in a Time of Perplexity. Essays in Honour of Shabtai Rosenne* (Dinstein and Tabory, eds.) (1989), p. 953, p. 975.
10. *Legal Consequences for States of the Continued Presence of South Africa in Namibia (South West Africa) notwithstanding Security Council Resolution 276 (1970), Advisory Opinion,* I.C.J. Reports 1971, p. 16.
11. I.C.J. Reports 1971, at pp. 18–19.
12. *Ibid.*, p. 3.
13. *Ibid.*, p. 6.
14. *Ibid.*, p. 9.
15. *Ibid.*, p. 309.
16. *Ibid.*, p. 324.
17. Court Statute, art. 17 (2): "No member [of the Court] may participate in the decision of any case in which he has previously taken part as agent, counsel, or advocate for one of the parties, or as a member of a national or international court, or of a commission of enquiry, or in any other capacity."
18. Compare the analogous controversy over the question of judicial disqualification for alleged "interest", in Comparative, national (West German) constitutional law, in the so-called Party Financing case: Decision of 2 March 1966, 20 B Verf GE 9 (1966) (Second Senate) (the "judicial disqualification" issue); Decision of 19 July 1966, 20 B Verf GE 56 (1966) (Second Senate) (the substantive, "Party Financing", issue). And see Friesenhahn, "Zur Ablehnung und Selbstablehnung eines Richters des Bundesverfassungsgericht wegen Besorgnis der Befangenheit", *Juristenzeitung*, (1966) p. 704; and see the present author's *Supreme Courts and Judicial Law-Making. Constitutional Tribunals and Constitutional Review* (1986), p. 39.
19. Court Statute, art. 31 (1).
20. *Ibid.*, art. 31 (2).
21. I.C.J. Reports 1971, pp. 299, 308–9.
22. *Ibid.*, pp. 25, 26–7.
23. *Ibid.*, p. 25.

24. Elias, in *Judicial Settlement of International Disputes* (Mosler and Bernhardt, eds., ) (1974), p. 23.
25. U.N. General Assembly Resolution 36/39, (para. 3), 18 November 1981.
26. I.C.J. Reports 1966, p. 6.
27. *Military and Paramilitary Activities in and against Nicaragua (Nicaragua v. United States of America), Provisional Measures, Order of 10 May 1984*, I.C.J. Reports 1984, p. 169; *Jurisdiction and Admissibility, Judgment*, I.C.J. Reports 1984, p. 392; *Merits, Judgment*, I.C.J. Reports 1986, p. 14.
28. Court Statute, art. 4.
29. von Mangoldt, "Arbitration and Conciliation", in *Judicial Settlement of International Disputes* (Mosler and Bernhardt, eds.), (1974), p. 417.
30. 36 Stat. 2199, T.S. no. 536, 1 Bevans 577.
31. 32 Stat. 1779, T.S. no. 392, 1 Bevans 230.
32. *Rapport du Conseil administratif de la Cour permanente d'Arbitrage* (1985), p. 4.
33. *Ibid.*, p. 8 *et seq.*
34. *Rapport du Conseil administratif de la Cour permanente d'Arbitrage* (1988), p. 4, p. 13 *et seq.*
35. Court Statute, art. 2.
36. *Ibid.*, art. 6.
37. Dominican Republic, Ecuador, Paraguay, Switzerland.
38. Austria (2), Brazil, El Salvador, Ecuador, France, Hungary, Italy, Japan, Poland, Spain. Appointments dating back to the 1960s extended, at that time, to almost half the states having formally-constituted National Groups, including the Soviet Union and Great Britain.
39. The members of the Soviet National Group – for the 1984 regular, triennial Court elections and again for the 1987 regular, triennial Court elections, all held academic-legal posts, but, in the Soviet tradition of cumulating professional-legal functions, also had substantial Governmental advising and counselling experience. The U.S. National Group, for 1984 and again for 1987, comprised (with one change in personnel) the then current Legal Adviser to the State Department and two former Legal Advisers, plus one practising lawyer. The French National Group, unchanged as between 1984 and 1987, comprised a Professor who was also a Member of the International Law Commission of the U.N., the Legal Adviser to the Foreign Ministry (who changed professional-legal hats, in late 1987, when he became a Judge of the International Court), plus two national judges. The British Group in 1984 was composed of the British Judge on the International Court, plus a former Legal Adviser to the Foreign Ministry, and two national judges; in 1987, one of the national judges had been replaced by another former Legal Adviser to the Foreign Ministry.
40. U.N. General Assembly A/42/589, A/42/590; Security Council S/19156, S/19157; 8 October 1987.
41. See, generally, Lee and McWhinney, "The 1987 Elections to the International Court of Justice", *Canadian Yearbook of International Law*, vol. 25 (1987), p. 379.
42. U.N. General Assembly A/43/1002, Security Council S/20552, 6 April 1989; A/43/1002/Rev. 1, S/20552/Rev. 1, 18 April 1989.
43. *Ibid.*
44. Court Statute, arts. 4, 6.
45. *Ibid.*, arts. 4 (1), 7 (2), 10 (1).
46. *Ibid.*, art. 10 (2).

47. Covenant of the League of Nations, art. 14.
48. Court Statute, art. 9.
49. Elias, Report, in *Judicial Settlement of International Disputes* (Mosler and Bernhardt, eds.) (1974), p. 23.
50. *Ibid.*, p. 24.
51. *Ibid.*
52. The discussion that follows draws upon the author's detailed study, "Law, Politics and 'Regionalism' in the Nomination and Election of World Court Judges", *Syracuse Journal of International Law and Commerce*, vol. 11 (1987), p. 1. And see, generally, Rosenne, *The International Court of Justice. An Essay in Political and Legal Theory* (1961); *Documents on the International Court of Justice* (Rosenne, ed.) (1974).
53. I.C.J. Reports 1966, p. 6.
54. See the comments by Elias, in *Judicial Settlement of International Disputes* (Mosler and Bernhardt, eds.) (1974), pp. 26–7.
55. Judge Shahabuddeen's scientific-legal publications, going back to the early 1970s, included *The Rôle of the Lawyer in a Developing Guyana* (1974); *Towards Industrial Justice in Guyana* (1974); *Constitutional Development in Guyana 1621–1978* (1978); *Nationalisation of Guyana's Bauxite. The Case of Alcan* (2nd ed., 1981); *From Plantocracy to Nationalisation. A Profile of Sugar in Guyana* (1983); *Long Though the Night* (*on the subject of the human condition in Southern Africa and Colonial Guyana* (1986); and other works.
56. Bedjaoui, in *La juridiction internationale permanente* (Philip, ed.), (1987), p. 73 *et seq.*
57. *Ibid.*, p. 75.
58. See, for example, in contemporary reformulation, Kokkini-Iatridou, "The *Tertium Comparationis* in the Micro-Comparative Research", in *Law in East and West, Recht in Ost und West* (Nakamura, ed.) (1988), p. 231.
59. *Supreme Courts and Judicial Law-Making, Constitutional Tribunals and Constitutional Review* (1986), p. 34 *et seq.*
60. See, generally, Briggs, *The International Law Commission* (1965), p. 54 *et seq.*; Rosenne, "The International Law Commission, 1949–1959, " *British Year Book of International Law* (1960), p. 122 *et seq.*
61. See, generally, the present author's discussion, *United Nations Law Making* (1984), p. 96 *et seq.*; Ramcharan, *The International Law Commission. Its Approach to Codification and Progressive Development of International Law* (1977), p. 38 *et seq.*; El Baradei, Franck and Trachtenberg, *The International Law Commission. The Need for a New Direction* (Unitar) (1981).
62. U.N. General Assembly Resolution A/RES/36/39, 20 November 1981 ("Enlargement of the International Law Commission: Amendments to Articles 2 and 9 of the Statute of the Commission.")
63. U.N. General Assembly, A/41/PV.71, 3 December 1986.
64. Court Statute, art. 10 (2).
65. See, for example, the 1981 regular, triennial elections (the most recent occasion on which the British and French seats were up for election) when, with a total of one hundred and fifty-five ballots cast, in the U.N. General Assembly, an excellent French candidate received one hundred and twenty-seven votes, and an equally excellent British candidate was down to one hundred and seven votes. In the Security Council, with fifteen ballots cast, the French candidate received eleven votes, and the British candidate ten votes. Both were elected. 36 U.N. GAOR (48th plen. mtg.), p. 6; U.N.

120 CHAPTER IV

Doc. A/36/PV.48 (1981); 36 U.N. SCOR (2306th Mtg.), p. 1, U.N. Doc. S/36/PV 2306 (1981).

66. As to the crucial procedural rulings in the General Assembly, consult Rosenne, *The International Court of Justice* (1961), p. 136.

67. U.N. General Assembly/Security Council, A/43/1002/Rev. 1, S20552/Rev. 1, 18 April 1989.

68. *Ibid.* (Belgium, Canada, Finland, France, Federal Republic of Germany, Greece, Ireland, The Netherlands, Sweden, U.S.A.)

69. See U.N. Charter, arts. 53, 107.

70. Japan, after having unsuccessfully contested the partial election of 1956 produced by the death of the incumbent Nationalist Chinese judge, nominated the distinguished and long-serving Chief Justice of the Supreme Court of Japan, Kotaro Tanaka, for the regular, 1960 elections to the Court, and Tanaka was elected. West Germany, after its long-delayed admission to the United Nations in 1973, presented Professor Hermann Mosler, (who had been an *ad hoc* judge named by the West German Government for *North Sea Continental Shelf* (I.C.J. Reports 1969, p. 3)), as its candidate in the 1978 regular elections to the Court, and Mosler was elected.

71. Elias, in *Judicial Settlement of International Disputes* (Mosler and Bernhardt, eds.) (1974), at p. 26.

72. Court Statute, art. 5 (2).

73. The disillusionment among De Visscher's admirers as to his electoral defeat was evidently considerable. See the comments made, almost four decades later, by ex-Judge Gros (France): Gros, "La Cour internationale de Justice 1946–1986: les reflexions d'un juge", in *International Law at a time of Perplexity. Essays in Honour of Shabtai Rosenne* (Dinstein and Tabory, eds.) (1989), p. 289, p. 293.

74. I.C.J. Reports 1966, p. 6.

75. Ex-Judge Gros (France) recalled, a quarter century afterwards, that at the Autumn, 1966, Annual Session of the U.N. General Assembly, immediately after the *South West Africa. Second Phase* decision, the then President of the Court (Spender) and his predecessor as President (Winiarski (Poland)) were "publicly insulted and defamed without the presiding officers of the sittings [of the General Assembly] ever intervening ...". Gros, *op. cit.*, in Dinstein and Tabory (eds.), *op. cit.*, at p. 295. Judge Gros further suggested that the internal dissension and disunion within the Court itself was so great, after *South West Africa. Second Phase*, that it cost both Fitzmaurice (a principal author of the majority decision) and also Jessup (who so brilliantly dissented from the majority decision) the Presidency of the Court, in 1967 (when Bustamante y Rivero (Peru) was elected President); and that it cost Fitzmaurice the Presidency of the Court again in 1970 (when Zafrullah Khan (Pakistan) was elected President instead). Judge Gros comments, acidly: "The best were excluded". Gros, *op. cit.*, at p. 297.

76. In the regular, triennial elections to the Court, held in November, 1990, the two incumbent judges from France and Great-Britain, Judges Guillaume and Jennings, who chose to run again, were re-elected. Three other incumbents – President Ruda (Argentina), and Judges M'Baye (Senegal) and Pathak (India), were not candidates for re-election, though for different reasons. Their seats were, however, filled with full respect for existing "regional" representation principles. The further principle, of *Alternation* (rotation) within a recognised "regional" grouping, was also vindicated. In the result, the Latin American seat was filled by an excellent candidate (Aquilar) from Venezuela (which had never before held a seat on the Court), after a diplomatic battle

with a candidate from Uruguay who withdrew before the actual vote. (Uruguay had, twice before, had judges on the Court). The Francophonic, sub-Sahara African seat was won by Madagascar, never before represented on the Court, over Senegal which had, twice before, had judges on the Court. The Asian seat went, finally, to Sri Lanka, though with a different candidate to the one who had finished so far back in the field in the April, 1989, partial election for the same seat. Incumbent Judge Pathak, who had made an excellent impression in his brief 18 months on the Court, was not re-nominated by his own Government, which apparently chose to concentrate on a Security Council seat battle (which it won). It had been expected that the seat would then go to the Pakistan candidate, Patel (the runner-up to Judge Pathak in the April, 1989 election), but the sudden change of Government in Pakistan – the new Government publicly disowned Patel's candidacy – effectively defeated his election chances.

## CHAPTER V

# A Contemporary, Operational Approach to Court Jurisdiction and Justiciability

## 1. THE NEW POPULARITY OF THE INTERNATIONAL COURT

Our examination of the International Court of Justice and its approach to Jurisdiction and Justiciability occurs when the Court, in its modern, reconstituted, post-World War II phase, approaches the completion of a half-century of *jurisprudence*. After a very lean period of the late 1960s and in the 1970s when the Court, in reaction in considerable measure to the public relations disaster of the *South West Africa. Second Phase* decision of 1966,[1] was effectively ignored by most of the member-states of the United Nations for purposes of concrete problem-solving, and when the Court, in consequence, had very few cases on its list, it has now rebounded remarkably in political popularity. In particular, the Court is today actively patronised by the very Third World state-clients that once boycotted its jurisdiction. The political paradox is that it is now the United States which, in the immediate post-World War II years, was the most vocal champion of the Court and of the principle of international judicial settlement, which has now turned its back on the Court, in a signal retreat from its erstwhile positive acceptance of Court jurisdiction.

The U.S. Administration's *volte face* on the Court, and also the extent of the latter-day U.S. disillusionment with an institution and with a process – international judicial settlement – that U.S. jurists often thought that they had pioneered or invented, is summed up in the title of a recent U.S., multi-authored, symposium volume, "The International Court of Justice at a Crossroads".[2] It is not unkind to suggest to the intellectually capable U.S. authors involved in that symposium that they are taking what amounts, in effect, to a pre-Copernican attitude to international adjudication. For it is not, it may be suggested, the International Court that is at a legal crossroads today. The Court's dilemma of choice was exposed in the *South West*

*Africa. Second Phase* decision in 1966 and resolved for the future, for all intents and purposes, with the Court's *Namibia* ruling of 1971.[3] Rather, it would appear to be U.S. foreign policy that was at a crossroads at the close of the decade of the 1980s, with the International Court and U.S. participation in its work as only one element in the larger, but purely internal, U.S., "great debate" over U.S. foreign policy and its long-range goals and objectives and the particular institutions and processes through which these could best be achieved. It is significant that no other Western state joined the U.S. Administration in its retreat from the International Court's jurisdiction in the mid-1980s, or in its public attacks on the Court's alleged "politicisation" and on the alleged political bias of the Full Court majority or of some at least of its members. Even the U.S. invocation of the Special Chamber jurisdiction of the International Court as a seemingly convenient device for at once maintaining a long-range historical commitment to the principle of international judicial settlement but, in practical terms, for escaping from the jurisdiction of a Full Court that one chose to characterise as too "political" for one's immediate purposes, benefits from cool analysis in its own special fact-context. *Gulf of Maine*,[4] the first such instance of recourse to the Special Chamber jurisdiction of the International Court, may have been so viewed by the U.S. Administration as a way of liberating itself from a particular philosophical-legal majority within the fifteen-member Full Court; but that was not the political *raison d'être* of the approach of the other party to the case, the Canadian Government. Indeed, at the very moment that the U.S. Administration was announcing the termination of the U.S. acceptance of the Compulsory Jurisdiction of the International Court under the Optional Clause, the Canadian Government moved, in the Autumn of 1985, to strike out a special exception that had been inserted in 1970 to the original Canadian full acceptance of Compulsory Jurisdiction, and to restore the Canadian acceptance to its original, unqualified form.

## 2. THE "INTERNATIONALISING" OF THE INSTITUTION OF JUDICIAL SETTLEMENT

Latter-day researches in Comparative International Legal History have corrected or at least provided more nuanced assessments of earlier, somewhat simplistic views of judicial settlement of disputes as being a distinctively Western –, and, even more, a distinctively Anglo-Saxon, Common Law, – legal institution that has no roots in other, non-Western societies and *a fortiori*, in an international society that has now become genuinely multicultural and legally multi-systemic in the wake of Decolonisation and the ending of Imperialism and the achievement of Self-Determination of Peoples on a World-wide scale. We are now reminded, for example, of the historical contribution of the late 19th century Imperial Russian jurists to the idea of Third Party settlement (arbitral and other) and to judicial settlement in particular, in the run-up to The Hague Peace Conferences of 1899 and 1907, and in the actual, detailed deliberations and debates at those Conferences.

In the post-World War II era in Continental Western Europe, judicial review of constitutionality of legislation and of executive-administrative decrees and practice, (*Verfassungsgerichtsbarkeit*), with some purely European antecedents or analogues (as in the French *Conseil d'Etat's* administrative law review *rôle*) and also a good deal of "received" American constitutional law learning, has taken firm root by now in the distinctively Continental Western European institution of the Special Constitutional Court (*Bundesverfassungsgericht*). This was introduced in the West German constitutional system in 1951 and it has been now widely copied throughout Europe. In addition, supranationalism and the movement for political and economic integration of Western Europe brought, with the step-by-step inauguration of the European Community, a functionally-specialised but highly operational High Court of Justice composed of judges from all of the Community member-states and necessarily developing a common, trans-systemic, *jurisprudence* in the process of hearing and deciding concrete cases from the different Community countries, involving interpretation and application of the Community's basic statute and law. It is hardly surprising that the empirical, trial-and-error testing and experience acquired over the years by Municipal, national judges and by supra-national, Community judges, in this way, and a resulting increasing judicial confidence and intellectual-legal sophistication in resolving the antinomies of judicial choice among competing theories of legal interpretation and of the *rôle* of Courts as community policy-makers, should carry over into the international arena to the work of the International Court.

The strong elements of intellectual-legal continuity between Imperial Russia and Soviet Russia are today sufficiently admitted and recognised, together with Imperial Russia and Soviet Russia's general intellectual-legal debts, in common, to Continental Western European legal science, – through the Civil Law of course, but also many aspects of Administrative Law and of Court organisation and procedure. Such a newly re-discovered Russian national legal-cultural base for judicial settlement of disputes, replacing the Vyshinsky-imposed orthodoxies of the 1930s with their denial of any judicial law-making *rôle*, when joined with the Continental Western European national and supra-national ("regional") applied practice, of the post-World War II era, in Court-based constitutional review, provides a powerfully trans-cultural, inter-systemic, pan-European support for the new, greatly expanded and more consciously policy-making *rôle* essayed by the International Court of Justice in the several decades and more since the *South West Africa. Second Phase* decision of 1966. That still leaves open the reconciliation of these new concepts of international judicial settlement with other, non-European legal cultures and legal systems, heavily influenced as many of these latter have been by European law, – Civil Law or Common Law, – depending on the particular vagaries and varieties of those non-European cultures' exposure, in past years, to European Imperial-Colonial institutions and law.

The institution of judicial review of the constitution was "received", with varying degrees of U.S. Common Law constitutional influence, in the post-World War II constitutional systems of Japan, which was militarily occupied by the U.S. at the time of adoption of the new, post-War Constitution in 1946; and of India which had become Decolonised and independent from the old British Empire at the time of adoption of the new Republican Constitution of 1950. In each of these countries, the institution of judicial review has taken firm root by now and is operated, confidently and easily, by the new constitutional judiciary, albeit with some procedural and general self-restraint on the part of the Japanese judges over the years, and with some more conscious and determined openings to judicial law-making on great social and economic issues in recent years on the part of the Indian judges. The carry-over of distinctive national judicial thought-ways and legal attitudes, – influenced as these may have been, in turn, by other, extrinsic, foreign law or Comparative Law elements – to the International Court is perhaps more readily perceptible in the case of Japan and India than it is with Western states. The first Japanese jurist elected to the International Court in the post-War period was the great, long-serving Chief Justice of the Supreme Court of Japan, Judge Tanaka; while the two most recent Indian representatives on the International Court, Judge Nagendra Singh and his successor, Judge Pathak, have been experienced constitutional lawyers, Singh having been a member of the Constituent Assembly charged with drawing up the post-Decolonisation national Constitution, and Pathak having been Justice and then Chief Justice of the Supreme Court of India.

Recent public debate in Japan over the concept of "Occidentalisation" (sometimes called "modernisation")[5] and its application in Japanese law, throws into relief some of the central problems today for an institution such as the International Court of Justice, and for a process such as judicial settlement of disputes – and, consequentially, judicial law-making – whose legal-cultural origins, at first sight, are unmistakably Western, and whose main political-legal impulse after 1945 is still conceived of as having been U.S. It is well-known that Imperial Japan, during the *Meiji* era, beginning in 1868, decided, as a conscious act-of-will and act-of-state, to "receive" Western institutions, processes and principles, including law, with the principal Western legal source, for both the private law and also constitutional law, being late 19th century Imperial German Law, symbolised in the adoption, in 1889, of a German-style *Rechtsstaat* constitution, and the adoption, later, of a Civil Code based on the then new German *Bürgerliches Gesetzbuch* of 1900. In the domain of International Law, after the inauguration of the *Meiji* era (1868-1912) and during the succeeding *Taisho* era (1912-26), there was a similar "reception" of Western-based International Law. That movement emphasised learning, faithfully, the positive law rules and theories of "classical" Western, Continental European-based International Law, and then simply applying them to events, as they might arise, in international society. It was only after the beginning of the *Showa* era in 1926, however, that Japanese studies in International Law really became established as a systematic juridical science in their own right, with a proper methodological foundation. This was the work, principally, of two very great scholars, Kisaburo Yokota and Ryoichi Taoka, who together built the scholastic foundation of modern International Law studies in Japan.[6] They applied a precise, positivist methodology based upon detailed historical analysis. Their approach is identified as historical positivism; although it bears obvious analogies to the method proposed by Cardozo in the U.S. for Municipal, national law testing, and there are also clear links to the first stages at least of that sociological enquiry in aid of law-making that is part of American Sociological Jurisprudence. The method employed by Yokota and Taoka emphasised the clarification of the socio-historical circumstances in which a claimed existing norm of International Law had first been formed, this on the premise that it was necessary to analyze the original social function of the norm in question and the limitation implied thereby on its practical operation.

Yokota traced the history of Japanese attitudes towards international adjudication,[7] and found such Japanese thinking to be originally, if briefly, sympathetic to that idea, in reflection of the enlightened European liberal internationalist thinking on International Law that was to culminate at the close of the 19th century in the establishment of the Permanent Court of Arbitration and in The Hague Conferences of 1899 and then 1907. During the period between the Russo-Japanese War of 1904-5 and World War II, however, Yokota found Japanese attitudes regarding international adjudication to be "negative, evasive and even antagonistic",[8] which he related directly to Japan's unhappy experience with the Permanent Court of Arbitration and its celebrated decision of 22 May 1905 in the so-called *House Tax* case. Yokota also acknowledged that the "marked tendency toward militarism appearing since the Russo-Japanese War" was hostile to the idea of international adjudication, since promoting opinion favouring the settlement of international disputes by force rather than peaceful methods.[9] Yokota and other Japanese jurists of his generation and general intellectual persuasion agreed, however, that World War II, in its cataclysmic break, for Japan, from its historical past through the agony of military defeat and the atomic bombings of Hiroshima and Nagasaki, brought a complete about-face in Japanese attitudes to international adjudication. This radical change was evidenced by Japan's acceptance, in 1958, of the Compulsory Jurisdiction of the International Court under the Optional Clause, and this without substantial reservations. Thus Japan, in the post-World War II era, in comparison even to Western states which were then the most vigorous vocal champions of international judicial settlement, had now become the "most advanced in the field of international adjudication, being ready to submit unconditionally all legal disputes to the I.C.J."[10]

What this suggests is that originally *Western* legal concepts, covering both substantive-legal ideas and also institutions and procedures, had, after their first "reception", sufficiently entered into *Japanese* legal discourse to become part of general *Japanese* legal culture and its specialised legal thought-ways and processes. It was the first Japanese judge on the International Court of Justice, Judge Tanaka, who defended the Court majority, in *South West Africa. Second Phase* in 1966, against charges, after that decision was rendered, of political bias; and who also affirmed, in neo-Positivist terms that the British judge, Sir Gerald Fitzmaurice, would certainly have approved, that the "essence" of the Court's function is "legal and not political disputes."[11] The Japanese "special legal community" in International Law (judges, University professors, Foreign Ministry legal advisers) is by now sufficiently acculturated in basic Western legal institutions like judicial review (including judicial policy-making, and its possibilities and also its prudent limits) to make judicial self-restraint, as represented by Judge Tanaka, fully consistent, in intellectual-legal terms, and also fully compatible, with more intrinsically and historically "Japanese" legal notions deriving from what Filmer Northrop identifies as the indigenous, local "living law". The Japanese jurist who later followed on Judge Tanaka, Judge Oda, had the dual training, Japanese Civil Law and Anglo-Saxon Common Law (U.S.-style) International Law; and one notes that, consistently with Judge Tanaka's general philosophical approach, Judge Oda, as one of the three dissenters in the International Court's 12-to-

3 *Merits* ruling in *Nicaragua*, bases his own Dissenting Opinion,[12] like his British colleague and co-Dissenter[13] (and unlike his U.S. colleague and co-Dissenter), on essentially technical grounds, thereby avoiding substantive law involvements and any temptation to canvass the political merits of the competing parties in the case. As an essentially neo-Positivist exercise, Judge Oda's Dissenting Opinion, it might be suggested, could well have been written by a judge with a wholly Western legal culture, since embracing that intellectually disciplined, logico-formal rationality that Max Weber conceived as being at the *apogée* of Western society and its legal development.

This is basically the point of the Indian jurist, Anand,[14] that Western legal philosophers like Northrop, and also Quincy Wright, and Jenks, and Röling, take much too static a view of the community "living law" in any society and its capacity *ipso facto* to frustrate or defeat borrowings, from outside, of other societies' distinctive legal institutions and processes and ideas. The process of foreign legal "reception" is, in itself, a dynamic act. It may either stimulate total rejection, thereby inevitably consolidating and extending existing, indigenous law and legal institutions; or else trigger a creative process of assimilation (and of refinement and adaptation and improvement) so that the "received", foreign law gradually acquires its own separate identity and integrity and may become, in the end, more rational and functionally effective and modern than the original foreign model from which it was first borrowed. In the international legal "Global Village" of today there is a sufficient interchange and interaction, between different legal systems, of jurists and of basic legal ideas, for the international legal culture to become increasingly homogenised, producing its own form of *Jus Gentium*-based common consensus on institutions like judicial review and its special modalities of operation. On this view, the judicial settlement of disputes is no longer a strictly "Western" concept, but has become truly international; and non-Western states that have participated in that creative evolution are not constrained by "classical" Western legal definitions prescribing or restricting the permissible limits of its concrete operation and application. Anand supplements his rejection of purely static, *Eurocentrist* attempts to limit the practical utility and efficacy of judicial settlement and judicial review to "Western" societies, by a persuasive argument that major non-Western societies, such as Hindu India, had, as part of their national legal cultures – and long before the arrival of the first Western European colonisers with their European Imperial law and court system, – their own highly developed network of courts for the administration of justice, dating back to very ancient times.[15] The conclusion is that there is nothing in the indigenous "living law" or legal traditions of Asian and African states inhibiting them from accepting international arbitration or international adjudication for purposes of international disputes-settlement. The empirical record of the International Court's dossier in the late 1970s and in the 1980s, with the impressive new *clientèle* of former Colonial, Asian and African states who are now positively invoking the Court's jurisdiction, would appear to confirm that.

## 3. THE "INTERNATIONALISING" OF THE INTERNATIONAL COURT AND ITS JUDGES

The debate of yesteryear over the "independence" or "neutrality" of the judges of the International Court is revealed, on empirical examination, to concern a false issue or at least one that is historically dated in contemporary terms. The contemporary national Special Constitutional Court or supra-national ("regional") tribunal is deliberately structured, in its basic rules on selection of judges, so as to secure political "balance" within the Court's ranks. This will, today, normally be done within the Court's Statute itself, and sometimes even in the national Constitutional Charter; but even in those states that have not reduced norms of "regional" (cultural-linguistic, legal-systemic, political-geographical) representation to positive law form, such principles tend to become effectively entrenched through Constitutional Custom or Convention as to judicial appointments and "reserved" seats on the Court. Where, as in France and West Germany, the judicial appointment/election power is dispersed and not concentrated in any one single authority, the Constitutional tribunal's membership will be chosen with significant inter-Party, political-ideological interaction. Supranational ("regional") tribunals like the High Court of Justice of the European Community countries, and indeed the International Court itself, are selected according to rules that guarantee "balanced" national representation. A key element in the contemporary Constitutional Court, – national, supra-national ("regional"), or international, – is now its political representativeness; and its claims to legitimacy in community decision-making terms necessarily relate back to that. Some current, intemperate political criticisms notwithstanding, charges of violation of judicial "independence" or judicial "neutrality" have not survived cool empirical examination. The special institution of the *ad hoc* judge, against which most of the public criticisms have been levelled,[16] is hardly important enough in itself, in simple numerical terms in a fifteen-member tribunal, to create too many practical problems.[17] In that great political *cause célèbre, South West Africa. Second Phase* in 1966, for example, with a closely divided Court that produced an 8-to-7 majority only on the second tie-breaking vote of the Court President, the two *ad hoc* judges' votes, quite predictably, cancelled each other out and did not affect the final outcome.

As for the issue of representativeness, even with the evidently more narrowly *Eurocentrist* or "Western" International Court of the late 1940s and the 1950s, the Court's membership more or less accurately mirrored the official World Community of the time, with its more limited, pre-Decolonisation, pre-Self-Determination, character. The Court membership has, in fact, kept pace in quite remarkable degree and with very little time lag, with the progressive expansion of the World Community to its presently genuinely inclusive, near universal basis. Such movement as now occurs in the regular, triennial elections to the Court, is of an incremental character only, refining the numerical balance between the different recognised "regions" (ethno-cultural, legal-systemic, political-ideological, as the case may be), along conceivedly more equitable lines; or else, within those "regions", developing and perfecting already existing ground rules or customs for rotating Court representation among the regional membership or for recognising special claims to more continuing representation on the part of some regional leaders.

Except perhaps on the part of the two superpowers who are Permanent Members of the Security Council and whose judicial candidates, by diplomatic courtesy, are not seriously contested, the professional-legal and also general intellectual or philosophical qualities of individual states' candidates, once perhaps considered marginal or secondary in relation to other, overriding political considerations, now assume an increasing importance. While states will hesitate to challenge existing equities as to allocation of seats between different "regions", when more than one state in a particular region is contesting a seat accepted as belonging to that region, Judge Elias' prophesy[18] that other states, in casting their votes in the judicial elections, will increasingly apply a thoughtful and critical analysis of individual candidates' scientific-legal qualifications and their degree of positive commitment, (as evidenced in their prior academic-scientific writings or in their official actions as government official or adviser), to the United Nations Charter mandate for the "progressive development of International Law", seems likely to be vindicated. Judge Elias was thinking, at the time, of the Third World states' scrutiny of Western states' candidates for claimed Western "regional" seats on the Court; but the principle is readily applicable in reverse, too, as we saw in the active and not necessarily well-counselled, Western states' positive intervention in the partial election to the International Court in April, 1989, to fill the vacancy in an Asian "regional" seat on the Court. The principle advanced by Judge Elias seems historically right and timely to the point, now, that even leading powers, Western and other, would be well advised not to take their existing seats for granted in the presence of other, intellectually better qualified and more attractive and open-minded, candidates from states in the same "region".

The "internationalising" of the International Court through the regular electoral processes, in this way, has not, unfortunately, been accompanied by any similar apparent change, in degree and in kind, in the Court's internal procedures and style of conducting cases coming before it, corresponding to the new, multi-cultural and plural-systemic quality of the Court's own membership. Judge Elias has referred to the inordinate costs of litigation before the International Court, whether contentious *inter-partes* suits or Advisory Opinion references,[19] and he relates this to unduly high lawyers' fees flowing from the sheer size of written pleadings and the length of oral statements before Court. Judge Elias' remedy:

> "Agents, counsel and advocates of parties to disputes before the Court should be implored to enact a self-denying ordinance so that fees charged for services rendered to relatively impecunious clients or in respect of disputes not involving complicated commercial and industrial enterprises could be kept within reasonable bounds. The idea of introducing a legal aid scheme for developing countries, which some have advocated in recent years, should be discountenanced, as these countries would view with suspicion and even resentment any offer of financial assistance or charity in the prosecution of their claim for redress before an international tribunal."[20]

One wonders, however, if the Court itself has done enough to limit the excesses, oral and written, and the consequent vastly expanded professional-legal fees, of states appearing before the Court. The Court's judges, so many of whom, – even those from non-Western states – are trained in part in Western Europe, have tolerated the emergence of a system of conducting cases before the Court that would seem to accentuate some of the worst elements of Western European national legal practice: unlimited oral argument conducted, successively, by the many lawyers in a state's team of counsel, and endless written briefs and supporting memoranda and documents that seem intended to pile Mount Pelion on Mount Ossa. Surely the legal issues in the vast majority of cases reaching the Court are sufficiently clear-cut, and the underlying social facts sufficiently a matter of public record (and subject, therefore, to judicial notice), – with *South West Africa. Second Phase*, and *Nicaragua*, as notable examples – for the Court to be able to cut through to the essentials, quickly and economically? One wonders if the U.S. Supreme Court's normal, one-hour maximum rule for oral argumentation for each side in a case might not sensibly be applied by the International Court, in furtherance of Judge Elias' basic recommendation.

There is another element, too, to the progressive "internationalising" of the International Court, and that concerns the choice of counsel appearing before the Court. A recent case before the Court, involving two North African, Islamic (Arab) states, *Tunisia/Libyan Arab Jamahiriya*,[21] had, as advocates pleading on the one side, one British lawyer, three French lawyers, one Arab jurist living in Switzerland, and one local lawyer; and, on the other side, two British lawyers, three U.S. lawyers, one French lawyer, one Italian lawyer, and one Arab jurist from Iraq (who died during the pendency of the case).[22] Another case, before the Court in 1988, and involving two Central American states, *Border and Transborder Armed Actions* (*Nicaragua* v. *Honduras*),[23] listed as Advocates pleading, on the one side, one British lawyer, one U.S. lawyer, and one French lawyer; and, on the other side, one British lawyer, one French lawyer, and one Spanish lawyer.[24] Even Nicaragua, for its ultimately successful legal complaint against the U.S.,[25] retained, as Advocates pleading the case, one British lawyer, two U.S. lawyers, and one French lawyer.[26]

In discussion with members of the International Court, it is suggested that not every state, and particularly those normally characterised as Third World states, will have its own local Bar of sufficient legal training and experience confidently to plead cases before the International Court. One wonders, however, if the Court's judges have themselves done enough to dispel the myth, dating back to the old Permanent Court of the pre-World War II era, that International Law as practised before the Court is an arcane, Western science that can be comprehended only by Western legal practitioners. In Municipal, national law, Common Law appellate tribunals traditionally extend a special indulgence, in the actual conduct of cases, to parties who are either not represented at all by legal counsel or else represented by manifestly young or inexperienced counsel. Why should not the International Court do the same, as a method of encouraging states to use their own nationals as counsel, or at least to include some of their own nationals in a team of counsel? Again, in municipal, national law, the French *Conseil d'Etat* supplies a perfect model of a determinedly contemporary tribunal anxious to maintain simplified, streamlined, and inexpensive processes, and perfectly capable of achieving those goals in rational fashion.

## 4. THE INTERNATIONAL COURT AS SUI GENERIS INSTITUTION

It should not be forgotten that the International Court, as lineal successor to the old Permanent Court of the between-the-two-World Wars era, now has seven decades of historical experience and trial-and-error testing and development, both as to its *jurisprudence* and also as to its procedures and internal regulation and practice concerning conduct and hearing of cases and modes of decision-making and of opinion-writing in support of Court decisions. By virtue of its current clear claims to universality, in the choice of its members and in the range of different legal cultures and legal systems that they now represent, the Court is in the position, if it wishes, to become a Comparative Law tribunal *par excellence*, integrating and synthesising diverse jurisprudential strains, for purposes of producing a new, pluralist, *Jus Gentium*-based International Law, both substantive and procedural.[27] But the Court does not have to take the Comparative Law route blindly and undiscriminatingly; and it should reject those forms of purely mechanical legal eclecticism, involving non-contextual use of particular rules or processes from particular Municipal, national legal systems, that are sometimes urged upon it by its critics. As has been suggested, comparisons between the International Court and national Supreme Courts like the British House of Lords or the U.S. Supreme Court, or even supra-national, "regional" tribunals like the High Court of Justice of the European Communities may be

> "inappropriate and constitute a disservice to the Court for the political framework in which these judicial bodies operate, the nature of their jurisdiction and their proceedings are quite different from those of the International Court of Justice".[28]

The recourse to Comparative Law, by way of analogy or model for direct and immediate adoption, thus needs to be critical and discriminating, with proper regard to the context in which selected rules and processes originated in the society or societies concerned and to the congruence or non-congruence of those societies with international society at the present stage of its development. While former Judge Pescatore of the European Communities Court[29] is right to look to that tribunal, above all, as a paradigm of a plural-systemic court in a rapidly evolving, plural-cultural society that has managed to achieve a high degree of operational efficacy in formulating common rules, derived from the various legal systems represented on the Court, to meet new societal problems, Judge Bedjaoui of the International Court[30] is clearly correct in offering a caveat as to the relevance and transferability of even the European Communities Court's experience to the International Court at the present day. Judge Bedjaoui reminds us of the historical distinctiveness of the organisation of the International Court and of the fact, for example, that unlike various Continental Western European tribunals that are claimed to be analogous, the International Court of Justice and the predecessor Permanent Court of International Justice were always built upon the concept of a *plenum* or Full Court operating for all cases or references before the Court; and not at all – in its practice, as distinct from the abstract, *a priori* statutory blueprints – upon any system of Chambers or Special Chambers operating within the Full Court. Seven decades of collegial experience by the Full Court, operating as such, plus the absence of any postulated *functional* justification for special panels or even any arguments of Court overload in actual number of cases (for which latter, of course, there would be other, alternative, less pathological solutions available), thus counselled against any latter-day attempt to sub-divide the Court's jurisdiction by way of Special Chambers.

The immediate origins of the recourse to Special Chambers at the end of the 1970s and the beginning of the 1980s, when the U.S. Administration's disillusionment with the International Court was marked, gave it the appearance of an *ad hoc* political ploy designed to evade the jurisdiction of the Full Court without the political opprobrium attaching to any overt and outright break with the Compulsory Jurisdiction of the Court. The International Court itself, after the initial trial-and-error testing in *Gulf of Maine*,[31] has now managed to refine the Special Chamber concept operationally and to harmonise it better with the Court's own ongoing historical traditions, by seemingly refusing the notion that the state parties have the legal right themselves to choose the Special Chamber judges and imposing, instead, a consensual, Court-and-parties process of selection in which, however, the Court's own preferred views will remain paramount and final for the parties. It is unlikely, however, that Judge Bedjaoui's critique of Special Chambers as being antithetical to the International Court's general historical development will be satisfactorily answered unless and until the International Court should opt to follow Judge Lachs' demonstration[32] that the original *raison d'être* and contemporary justification for such Chambers must reside in functional specialisation and in the creation of panels based on expertise in particular subject matters not generally represented within the Court's ranks.

## 5. THE COURT AND "POLITICAL QUESTIONS"

The "Law"/"Politics" dichotomy, as an *a priori* legal category, is itself a product of a particularist, and spatially and temporally relativist, body of legal theory involving particularist conceptions of the judicial process and of the constitutional *rôle* of the judge in community policy-making, that have no claims to universality of application today. Reflecting the aspirations of late 19th century liberal democratic society for clarity and certainty in law to the exclusion of other values, and for precise delimitation and separation of governmental functions and decision-making, the "Law"/"Politics" dichotomy corresponded, in legal terms, to the "hands-off" approach of the *laissez-faire* state to issues of economic policy-making and regulation which were, by definition, to be left to the uncontrolled play of market forces. Legal Positivism, as a philosophy of law, is not necessarily good for all times and all places, or for international society at its present stage of historical development. Besides, the postulated political "neutrality" of approaches such as that of the Court majority in the 8-to-7 decision in *South West Africa. Second Phase* in 1966,[33] ignores the obvious fact that, in its consequences when applied, that decision was anything but politically neutral, in effectively licensing the continuance of the white minority-ruled Republic of South Africa's hegemony over the U.N. Trust Territory of Namibia (South West Africa) and the extension of its racially discriminatory legal *régime* of *Apartheid* to that Trust Territory. Every legal case or Advisory Opinion reference of the International Court, in this dimension, necessarily takes on a political character, of varying degree or intensity. Just as Municipal, national Constitutional tribunals had increasingly abandoned the asserted distinction between Law and Politics, under its various synonyms, as a false dichotomy, so the International Court's abandonment of the Court majority's earlier neo-Positivist conception of the judicial *rôle* as expressed in *South West Africa. Second Phase* in 1966, with the Court ruling in *Namibia* in 1971,[34] was no doubt historically inevitable in its own right. This was because of the evolution of the Court's own philosophy of law, going hand-in-hand with the evolution of the Court's legal-cultural and legal-systemic representativeness, – quite apart from the World-wide political back-lash to the *South West Africa. Second Phase* rationale and any to-be-expected *ad hoc* Court reactions to that.

Thereafter, the International Court, in rejecting the claimed "Law"/"Politics" dichotomy as inappropriate and inapplicable to its own *jurisprudence*, would appear to be evolving, like Municipal, national Constitutional tribunals, to a highly nuanced, cases-oriented approach in which the two different categories are seen merely as points in a factual continuum, with the judges free to decide in the individual case, on essentially pragmatic considerations, whether or not to exercise jurisdiction and to rule on the substantive-legal issues inherent in it. The question of justiciability is better seen, then, in the context of the Judicial Self-Restraint/Judicial Activism antinomy, with the decision whether or not the judges should intervene and rule in a substantive way being resolved by application of the same range of criteria looked to in other, more general arenas for community policy-making. Among these, the issue of timing, and whether a particular problem is really "ripe" for judicial settlement at that particular moment; and the availability of other, alternative arenas for community problem-solving, and whether these might be more appropriate or useful than Court-based action in the particular case; and also the problem-solving capacities of judges, and their practical limits, if any, in the particular context of the case before the Court. In its own way, on an empirical, case-by-case basis, and as it seems, in retrospect, through a testing, sometimes trial-and-error method, the International Court has developed, in its *jurisprudence*, its own operational indices[35] to guide it for its decision-making for the future. These look, on the one hand, to situations or categories of events where the Court may opt, prudently, to exercise self-restraint in regard to great political *causes célèbres*, and thus to apply a politic of judicial non-involvement either by declining jurisdiction altogether, or, where this is hardly possible on the past precedents, then by consciously avoiding, in the actual decision and opinion-writing, the substantive, high policy issues in favour of rulings given on essentially procedural or adjectival-law grounds.

The guide-posts, on the other hand, for judicial interventionism and for the exercise of an activist, policy-making, legislative *rôle* in relation to old International Law *doctrines* as sought to be applied to new societal problems of the World Community, are rather less explicit in the Court's *jurisprudence*. They tend to be derived, inferentially, from examination of the canons of judicial self-restraint, as established in the Court *jurisprudence*, so that if the tests for the latter are not offended, then the Court may sensibly go ahead to canvass the high policy issues involved in a case. The actual record of the International Court's *jurisprudence* in the post-*South West Africa. Second Phase* era, shows a tribunal that is increasingly confident in its new, community policy-making *rôle*; but a tribunal, nevertheless, that as an important element in that new judicial and legal sophistication, will still be cautious about venturing into policy pronouncements in law unless the essential procedural, adjectival law pre-conditions for a Court ruling are properly met, and unless the occasion really does seem to be legally and politically timely and helpful for an exercise in judicial policy-making, in cooperation with or separately from other coordinate institutions of community policy-making, like the General Assembly or the Security Council.

## 6. OPERATIONAL INDICES AS TO JUSTICIABILITY IN CONTEMPORARY INTERNATIONAL LAW PROBLEM-SITUATIONS

### A. The issue of timing

Are some international legal problem-situations simply not "ripe" for judicial settlement at the particular time in which they are raised before the International Court? Or, putting it more directly, is judicial intervention, in the particular context, more likely to impede rather than to assist international problem-solving and conflicts-resolution?

In *Certain Expenses of the United Nations* in 1962,[36] the Advisory Opinion ruling, by 9-to-5 majority of the Court, in the dispute over the United Nations Congo operation and the use of the U.N. Secretary-General's Office in the particular political solution to the post-Decolonisation Congo succession that finally emerged in the United Nations, undoubtedly clarified the meaning of Article 17(2) of the U.N. Charter,[37] the technical point involved in the reference to the Court. But in confirming one of the state parties to the political dispute within the United Nations in the legal rightness of its cause, the Court's majority ruling, as its practical result, encouraged that particular state party in the politically intransigent strategy of forcing the matter to a political show-down in the United Nations General Assembly. The ineluctable political consequence in the General Assembly, once Article 19 of the United Nations Charter had there been invoked by the winning party in the International Court[38] – depriving the Soviet Union, (and also France), of their votes in the General Assembly – was generally accepted as amounting, if accepted by the General Assembly, to an unmitigated political disaster for the United Nations as a whole at that time. The only practical political way out of the legal dilemma created by the Court's ruling was, in effect, to adjourn the General Assembly *sine die*, before it could enter upon the issue, thereby postponing all the General Assembly's substantive agenda until the next Annual Session, twelve months away, when the issue of application of Article 19 of the Charter, was, by general consent and to a near universal satisfaction, allowed quietly to drop. In historical retrospect, an untimely, premature ruling by the Court, purportedly restricted to the "legal" issues, but occurring before the processes of diplomatic negotiation and give-and-take had been properly tried and exhausted, hardened the rival state parties in their politically antagonistic positions, thereby exacerbating the conflict and delaying its final solution. A Constitutional tribunal, – as leading Municipal, national legal systems have amply recognised, – is always entitled to "make an ally of time" and delay its ruling until political circumstances are more propitious than they clearly were in *Certain Expenses of the United Nations* in 1962.

In a number of other cases – *Nuclear Tests*,[39] *Iranian Hostages*,[40] as examples – the issue of timing, though not central, appears to have entered into the Court's approach to decision-making. In *Nuclear Tests*, the Court majority evidently concluded that, at the particular stage then reached in the on-going diplomatic negotiations over nuclear disarmament, between the two superpowers and also more generally within the United Nations, no useful purpose would be served by an International Court ruling on the substantive legality of nuclear armaments or nuclear test explosions. The Court majority in *Nuclear Tests* managed, however, elegantly and easily, to place the Court on the side of the Angels. The Court's decision effectively ensured an end to the French Government's high-level nuclear tests in the South Pacific; but in avoiding substantive-legal issues, consciously and purposefully, the Court did so by the procedural device of estoppel, holding the French Government legally bound by its own previous Unilateral Declarations of Intention to cease such nuclear tests for the future.[41]

In *Iranian Hostages*,[42] the Court seems to have been sufficiently disturbed by the blow to some of the very oldest and best applied rules of International Law, the Privileges and Immunities of Diplomats and Consuls –, to move quickly to a judgment on the general principle. However, such a Court ruling, given *tout court* and without some Court openings to the underlying major political conflicts between Iran and the U.S., going back to the U.S. Government-backed military coup against the Mossadeq Government of Iran a quarter century earlier, could not ensure, in the end result, that there would be cooperation by the Iranian Government in the implementation of the Court decision. The practical follow-up – release of the detained U.S. Diplomatic and Consular personnel – would have to wait several years and then be achieved by other, non-judicial, diplomatic negotiating techniques, and by other, non-judicial, diplomatic players. The Court majority ruling, limited as it was to the abstract general principle, was no doubt admirable as a re-affirmation of "old", "classical" International Law principles so recently repeated as "new", treaty-based, International Law; but it may properly be questioned as to how much it itself positively contributed to the contemporary international problem-solving in the particular case and to the time dimension of such problem-solving. Would a more nuanced Court approach, that affirmed the general principle of Diplomatic and Consular Privileges and also the receiving, host state's clear and unequivocal legal obligations to uphold them, but that then went on to include, in terms, some of the types of legal reservations expressed in the Special and Dissenting Opinions[43] as to the contribution of the conduct of both state parties in the escalation and exacerbation of their dispute, have been operationally more helpful and useful in producing an effective and timely solution?

## B. The issue of fact-finding

Underlying issues of fact, as Municipal, national Constitutional tribunals have also amply recognised, do indeed condition or determine questions of ultimate legality, especially where what is involved are general legal concepts or legal standards. The fact-finding issue was one of the grounds of complaint advanced by the United States Administration for its withdrawal, in mid-passage, from the proceedings before the International Court in *Nicaragua*,[44] and then for termination of the U.S. acceptance of the Compulsory Jurisdiction of the Court under the Optional Clause. The fact-finding problem, to the extent that it was influential or controlling in the final, *Merits* decision of the Court in *Nicaragua*, was undoubtedly contributed to by the U.S. Administration's own decision to quit the case before the actual hearings on *Merits*. A good deal of the U.S. Administration's anger on this point was undoubtedly provoked by the Court's summary rejection, in October, 1984, of the request by the Government of El Salvador[45] to be allowed to intervene, under Article 63 of the Court Statute,[46] in the dispute in *Nicaragua* v. *United States*. That was the occasion, two years later, for a sharp verbal exchange between the U.S. judge on the Court[47] and the then President of the Court, Judge Elias.[48] The Court as a whole was sufficiently unimpressed by El Salvador's legal claims to be allowed to intervene, for it to decide to reject the El Salvador application by a 14-to-1 majority, with only the U.S. judge dissenting.[49] This was immediately following upon the Court's ruling, in the same process, by 9-to-6 vote, not to allow an oral hearing of the El Salvador application.[50] At the later, *Merits* stage of the *Nicaragua* case, Judge Lachs, while having no doubts as to the *legal* correctness of the Court's earlier decision to reject El Salvador's claim to intervene, seems to have had some second thoughts as to its *political* wisdom in the light of subsequent U.S. Administration actions, Judge Lachs here citing the old legal maxim that Justice must not only be done, but also be "seen to be done".[51]

The International Court's approach to fact-finding in the *Nicaragua* complex of cases over the period 1984-1986 seems to have been to rely very heavily on the concept, well-accepted and well-applied in Municipal, national Constitutional Law, of Judicial Notice, which allows Courts to act, without any need for special enquiry, upon facts of general public knowledge. It would, in this respect, be very difficult to find a case, in the *jurisprudence* of the old Permanent Court and of the new International Court, as well publicised, as to its essential elements and also the motivations and actions of the various state players involved, as the *Nicaragua* conflict. The U.S. mass media (television, radio, and newspapers) had given maximum coverage, on a day-to-day basis, to the facts of U.S. Government direct involvement in Nicaraguan affairs and to the U.S. Government direct financial aid and military-logistical support for the so-called *Contra* rebels who were operating from "safe haven" bases in neighbouring, Central American states, against Nicaraguan territory.

A legally apparently more subtle and more demanding problem of fact-finding is that offered by former International Court judge and sometime Court President, Jiménez de Aréchaga in the suggested distinction between "frontier disputes" and "disputes as to the attribution of territory".[52] The first category is explained as involving "delimitation disputes [in which] the Court is asked to draw a boundary line or interpret a boundary treaty or an arbitral award", with the enquiry "subordinated to the legal titles such as relevant delimitation treaties, arbitral awards or maps accepted or not contested by the parties."[53] The prime example offered of this category, – reflecting, perhaps, Dr. Jiménez de Aréchaga's own personal legal-culture – is of Latin American frontier disputes: "When the principle of *uti possidetis juris* is applicable, decisive importance is assigned to delimitation documents issued in colonial times by the former common sovereign".[54]

The second category, – "disputes as to the attribution of territory" – is perhaps not clarified too much by the further explanation that it involves cases in which the "Court must determine ... which State has sovereignty over an island, a group of islands, or another whole territory".[55] Perhaps the purported distinction is better offered not in *a priori*, verbal terms, but experientially in terms of the Court's own past *jurisprudence* and the sort of cases in which the Court's intervention has been actively invited by the rival state parties; and those, clearly, in which it has clearly not been welcomed by *both* parties but only sought by one. The first sort of case of an essentially friendly, non-adversary proceeding between two states with long-continuing stable relations in territorial matters, is evidenced in the *Minquiers and Écrehos* dispute[56] between France and Great Britain; and more recently, perhaps, by the post-Decolonisation frontier disputes between "succession" states to the old European Imperial powers in sub-Sahara Africa, once those "succession" states had realistically accepted as ultimate *Grundnorm* of their mutual relations the legitimacy, and hence inviolability *inter se*, of their respective, inherited Imperial Colonial boundaries.[57] On this basis, there is no difficulty in assigning *Frontier Dispute (Burkina Faso/Mali)*,[58] a difference between two former French

Colonies in Africa, to the first category. Such cases, because of the prior consensus between the parties that their vital interests are not involved, can sensibly be confined to narrow, technical, non-policy issues, to which the "classical", Positivist legal skills are clearly relevant. The only question, here, would be whether the International Court, in its contemporary, consciously policy-making *rôle*, is best occupied with such questions which inevitably require a great deal of valuable time and patience and concern with low-level detail and culling of old historical sources, in comparison, for example, to a non-judicial, expert fact-finding commission designated by the rival parties themselves or else chosen by some process agreed upon by them.

The second sort of case has potentially far more explosive political implications, since the quest for legal truth, in the end, may involve not merely the attempted ascertainment or definition of a pre-existing legal *status quo*, but active involvement by the Court or other tribunal that is charged with the problem in changing that situation in response to new societal conditions or demands. Most of the "little" wars between the European states in the "classical" era of International Law, both in Europe itself and also when projected to the new territories in Asia and Africa and the Caribbean deemed ripe for Colonising, were of this character. The quest for national *Lebensraum*, or for "natural frontiers", was inevitably adversarial; and only one party could expect to emerge the victor from the resultant political-diplomatic or military conflict. In the post-Decolonisation era, it might make sense for a European Imperial power or its Colonial surrogate to seek a Court ruling on its territorial claims if the tribunal, as in *South West Africa. Second Phase*,[59] could confidently be expected to apply a "fortress Positivism" approach to International Law and, in the result, simply confirm and ratify the already existing Colonial title. Once, however, the Court should venture, as with some of the more imaginative Special Opinions in *Western Sahara*,[60] to re-examine the original legal foundations of the claimed Colonial title, then the attractions of seeking a legal interpretation of title from the Court, in the first place, would tend to disappear for Imperial powers and for their latter-day surrogates like the white minority-ruled Republic of South Africa. The switch in majority judicial philosophy on the International Court, as between *South West Africa. Second Phase* in 1966,[61] and in *Namibia* in 1971,[62] had, in this respect, dramatic and predictable consequences for the attitudes and expectations of the different classes of potential client-states of the International Court.

Sometimes the state parties, since not well briefed by their Foreign Ministries both as to their ultimate objectives themselves and also as to the best arenas and processes for achieving them, may make a misstep in choice of these. Sometimes, it may be a particular tribunal that misconceives its own proper *rôle* in problem-solving and that, thereby, adds to the problem rather than helping to resolve it. The *Beagle Channel* Arbitration has been cited as just such an example;[63] for there an Arbitral tribunal, forgetting that arbitration, far more than judicial decision-making (at least as far as the latter is "classically" defined and limited) has a mandate to reach equitable as distinct from narrowly legalistic decisions, seemed to try to act as an expert fact-finding commission only and to eschew any concern for the substantial merits of the rival state claims.

Once the Court's jurisdiction has been properly invoked, however, whether *inter partes* or by way of Advisory Opinion reference, it is the Court's decision, and not that of the parties, whether ruling the matter to be justiciable and so proceeding on to judgment on the substantive issues of International Law involved is, on balance, useful in international conflicts-resolution or in contribution to the progressive development of International Law. The Court, with a broader legal perspective and certainly a more plural legal-cultural background than the rival parties, may sensibly differ from either or both of them on that point. In continuing disputes such as those between Great Britain and Spain over Gibraltar,[64] or between Great Britain and Argentina over the Falklands (Malvinas), where one party, clearly, would benefit from the "old", "classical" International Law mechanically and unimaginatively restated, and the other from the "new" International Law, the conclusion of the individual parties whether or not to resort to international judicial settlement will turn on their own individual appraisals or informed predictions of just how the Court majority can be expected to react today in the light of its *jurisprudence constante*, and also as evidenced in the trends in the Court's more recent case law. For the Court, the decision to intervene or not to intervene, by ruling the dispute to be justiciable or else non-justiciable, turns on other, more long-range, pragmatic considerations, here including the availability of other, alternative international problem-solving arenas and processes and their degree of relevance or competence for the particular issue at hand.

C. "Judge and Company": the issue of a constitutional separation-of-powers

"The law", in Jeremy Bentham's phrase, "is not made by Judge alone, but by Judge and Company." After an early period, in Municipal, national constitutional law dominated by overly rigid conceptions of the triadic separation or division of governmental decision-making authority, – in ways never intended by Montesquieu himself, – into watertight compartments of executive, legislative, and judicial power, with no possibility of any mutual cooperation or sharing between those different institutions, we have, in modern times, seen a new, pragmatic evolution towards full complementarity of legal authority, with the informed constitutional emphasis today being on saving and not frustrating community problem-solving. While the United Nations Charter, in its Article 12, forbids, in terms, the General Assembly from acting on any dispute or situation while the Security Council is exercising its own Charter-assigned functions in the matter, – "unless the Security Council so requests", no such prohibition is established under the Charter in regard to Court action or Court initiatives concurrent with Security Council, or for that matter General Assembly action. In other words, the issue of the Court's acting on a matter that is before one of the political organs of the U.N. (Security Council/General Assembly) is different, in Constitutional-legal, Charter terms, from one of possible conflicts of those political organs *inter se*. As Judge Lachs has commented, sagely:

"There is an old Roman law principle that if you resort to one method you cannot resort to other methods. Well, we have abandoned this – I was very active in abandoning it – and if there is a dispute, now you have to seek all methods, perhaps simultaneously, in order to solve it."[65]

Judge Lachs indicated *Aegean Sea Continental Shelf*[66] as a leading instance of the International Court's new flexibility as to the location and, if you wish, pluralisation of international legal problem-solving capacity. The two state parties, Greece and Turkey, were before the United Nations Security Council, on a complaint from Greece; and Greece, at the same time, had instituted proceedings against Turkey before the International Court of Justice. In ruling, in 1976, on the Greek request, in the first instance, for Interim Measures of protection under Article 41 of the Court Statute, pending final determination by the Court of the substantive-legal issues involved, the Court took notice that, simultaneously with the proceedings before it, the Security Council was also seized of the dispute, and that the Security Council had held a number of meetings with the participation of representatives of both Greece and Turkey and had adopted, by consensus, a Resolution[67] that, *inter alia*, urged the parties to resume diplomatic negotiations. In the light of its own *résumé* of the course of the parallel action before the Security Council, the Court concluded that it was not necessary to examine the question of Interim Measures, the Court deciding accordingly by a 12-to-1 vote.[68] In an interesting Separate Opinion, Judge Lachs[69] specifically examined the question of whether the fact of the parallel proceedings before the Security Council should constitutionally inhibit the Court from pronouncing on the Greek complaint. Judge Lachs

thought not, here adopting several instances of the practice of the old
Permanent Court of International Justice:

">... The present Court, whose Statute is much more intimately bound up
with the United Nations Charter than that of its predecessor with the
Covenant of the League, should the more readily seize the opportunity of
reminding the member States concerned in a dispute referred to it of
certain obligations deriving from general international law or flowing
from the Charter .... There was in my view no statutory bar to its
spelling out the legal consequences of the Security Council's resolution
and the official statements of the representatives of the two States. The
pronouncements of the Council did not dispense the Court, an independent judicial organ, from expressing its own view on the serious situation
in the disputed area .... In going further than it has, the Court, with all
the weight of its judicial office, could have made its own constructive,
albeit indirect, contribution, helping to pave the way to the friendly
resolution of a dangerous dispute."[70]

Judge Tarazi, in his Separate Opinion,[71] took the same beneficial, expansive
view of the Court's powers, rejecting any negative implication flowing
from the simultaneous presence of the problem-situation before the Court
and other U.N. organs. Judge Tarazi noted that the International Court,
unlike the predecessor Permanent Court, is expressly stipulated in Article
7(1) of the U.N. Charter as one of the "principal organs of the United
Nations"; while Article 92 of the Charter indicates that the Court Statute is
annexed to and "forms an integral part" of the Charter. It flowed from this
that if, by virtue of the Charter, – "the Security Council bears an essential
responsibility for the maintenance of peace and security", nevertheless –
"the Court, if the circumstances so require, ought to collaborate in the
accomplishment of this fundamental mission".[72]

Judge Mosler, in his Separate Opinion, also felt no particular problem to
be created for the Court by the simultaneity of action in the Court and in the
Security Council, holding that the Court had an – "overall responsibility to
consider the situation as a whole, quite apart from its assessment of the
Security Council's resolution and the reaction thereto of Greece and
Turkey".[73]

Having declined to grant Interim Measures of protection under Article 41
of the Court Statute, pending any final determination, the Court then went
on, in its further, 1978, Judgment in the same cause,[74] to deny jurisdiction
to hear the Greek complaint against Turkey, this by a 12-to-2 vote based on
the Court's interpretation both of the 1928 General Act for the Pacific
Settlement of International Disputes, and also of a joint *communiqué* issued
by the two parties in 1975 and alleged by Greece to constitute an agreement

to refer the matter to the Court. The Opinion of Court did reject, in passing, a somewhat analogous argument to the earlier objection, advanced at the Interim Proceedings stage, that the Court proceedings should be stopped because of the simultaneous action in the Security Council. Here, the Opinion of Court responded to an objection to the further Court proceedings based on the argument that –

"the existence of active negotiations in progress constitutes an impediment to the Court's exercise of jurisdiction in the present case. The Court is unable to share this view. Negotiation and judicial settlement are enumerated together in Article 33 of the Charter of the United Nations as means for the peaceful settlement of disputes. The jurisprudence of the Court provides various examples of cases in which negotiations and recourse to judicial settlement have been pursued *pari passu* .... The fact that negotiations are being actively pursued during the present proceedings is not, legally, any obstacle to the exercise by the Court of its official function."[75]

In *Aegean Sea Continental Shelf* the International Court thus effectively disposed of old-fashioned, separation-of-powers arguments that would legally inhibit the Court from acting when the Security Council is also acting, and that would involve deference to a constitutional concept of a necessary, absolute divorcement of the functions of the two institutions.

In its earlier ruling in the *Namibia* Advisory Opinion in 1971,[76] the International Court had also rejected similar arguments of a constitutional separation-of-powers between the judicial and legislative organs of the United Nations, and specifically the argument that the U.N. General Assembly was illegally usurping judicial functions. In a written statement submitted to the Court and also in the oral arguments made by the Republic of South Africa in the hearings by the Court, it was contended that the U.N. General Assembly had acted *ultra vires* in adopting its Resolution 2145 (XXI) in 1966,[77] immediately after the Court's *South West Africa. Second Phase* decision.[78] This was the Resolution that, in reaction to that 8-to-7 Court decision, had declared "terminated" the Republic of South Africa Mandate over Namibia. The objections therein advanced by the Governments of France and South Africa were repeated, succinctly, in the Annex to the Dissenting Opinion of Judge Fitzmaurice, in *Namibia*:[79]

"When, by its Resolution 2145 of 1966, the Assembly purported to declare the termination of South Africa's mandate, on the basis of alleged fundamental breaches of it, ... it was making pronouncements of an essentially juridical character which the Assembly, not being a judicial organ, and not having previously referred the matter to any such organ, was not competent to make.

"... A separation of functions is the rule. Thus the legislature is alone
competent to enact a law, – the executive or administration alone
competent to apply or enforce it, – the judiciary alone competent to
interpret it and decide whether its application or enforcement is justified
in the particular case..."[80]

The response of the Court majority, in *Namibia*, to this constitutional law-
based, absolute separation-of-powers argument, was direct and categorical.
First, on the question whether the Court could examine the validity of the
U.N. General Assembly Resolution (and also the related Security Council
Resolution) and, in effect, "act as a court of appeal from their decisions",[81]
the Opinion of Court affirmed that – "the Court does not possess powers of
judicial review or appeal in respect of the decisions taken by the United
Nations organs concerned".[82]

Examining these arguments, nevertheless, – "in the exercise of its
judicial function and since objections have been advanced",[83] the Opinion
of Court in *Namibia* returned, logically and inevitably, to the 8-to-7
majority decision in *South West Africa. Second Phase* in 1966:

"Without dwelling on the conclusions reached in the 1966 Judgment in
the *South West Africa* contentious cases, it is worth recalling that in those
cases the applicant States, which complained of material breaches of
substantive provisions of the Mandate, were held not to 'possess any
separate self-contained right which they could assert ... to require the
due performance of the Mandate in discharge of the 'sacred trust''.
[I.C.J. Reports 1966, pp. 29 and 51]. On the other hand, the Court
declared that: '... any divergences of view concerning the conduct of a
mandate were regarded as being matters that had their place in the
political field, the settlement of which lay between the mandatory and the
competent organs of the League [of Nations]'. [ibid., p. 45]. To deny to a
political organ of the United Nations which is a successor of the League
in this respect the right to act, on the argument that it lacks competence
to render what is described as a judicial decision, would not only be
inconsistent but would amount to a complete denial of the remedies
available against fundamental breaches of an international under-
taking."[84]

The Court, in *Namibia*, thus concluded against the existence of any formal
separation-of-powers barrier, – "classical" Western constitutional law-style
– to the operation and interaction of the decision-making competences of
the principal organs of the United Nations, – General Assembly, Security
Council, and International Court. For these institutions all partake of the
general constitutional competence of the United Nations and share responsibility for the exercise of its international problem-solving powers. If the

international problem-solving process should break down or otherwise become clogged – as happened, evidently, as a consequence of the Court's decision in *South West Africa. Second Phase* in 1966, – then it would be quite unreasonable to stand on ceremony and insist on trying to maintain some particularist Western, abstract, *a priori*, "watertight compartments"-style division of decision-making powers, at the expense of substantive problem-solving. On this approach, the extreme judicial self-restraint consciously applied by the Court majority in the 8-to-7 decision in *South West Africa. Second Phase* in 1966, compelled some reciprocal, compensatory action by the other, coordinate United Nations institutions, the General Assembly and Security Council, to fill the gap as to effective community problem-solving in a political and legal crisis-situation.

It was in this same spirit that the Court, in *Nicaragua. Jurisdiction and Admissibility. Judgment,* in 1984, rejected the U.S. argument that the conflict there in question was non-justiciable as belonging to the competence of the Security Council and not of the Court, or "as being in effect an appeal to the Court from an adverse decision of the Security Council".[85]

## 7. THE NEW CONSTITUTIONAL LEGITIMACY OF THE INTERNATIONAL COURT AND OF JUDICIAL LAW-MAKING

We have seen a progressive evolution, over the post-World War II era, in the character and composition, and also the public image, of the International Court, from its being a narrowly Western, "Eurocentrist" institution to one that is genuinely representative of the larger, pluralistic World Community that has emerged in the wake of Decolonisation and Self-Determination of Peoples. Corresponding to the change in the Court's membership, there has been a profound change in the dominant philosophy of law within the Court from an essentially Positivist, abstract jurisprudence-of-concepts and strict-and-literal interpretation approach, that seemed to lead, inevitably, to a mechanical restatement of the old, "classical" International Law and, as a practical consequence, to the maintenance of the legal and political *status quo* in the World Community. In the field of Jurisdiction and Justiciability, the resulting self-denying ordinance of the Court meant passing up the opportunity and also the responsibility for assisting in the solution of the great political-legal *causes célèbres* stemming from the unbearable tensions between an old and increasingly out-dated positive law International Law and the new societal demands and expectations of a World Community undergoing fundamental change in an era of transition in International Relations.

The new, community policy-making, legislative *rôle* that the Court majority increasingly sees for itself, since the epochal ruling in *Namibia* in 1971, has its dangers as well as its opportunities. On the positive side, with a bench of the Full Court that is now remarkably representative in ethno-cultural, legal-systemic, and political-ideological terms, and that has a political and legal mandate flowing from the election of its members by the Security Council and General Assembly and from election for a term-of-years that must be renewed at regular intervals, the International Court's claims to constitutional legitimacy for its ventures in new law-making seem at least as great, within the United Nations legal system, as those of modern Constitutional tribunals like those of West Germany and France and the United States are within their own Municipal, national legal systems. On the other hand, the conscious eschewing of abstract, *a priori* categories of Jurisdiction and Justiciability in favour of pragmatic tests that emphasise the Court's common international problem-solving responsibilities and common mandate for the progressive development of International Law with other, coordinate United Nations institutions like the General Assembly and Security Council, could easily deteriorate into a series of purely *ad hoc* rulings unless the Court also takes the time to develop and then explain its own, experientially-based ground rules or guide-lines as to when it will venture to exercise jurisdiction and enter on substantive law rulings, and when, by contrast, it will sensibly opt for judicial self-restraint and judicial non-intervention.

The suggestion by the current U.S. judge, Judge Schwebel,[86] with echoes perhaps of his own, then recent Dissenting Opinion in *Nicaragua*,[87] that the Court should avoid ruling on what are, in effect, issues of Superpower conflict or at least issues touching on the vital interests of one or other of them, has, on the empirical record of the Court's past *jurisprudence* and its consequences in action, much to commend it. The Court's Advisory Opinion in *Certain Expenses of the United Nations* in 1962,[88] in historical retrospect, not merely did *not* advance solution of the then Soviet-U.S. political-ideological conflict that was at its core but also considerably exacerbated the problem when it had to be resolved, inevitably, by the other, coordinate United Nations organs, the General Assembly and the Secretariat.

That would raise the question whether, applying these particular criteria, the Court should sensibly have taken itself out of any substantive, *Merits* ruling in *Nicaragua*,[89] either by applying an extremely restrictive view (of the sort presaged by Judge Oda)[90] of the nature of acceptance, and main-tenance of acceptance, of the Court's Compulsory Jurisdiction on the part of the respondent United States; or else, (with the Court having concluded that it should exercise jurisdiction), by going on to hold that the issues involved were simply not "ripe" for judicial settlement at that particular time.

The first type of approach might run the risk of being criticised as the sort of contrived, legal "nit-picking", as a means of avoiding judicial responsibilities for the progressive development of International Law, that the Court majority resorted to in the much-criticised 8-to-7 majority decision in *South West Africa. Second Phase* in 1966.

The second type of approach would have the additional virtue of public frankness, for it would allow thoughtful students of the Court to enter into the same sort of identification and weighing of policy considerations as actually undertaken by the Court, if the Court should, indeed, decide on balance to eschew the opportunity for judicial law-making, and to leave the responsibility, instead, to the U.N. General Assembly, or else to tolerate a potential gap in World Community problem-solving. The distinguished U.S. academic jurist and Under Secretary of State in President Johnson's Administration, Eugene Rostow, has attacked the International Court's decision to accept justiciability of the Nicaraguan complaint against the U.S. on the score that it interfered with the security of the U.S., as determined by the U.S.[91] As against this particular criticism, and in support of the positions taken in *Nicaragua* by the lop-sided, multi-systemic (Western and non-Western), Court majorities, at both the Preliminary[92] and also the *Merits* stages,[93] it might be suggested that, on the particular facts, the security of the United States and its vital interests hardly seemed involved or threatened by the internal political conflicts in a small Central American republic, in regard to which the relevant "regional", Latin American organisation's principal concern was apparently always the element of outside, (U.S.) involvement. In the immediate context, the International Court appears to have reasoned that the U.S. intrusions into Nicaraguan internal affairs, through the covert and also public aid, (military, paramilitary), to the various (so-called "Contra") rebel groups claiming to act against the Nicaraguan Government, were sufficiently blatant and sufficiently in conflict with general International Law to warrant legal rebuke by the Court, and this even or perhaps especially because it involved the Court's legally chastising a Superpower. The Court judgment, on the *Merits*, thus tends to emerge as something akin to Chief Justice Coke's celebrated, early 17th Century reminder to King James I, that even a King may be "under God and the Law".[94] There was a certain, no doubt unconscious, irony, which the judges of the International Court, in *Nicaragua*, in its Preliminary phase in 1984, could hardly have been unaware of, (even if they refrained from expressly commenting on it in their ruling), that the particular argument advanced by the U.S. Administration that the U.S./Nicaragua conflict was part of a larger political situation in Central America to which other states in the region necessarily belonged,[95] replicated the Iranian Government's objection, in the *Hostages* case, that the Iranian/U.S. conflict there involved could not properly be – "divorced from its proper context, namely the whole political dossier of the relations between Iran and the United States over the last 25 years".[96]

It seems not unreasonable to conclude that the new "judicial politic" of the Court and its highly pragmatic, functional approach to issues of justiciability today is inspired by the exigencies of the maintenance of international peace.[97]

## NOTES

1. I.C.J. Reports 1966, p. 6.
2. *The International Court of Justice at a Crossroads* (Damrosch, ed.) (1987).
3. I.C.J. Reports 1971, p. 16.
4. *Delimitation of the Maritime Boundary in the Gulf of Maine Area, Constitution of Chamber, Order of 20 January 1982*, I.C.J. Reports 1982, p. 3; *Judgment*, I.C.J. Reports 1984, p. 246.
5. Kensaburo, "Occidentalisation et Japonisation", in *L'avenir de la culture: Sommet culturel franco-japonais* (1984), p. 39.
6. Tabata, "The late Professor Ryoichi Taoka: his contributions to the study of International Law", *Japanese Annual of International Law*, vol. 28 (1985), p. 1.
7. Yokota, "International Adjudication and Japan", *Japanese Annual of International Law*, vol. 17 (1973), p. 1.
8. *Ibid.*
9. *Ibid.*, p. 4.
10. *Ibid.*, p. 15.
11. Tanaka, "The changing character of World Law in the International Court of Justice", *Japanese Annual of International Law*, vol. 15 (1971), p. 1, pp. 7–8. In similar, general vein, see the views of the late Takeshi Minagawa, (who acknowledged the influence of the British jurist, Brierly), that the – "task for the Court ... is to interpret and apply, but not to create and modify, law": Sato, "Review of Professor Takeshi Minagawa's *Kokusaiho Kenkyu* with some general observations on his contribution to the science of International Law", *Hitotsubashi Journal of Law and Politics*, vol. 15 (1987), p. 13, p. 25.
12. *Merits, Judgment*, I.C.J. Reports 1986, p. 14, p. 212 (Oda J., Dissenting Opinion).
13. I.C.J. Reports 1986, p. 14, p. 528 (Jennings J., Dissenting Opinion).
14. Anand, "Rôle of International Adjudication", in *The Future of the International Court of Justice*, (Gross, ed.), (vol. 1) (1976), pp. 4–5.
15. *Ibid.*, p. 4.
16. See, for example, McNair, *The Development of International Justice* (1956), p. 12; Corbett, *Law and Society in the Relations of States* (1951), p. 234.
17. Thus Anand, in a survey of the first half century of the work of the Court (the "old"

Permanent Court, and the "new" International Court) concluded that in only one case, the *Austro-German Customs Union* case (Series A./B., No. 41 (1931) p. 42), (where there were four interested parties on one side, three of whom had their own nationals on the bench, and two parties on the other side, only one of whom had its own national on the bench), would the absence of a national judge, regularly elected to the Court in the usual way or appointed *ad hoc*, have changed the final decision in the case. (The *Austro-German Customs Union* decision was rendered by an 8-to-7 vote). Anand, *Studies in International Adjudication* (1969), p. 104.

18. Elias, *New Horizons in International Law* (1979), p. 78.

19. Elias, in *Judicial Settlement of International Disputes* (Mosler and Bernhardt, *eds.*) (1974), p. 23, p. 31.

20. *Ibid.*

21. *Continental Shelf (Tunisia/Libyan Arab Jamahiriya), Judgment*, I.C.J. Reports 1982, p. 18.

22. *Ibid.*, pp. 19–20.

23. *Border and Transborder Armed Actions (Nicaragua v. Honduras), Jurisdiction and Admissibility, Judgment*, I.C.J. Reports 1988, p. 69.

24. *Ibid.*, p. 70.

25. *Military and Paramilitary Activities in and against Nicaragua (Nicaragua v. United States of America), Jurisdiction and Admissibility, Judgment*, I.C.J. Reports 1984, p. 392.

26. *Ibid.*, p. 393.

27. Compare Falk, whose "pluralist" jurisprudence, which he sets up in opposition to a "provincial (that is, Western) jurisprudence" and in contradistinction to an ideal but seemingly unattainable "universalist" jurisprudence, is predicated upon the triadic scheme of division – much discussed in a more general United Nations context in the 1960s and the 1970s in connection with the debate over the legally normative, law-making quality of U.N. General Assembly Resolutions, – of Western, Marxist, and non-Western. Falk, *Reviving the World Court* (1986).

28. Weissberg, "The *rôle* of the International Court of Justice in the United Nations system: the first quarter century", in *The Future of the International Court of Justice*, (Gross ed.) (vol. 1) (1976), p. 131, p. 176. And compare Schwarzenberger, *International Law*, vol. 4, *International Judicial Law* (1986), p. 6.

29. Pescatore, "Les mesures conservatoires et les référés", in *La juridiction internationale permanente* (Société Française pour le Droit International, Colloque de Lyon), (Philip, ed.), (1987), p. 315 *et seq.*

30. Bedjaoui, "Remarques sur la création de Chambres *ad hoc* au sein de la Cour internationale de Justice", in *La juridiction internationale permanente* (Philip, ed.), (1987), p. 73, p. 75:

> "Arrêtons-nous quelques instants sur les deux premiers types de Chambres [Chambres *spécialisées* et *preconstituées*, et Chambres *ad hoc*] qui montrent déjà combien la Cour mondiale n'est pas bâtie du tout sur le système caméraliste.
>
> "C'est une première observation importante: la Cour internationale de justice n'a pas été conçue constitutionellement et organiquement à l'image d'autres juridictions permanentes internationales ... [qui] siègent en formations restreintes. Or la Cour internationale de justice ne répond constitutionnellement pas du tout à ce schéma; c'est par construction initiale.
>
> "Il n'existe pas de division du travail, il n'existe pas de répartition des tâches, il

n'existe pas de section; bref il n'existe pas de Chambres ordinaires au sein de la Cour internationale de Justice...

"Or, il est impossible de reproduire à travers un juge, ou même trois ou cinq, l'équilibre géographique laborieusement obtenu à travers les 15 juges de la Cour. Laborieusement obtenu et toujours contesté de façon latente comme déjà non satisfaisant. Si la composition actuelle de la Cour, dans son kaléidoscope géographique, et dans ses équilibres internationaux, n'est pas encore jugée par certains tout à fait satisfaisante, à plus forte raison y avail-il lieu de craindre, semble-t-il, qu'une formation restreinte telle une Chambre de la Cour, ne puisse pas répondre au voeu d'universalité."

31. I.C.J. Reports 1982, p. 3; I.C.J. Reports 1984, p. 246.
32. Lachs, "The Revised Procedure of the International Court of Justice", in *Essays on the Development of the International Legal Order*, (Kalshoven, Kuyper, and Lammers, eds.) (1980), p. 44.
33. I.C.J. Reports 1966, p. 6.
34. I.C.J. Reports 1971, p. 16.
35. The identification, Operational Indices, is Harold Lasswell's. See, generally, Lasswell and Kaplan, *Power and Society. A Framework for Political Inquiry* (1950).
36. I.C.J. Reports 1962, p. 151.
37. U.N. Charter, Article 17: "(1) The General Assembly shall consider and approve the budget of the Organisation. "(2) The expenses of the Organisation shall be borne by the Members as apportioned by the General Assembly."
38. U.N. Charter, Article 19: "A Member of the United Nations which is in arrears in the payment of its financial contributions to the Organisation shall have no vote in the General Assembly if the amount of its arrears equals or exceeds the amount of the contributions due from it for the preceding two full years. The General Assembly may, nevertheless, permit such a Member to vote if it is satisfied that the failure to pay is due to conditions beyond the control of the Member."
39. I.C.J. Reports 1973, p. 99; I.C.J. Reports 1974, p. 253.
40. I.C.J. Reports 1979, p. 7; I.C.J. Reports 1980, p. 3.
41. I.C.J. Reports 1974, p. 253, pp. 264–8, pp. 271–2.
42. *United States Diplomatic and Consular Staff in Tehran (United States of America v. Iran), Provisional Measures*, I.C.J. Reports 1979, p. 7; *Judgment*, I.C.J. Reports 1980, p. 3.
43. *Ibid., Judgment*, I.C.J. Reports 1980, p. 3. (Judge Lachs, Separate Opinion; Judge Morozov, Dissenting Opinion; Judge Tarazi, Dissenting Opinion).
44. I.C.J. Reports 1984, p. 169; I.C.J. Reports 1984, p. 392; I.C.J. Reports 1986, p. 14.
45. *Declaration of Intervention of the Republic of El Salvador*, I.C.J. Reports 1984, p. 215.
46. Court Statute, Article 63:
"1. Whenever the construction of a convention to which states other than those concerned in the case are parties is in question, the Registrar shall notify all such states forthwith.
"2. Every state so notified has the right to intervene in the proceedings; but if it uses this right, the construction given by the judgment will be equally binding upon it."
47. I.C.J. Reports 1986, p. 14, pp. 312–5.
48. I.C.J. Reports 1986, p. 14, pp. 178–80.
49. I.C.J. Reports 1984, p. 215.
50. *Ibid.*

51. I.C.J. Reports 1986, p. 14, pp. 170–1.
52. Jiménez de Aréchaga, "The Work and the Jurisprudence of the International Court of Justice 1947–1986", *British Year Book of International Law*, vol. 58 (1987), p. 1, pp. 23–7.
53. *Ibid.*, p. 23.
54. *Ibid.*, p. 23, pp. 25–7.
55. *Ibid.*, p. 23.
56. *Minquiers and Écrehos, Judgment*, I.C.J. Reports 1953, p. 47.
57. Ofosu-Amaah, "Regional Enforcement of International Obligations", *Zeitschrift für ausländisches öffentliches Recht und Völkerrecht*, vol. 47 (1987), p. 80, pp. 85–6.
58. I.C.J. Reports 1986, p. 554, p. 563, Jiménez de Aréchaga, *op. cit.*, at p. 23.
59. I.C.J. Reports 1966, p. 6.
60. *Western Sahara, Advisory Opinion*, I.C.J. Reports 1975, p. 12.
61. I.C.J. Reports 1966, p. 6.
62. I.C.J. Reports 1971, p. 16.
63. Bilder, "Some Limitations of Adjudication as an International Dispute Settlement Technique", *Virginia Journal of International Law*, vol. 23 (1982), p. 1, p. 8, citing the award and the subsequent Argentine Government Declaration of Nullity. And see also "La questione del Canale Beagle (Lodo Arbitrale Britannico), Argentina-Cile, 18 aprile 1977", *Jus Gentium* (Roma), vol. 1 (N.S.), N. 3B, p. 137. And see also Salazar Sánchez, "Der argentinisch-chilenische Grenzstreit und die Mittel friedlicher Streitbeilegung", *Archiv des Völkerrechts*, vol. 27 (1989), p. 455.
64. Jessup, *The Price of International Justice* (1971), p. 31 *et seq.*; Weissberg, "The *rôle* of the International Court of Justice in the United Nations system: the first quarter century", in *The Future of the International Court of Justice*, vol. 1 (1976), p. 131, pp. 176–7.
65. Cited in Sturgess and Chubb, *Judging the World: Law and Politics in the World's Leading Courts* (1988), at p. 463.
66. *Aegean Sea Continental Shelf, Interim Protection, Order*, I.C.J. Reports 1976, p. 3; *Judgment*, I.C.J. Reports 1978, p. 3. And see Bernhardt, "Das Urteil des Internationalen Gerichtshof im Ägäis-Streit", *Festschrift für Hans-Jürgen Schlochauer* (von Münch, ed.), (1981), p. 167.
67. U.N. Security Council Resolution 395 (1976).
68. I.C.J. Reports 1976, p. 3.
69. *Ibid.*, p. 19.
70. *Ibid.*, p. 20.
71. *Ibid.*, p. 33.
72. *Ibid.*
73. *Ibid.*, p. 26. And see generally Klein, "Paralleles Tätigwerden von Sicherheitsrat und Internationalen Gerichtshof bei Friedensbedrohenden Streitigkeiten, Zu Fragen der Zuständigkeit und Organtreue", in *Völkerrecht als Rechtsordnung. Festschrift für Hermann Mosler*, (Bernhardt, Geck, Jaenicke, Steinberger, (eds.), (1983), p. 467, p. 469.
74. *Judgment*, I.C.J. Reports 1978, p. 3.
75. *Ibid.* In *United States Diplomatic and Consular Staff in Tehran, Judgment*, I.C.J. Reports 1980, p. 3, the Court applied similar principles in rejecting, as a purported bar to Court jurisdiction, the simultaneity of the seising of the Court and the seising of the U.N. Security Council with a problem.

76. I.C.J. Reports 1971, p. 16.
77. U.N. General Assembly Resolution 2145 (XXI), 27 October 1966.
78. I.C.J. Reports 1966, p. 6.
79. I.C.J. Reports 1971, p. 16.
80. *Ibid.* pp. 299–300.
81. *Ibid.*, p. 45.
82. *Ibid.*
83. *Ibid.*
84. *Ibid.*, p. 49.
85. I.C.J. Reports 1984, p. 392, p. 436. Some commentators, in reviewing the issue of concurrent action in the political organs (Security Council, General Assembly), and in the principal judicial organ (International Court), of the United Nations, and the resulting competence-problematic, seek to make the analogy to the problem of *Litispendence* under Municipal, national law. The attempted analogy would not appear to be legally well-founded, since the Municipal law doctrine is limited to a denial of simultaneous processes before more than one *Court* at the same time. The old Permanent Court of International Justice took a very restrictive view of the alleged *Litispendence* barrier, rejecting its application in *German Settlers in Upper Silesia* and ruling that, to be relevant, it must involve identical action, and the same parties, and a court of the same character. (PCIJ, Ser. A no. 6 (1925), p. 20). See generally, Klein, *op. cit.*, in *Festschrift für Hermann Mosler* (Bernhardt, Geck, Jaenicke, Steinberger, (eds.)), p. 467, p. 474; Ciobanu, "*Litispendence* between the International Court of Justice and the Political Organs of the United Nations", in *The Future of the International Court of Justice* (Gross, (ed.)), (1976), p. 209; Pellet, "Le glaive et la balance", in *Essays in Honour of Shabtai Rosenne* (Dinstein, (ed.)) (1989), p. 529, p. 545. Taking account of the contemporary constitutional evolution of the United Nations and of the International Court, the constitutional separation-of-powers analogy, interpreted in its contemporary, neo-Montesquieuan sense as implying a cooperation and complementarity of the principal U.N. organs in their problem-solving, and not any old-fashioned, artificial division and allocation of competences into abstract, *a priori* categories, seems more appropriate today. Klein, *op. cit.*, at p. 481, would appear right in stressing the principle of institutional Comity (*Organtreue*) and the obligations of mutual restraint, *inter se*, on the part of the principal U.N. organs in exercising their new, cooperative approach.
86. Cited in Sturgess and Chubb, *op. cit.*, p. 473.
87. *Merits*, I.C.J. Reports 1986, p. 14, p. 259, especially pp. 284–7.
88. I.C.J. Reports 1962, p. 151.
89. I.C.J. Reports 1986, p. 14.
90. *Jurisdiction and Admissibility, Judgment*, I.C.J. Reports 1984, p. 392, p. 471, p. 510 *et seq.*; *Merits. Judgment*, I.C.J. Reports 1986, p. 14, p. 212, p. 216 *et seq.*
91. Rostow, "Disputes involving the Inherent Right of Self-Defence", in *The International Court of Justice at a Crossroads* (Damrosch, ed.) (1987), p. 264.
92. *Provisional Measures, Order of 10 May 1984*, (I.C.J. Reports 1984, p. 169), was decided by a vote of 14-to-1 (Judge Schwebel dissenting); *Jurisdiction and Admissibility, Judgment*, (I.C.J. Reports 1984, p. 392), by votes of 11-to-5 (Mosler, Oda, Ago, Jennings, and Schwebel, JJ., dissenting), 14-to-2 (Ruda and Schwebel, JJ., dissenting), 15-to-1 (Schwebel J., dissenting) and 16-to-0, on its separate issues.
93. *Merits, Judgment*, I.C.J. Reports 1986, p. 14, was decided, as to its main substantive-legal issues, by votes of 12-to-3 (Oda, Jennings, and Schwebel, JJ., dissenting).

94. *Case of Prohibitions*, 12 Rep. 65.
95. I.C.J. Reports 1984, p. 392, at p. 430.
96. *United States Diplomatic and Consular Staff in Tehran*, I.C.J. Reports 1980, p. 3, p. 19. See the remarks, in this regard, by ex-Judge Mosler, in *Festschrift für Karl Doehring* (Hailbronner, Ress, Stein (eds.)), (1989), p. 607, p. 619.
97. Pellet, "Le glaive et la balance. Remarques sur le rôle de la C.I.J. en matière de maintien de la paix et de la sécurité internationales", in *Essays in Honour of Shabtai Rosenne* (Dinstein, (ed.)), (1989), p. 539, p. 559.

CONCLUSION

# New Agenda, and New Client-States
# for the International Court

International Judicial Settlement, as a prime mode of international conflicts-resolution, was launched as a legal concept by Continental European (including Imperial Russian) jurists towards the close of the 19th century. Concretised in international legal form in the "old", Permanent Court of International Justice, it acquired an essentially *Eurocentrist* image in the between-the-two-World-Wars era, with a *clientèle* drawn largely from the Western European states and a docket that was limited essentially to *intra*-European cases, – very often cases involving the application and enforcement of the Treaty of Versailles and the related European Peace Treaties of 1919 that established the between-the-World Wars, European-based, World political system and World political balance of power.

In the post-World War II era, the "new" International Court of Justice, reconstituted from the old, Permanent Court of the inter-War period as the "principal judicial organ of the United Nations", began in the traditions and legal thought-ways established by the old Permanent Court. But, after the political watershed decision of the Court, by single-vote-majority, in *South West Africa. Second Phase* in 1966, and the intellectual-legal debate and controversy unloosed by that decision as to the proper *rôles* and missions of international adjudication, the International Court has moved increasingly into a highly functional, problem-solving approach that emphasises the spirit of the law and the main trends in its historical unfolding, in contradistinction to an abstract, *a priori* legal logic and strict-and-literal interpretation of international acts and of the Court's own past *jurisprudence*.

The revolution in the Court's thinking and practice, since 1966, has been assisted by the rapidly changing character of the membership of the Court and its evolution, today, into a fully representative, plural tribunal, viewed in ethno-cultural, legal-systemic, and political-ideological terms. This reflects, more or less accurately, the historical transformation of the World

156

Community as a whole over the same time period, with the progressive achievement of Decolonisation and Independence and Self-Determination of Peoples on a World-wide scale. The International Court's claims to constitutional-legal legitimacy for its new, policy-making approach are now at least as persuasive as those of the great, Municipal, national tribunals claiming to exercise a similar legislative, law-making *rôle* – the Special Constitutional Courts (whether *de jure* or *de facto*) of so many contemporary Western societies, as the prime examples of this.

The intellectual-legal changes in the International Court's own thinking and in its basic philosophy of law have been strongly influenced by developments in Municipal, national legal systems away from Legal Positivism and towards more consciously instrumental, Sociological or "social engineering", conceptions of the judicial process. Among these Municipal, national legal systems, the "reception" of modern American constitutional law thinking, with its Legal Realist and Sociological Schools' emphasis on the imaginative or creative restatement of old legal *doctrines* to meet new societal problems, has been most noticeable. The International Court remains at the same time, however, the heir to seven decades of empirical, trial-and-error legal testing and experience, in the *jurisprudence* and practice of both the "old" and the "new" Courts. This means that arguments for a purely mechanical form of legal "reception" or borrowing from other and different Courts in other and different legal systems, national or supra-national – as with the latter-day sponsorship by the United States Administration of the institution of a numerically-limited, Special Chamber or Senate within the *plenum* or Full Court of the International Court – may properly be questioned or contested (quite apart from the political motives that may have inspired them), unless a sufficient minimum congruence of underlying societal conditions can be demonstrated as between the particular national or supra-national community selected for purposes of analogy and the contemporary World Community.

In terms of concepts of justiciability, the rejection of the old, abstract, *a priori* distinction between Law and Politics, and of the claimed "Political Questions" exception to any exercise of jurisdiction that was supposed to flow from it, is another consequence of the International Court's latter-day abandonment of Legal Positivism as dominant judicial philosophy. Henceforth, the approach to justiciability will be better ascertained according to a Judicial Self-Restraint/Judicial Activism continuum, with the line of demarcation as to Court acceptance or Court non-acceptance of a case as "ripe" for substantive legal decision, being established according to essentially pragmatic considerations. These may include whether or not judicial intervention in the instant case will help, rather than hinder, international conflicts-resolution; and also the relation of any contemplated Court action to action already taken, or pending, on the part of the other, coordinate United Nations policy-making organs, the Security Council and General Assembly. In approaching the latter question, the International Court will now reject old-fashioned, Municipal, national law-derived, constitutional separation-of-powers arguments that insisted on artificially dividing up the competences of Court, Security Council, and General Assembly, and that emphasised the mutual conflict or mutual exclusiveness of these three main United Nations organs. The new acceptance of a complementarity of problem-solving competences of the main, coordinate international institutions, has brought a correlative understanding of their capacity for joint, cooperative problem-solving in initiatives that may be both contemporaneous and also fully interdependent. This means that action by any one of Court, Security Council, and General Assembly will be no necessary bar to action by the other, coordinate institutions at any time, subject only to the ordinary constitutional principles of mutual self-restraint or mutual deference (*Organtreue*).

The new public confidence that the International Court now enjoys, as a fully representative tribunal, in the contemporary, plural World Community is amply evidenced in the new popularity of recourse to the Court's jurisdiction on the part of States from outside the more traditional, Western client-states of yesteryear. In the period leading up to the Court's single-vote-majority decision in *South West Africa. Second Phase* in 1966, and in the strong political controversy that succeeded that decision, non-Western states tended to be suspicious of the Court's degree of commitment to the progressive development of International Law, and hostile in consequence to acceptance of the Court's contentious jurisdiction. What may have been lost, in terms of any current withdrawals from, or cutting down on, acceptances of the Court's Compulsory Jurisdiction, under the Optional Clause on the part of some more traditional, Western client-States, seems to have been more than compensated for by the emergence of the new groups of non-Western client-States and by the opening to new, "regional" systems of International Law involved in that.

The Advisory Opinion jurisdiction of the Court, resorted to, with ordinary civil courage, by the United Nations, and applied with a high degree of flexibility and pragmatism by a present Court majority that also finds no place here for old-fashioned, abstract, *a priori* distinctions of the Law/Politics variety, will help to avoid any threat of a constitutional vacuum within the United Nations as a whole, as to international law-making capacity to meet crisis-situations. On the historical analogy of the U.N. General Assembly's celebrated "Uniting for Peace" Resolution, adopted in the Korean crisis of 1950, the International Court may itself choose to move boldly to fill the gap in similar Peace and Security situations, in the absence of appropriate problem-solving initiatives by the other, coordinate institutions of the United Nations or a blockage of the exercise of their constitutional powers as, for example, by arbitrary and capricious user of the Permanent Members' veto in the Security Council. The emphasis, here, is on saving, and not frustrating, the exercise of World Community powers designed to implement and achieve the larger purposes and goal values established by the United Nations Charter in its Preamble and in its main operative sections – in the full spirit of the old, Anglo-Saxon Common Law, *ut res magis valeat quam pereat.*

The monumental political events in Eastern Europe in the *annus mirabilis*, 1989, and the rightly celebrated Soviet "New Thinking" on Law and Society (international and national) that contributed so markedly to those processes of peaceful change, have provided new opportunities for the International Court. One incidental, minor consequence of the disappearance of the *post-War* public order system, with its rigid division of the World Community into the two rival, political-military blocs (Soviet and U.S.) is the opportunity to re-examine whether, for purposes of nominations and elections to the International Court, it is still useful or helpful to preserve notional *Western* and *Eastern* European "regional" blocs of reserved seats on the Court. Another, much more important consequence of the "New Thinking" is the new, highly supportive approach to the Soviet Government to the United Nations and to the International Court, thereby reversing traditional historically-based Soviet attitudes. This is already evidenced, concretely, in the Soviet Government's Decree accepting the principle of Court Jurisdiction in relation to a number of Human Rights accords. It helps to offset or balance the U.S. Administration's conscious and concerted retreat from Court Jurisdiction in the early and middle 1980's. Perhaps a "kinder and gentler" U.S. Administration in the future may see fit to embrace, again, the principle of judicial settlement of international disputes so warmly championed by U.S. leaders in the early, post-war years.

# Table of Principal Cases

# A. Covenant of the League of Nations (1920)

## Article 12. Disputes

1. The Members of the League agree that, if there should arise between them any dispute likely to lead to a rupture, they will submit the matter either to arbitration or judicial settlement or to inquiry by the Council, and they agree in no case to resort to war until three months after the award by the arbitrators or the judicial decision, or the report by the Council.

2. In any case under this Article the award of the arbitrators or the judicial decision shall be made within a reasonable time, and the report of the Council shall be made within six months after the submission of the dispute.

## Article 13. Arbitration or Judicial Settlement

1. The Members of the League agree that, whenever any dispute shall arise between them which they recognize to be suitable for submission to arbitration or judicial settlement, and which can not be satisfactorily settled by diplomacy, they will submit the whole subject-matter to arbitration or judicial settlement.

2. Disputes as to the interpretation of a treaty, as to any question of international law, as to the existence of any fact which, if established, would constitute a breach of any international obligation, or as to the extent and nature of the reparation to be made for any such breach, are declared to be among those which are generally suitable for submission to arbitration or judicial settlement.

3. For the consideration of any such dispute, the court to which the case is referred shall be the Permanent Court of International Justice, established

in accordance with Article 14, or any tribunal agreed on by the parties to the dispute or stipulated in any convention existing between them.

4. The Members of the League agree that they will carry out in full good faith any award or decision that may be rendered, and that they will not resort to war against a Member of the League which complies therewith. In the event of any failure to carry out such an award or decision, the Council shall propose what steps should be taken to give effect thereto.

## Article 14. Permanent Court of International Justice

The Council shall formulate and submit to the Members of the League for adoption plans for the establishment of a Permanent Court of International Justice. The Court shall be competent to hear and determine any dispute of an international character which the parties thereto submit to it. The Court may also give an advisory opinion upon any dispute or question referred to it by the Council or by the Assembly.

## Article 15. Disputes not Submitted to Arbitration or Judicial Settlement

1. If there should arise between Members of the League any dispute likely to lead to a rupture, which is not submitted to arbitration or judicial settlement in accordance with Article 13, the Members of the League agree that they will submit the matter to the Council. Any party to the dispute may effect such submission by giving notice of the existence of the dispute to the Secretary-General, who will make all necessary arrangements for a full investigation and consideration thereof.

2. For this purpose, the parties to the dispute will communicate to the Secretary-General, as promptly as possible, statements of their case with all the relevant facts and papers, and the Council may forthwith direct the publication thereof.

3. The Council shall endeavor to effect a settlement of the dispute, and, if such efforts are successful, a statement shall be made public giving such facts and explanations regarding the dispute and the terms of settlement thereof as the Council may deem appropriate.

4. If the dispute is not thus settled, the Council either unanimously or by a majority vote shall make and publish a report containing a statement of the facts of the dispute and the recommendations which are deemed just and proper in regard thereto.

5. Any member of the League represented on the Council may make public a statement of the facts of the dispute and of its conclusions regarding the same.

6. If a report by the Council is unanimously agreed to by the Members thereof other than the Representatives of one or more of the parties to the dispute, the Members of the League agree that they will not go to war with any party to the dispute which complies with the recommendations of the report.

7. If the Council fails to reach a report which is unanimously agreed to by the members thereof, other than the Representatives of one or more of the parties to the dispute, the Members of the League reserve to themselves the right to take such action as they shall consider necessary for the maintenance of right and justice.

8. If the dispute between the parties is claimed by one of them, and is found by the Council, to arise out of a matter which by international law is solely within the domestic jurisdiction of that party, the Council shall so report, and shall make no recommendation as to its settlement.

9. The Council may in any case under this Article refer the dispute to the Assembly. The dispute shall be so referred at the request of either party to the dispute, provided that such request be made within 14 days after the submission of the dispute to the Council.

10. In any case referred to the Assembly, all the provisions of this Article and of Article 12 relating to the action and powers of the Council shall apply to the action and powers of the Assembly, provided that a report made by the Assembly, if concurred in by the Representatives of those Members of the League represented on the Council and of a majority of the other Members of the League, exclusive in each case of the Representatives of the parties to the dispute, shall have the same force as a report by the Council concurred in by all the members thereof other than the Representatives of one or more of the parties to the dispute.

. . . . . .

## Article 19. Review of Treaties

The Assembly may from time to time advise the reconsideration by Members of the League of treaties which have become inapplicable, and the consideration of international conditions whose continuance might endanger the peace of the world.

# B. Charter of the United Nations (1945)

## CHAPTER XIV

## THE INTERNATIONAL COURT OF JUSTICE

### Article 92

The International Court of Justice shall be the principal judicial organ of the United Nations. It shall function in accordance with the annexed Statute, which is based upon the Statute of the Permanent Court of International Justice and forms an integral part of the present Charter.

### Article 93

1. All Members of the United Nations are *ipso facto* parties to the Statute of the International Court of Justice.
2. A state which is not a Member of the United Nations may become a party to the Statute of the International Court of Justice on conditions to be determined in each case by the General Assembly upon the recommendation of the Security Council.

### Article 94

1. Each Member of the United Nations undertakes to comply with the decision of the International Court of Justice in any case to which it is a party.
2. If any party to a case fails to perform the obligations incumbent upon it under a judgment rendered by the Court, the other party may have recourse to the Security Council, which may, if it deems necessary, make recommen-

dations or decide upon measures to be taken to give effect to the judgment.

## *Article 95*

Nothing in the present Charter shall prevent Members of the United Nations from entrusting the solution of their differences to other tribunals by virtue of agreements already in existence or which may be concluded in the future.

## *Article 96*

1. The General Assembly or the Security Council may request the International Court of Justice to give an advisory opinion on any legal question.
2. Other organs of the United Nations and specialized agencies, which may at any time be so authorized by the General Assembly, may also request advisory opinions of the Court on legal questions arising within the scope of their activities.

# C. Statute of the International Court of Justice

### *Article 1*

The International Court of Justice established by the Charter of the United Nations as the principal judicial organ of the United Nations shall be constituted and shall function in accordance with the provisions of the present Statute.

## Chapter I
## Organization of the Court

### *Article 2*

The Court shall be composed of a body of independent judges, elected regardless of their nationality from among persons of high moral character, who possess the qualifications required in their respective countries for appointment to the highest judicial offices, or are jurisconsults of recognized competence in international law.

### *Article 3*

1. The Court shall consist of fifteen members, no two of whom may be nationals of the same state.

2. A person who for the purposes of membership in the Court could be regarded as a national of more than one state shall be deemed to be a national of the one in which he ordinarily exercises civil and political rights.

## Article 4

1. The members of the Court shall be elected by the General Assembly and by the Security Council from a list of persons nominated by the national groups in the Permanent Court of Arbitration, in accordance with the following provisions.

2. In the case of Members of the United Nations not represented in the Permanent Court of Arbitration, candidates shall be nominated by national groups appointed for this purpose by their governments under the same conditions as those prescribed for members of the Permanent Court of Arbitration by Article 44 of the Convention of The Hague of 1907 for the pacific settlement of international disputes.

3. The conditions under which a state which is a party to the present Statute but is not a Member of the United Nations may participate in electing the members of the Court shall, in the absence of a special agreement, be laid down by the General Assembly upon recommendation of the Security Council.

## Article 5

1. At least three months before the date of the election, the Secretary-General of the United Nations shall address a written request to the members of the Permanent Court of Arbitration belonging to the states which are parties to the present Statute, and to the members of the national groups appointed under Article 4, paragraph 2, inviting them to undertake, within a given time, by national groups, the nomination of persons in a position to accept the duties of a member of the Court.

2. No group may nominate more than four persons, not more than two of whom shall be of their own nationality. In no case may the number of candidates nominated by a group be more than double the number of seats to be filled.

## Article 6

Before making these nominations, each national group is recommended to consult its highest court of justice, its legal faculties and schools of law, and its national academies and national sections of international academies devoted to the study of law.

*Article 7*

1. The Secretary-General shall prepare a list in alphabetical order of all the persons thus nominated. Save as provided in Article 12, paragraph 2, these shall be the only persons eligible.

2. The Secretary-General shall submit this list to the General Assembly and to the Security Council.

*Article 8*

The General Assembly and the Security Council shall proceed independently of one another to elect the members of the Court.

*Article 9*

At every election, the electors shall bear in mind not only that the persons to be elected should individually possess the qualifications required, but also that in the body as a whole the representation of the main forms of civilization and of the principal legal systems of the world should be assured.

*Article 10*

1. Those candidates who obtain an absolute majority of votes in the General Assembly and in the Security Council shall be considered as elected.

2. Any vote of the Security Council, whether for the election of judges or for the appointment of members of the conference envisaged in Article 12, shall be taken without any distinction between permanent and non-permanent members of the Security Council.

3. In the event of more than one national of the same state obtaining an absolute majority of the votes both of the General Assembly and of the Security Council, the eldest of these only shall be considered as elected.

*Article 11*

If, after, the first meeting held for the purpose of the election, one or more seats remain to be filled, a second and, if necessary, a third meeting shall take place.

## Article 12

1. If, after the third meeting, one or more seats still remain unfilled, a joint conference consisting of six members, three appointed by the General Assembly and three by the Security Council, may be formed at any time at the request of either the General Assembly or the Security Council, for the purpose of choosing by the vote of an absolute majority one name for each seat still vacant, to submit to the General Assembly and the Security Council for their respective acceptance.

2. If the joint conference is unanimously agreed upon any person who fulfils the required conditions, he may be included in its list, even though he was not included in the list of nominations referred to in Article 7.

3. If the joint conference is satisfied that it will not be successful in procuring an election, those members of the Court who have already been elected shall, within a period to be fixed by the Security Council, proceed to full the vacant seats by selection from among those candidates who have obtained votes either in the General Assembly or in the Security Council.

4. In the event of an equality of votes among the judges, the eldest judge shall have a casting vote.

## Article 13

1. The members of the Court shall be elected for nine years and may be re-elected; provided, however, that of the judges elected at the first election, the terms of five judges shall expire at the end of three years and the terms of five more judges shall expire at the end of six years.

2. The judges whose terms are to expire at the end of the above-mentioned initial periods of three and six years shall be chosen by lot to be drawn by the Security-General immediately after the first election has been completed.

3. The members of the Court shall continue to discharge their duties until their places have been filled. Though replaced, they shall finish any cases which they may have begun.

4. In the case of the resignation of a member of the Court, the resignation shall be addressed to the President of the Court for transmission to the Secretary-General. This last notification makes the place vacant.

## Article 14

Vacancies shall be filled by the same method as that laid down for the first election, subject to the following provision: the Secretary-General shall, within one month of the occurrence of the vacancy, proceed to issue the invitations provided for in Article 5, and the date of the election shall be fixed by the Security Council.

## Article 15

A member of the court elected to replace a member whose term of office has not expired shall hold office for the remainder of his predecessor's term.

## Article 16

1. No member of the Court may exercise any political or administrative function, or engage in any other occupation of a professional nature.

2. Any doubt on this point shall be settled by the decision of the Court.

## Article 17

1. No member of the Court may act as agent, counsel, or advocate in any case.

2. No member may participate in the decision of any case in which he has previously taken part as agent, counsel, or advocate for one of the parties, or as a member of a national or international court, or of a commission of enquiry, or in any other capacity.

3. Any doubt on this point shall be settled by the decision of the Court.

## Article 18

1. No member of the Court can be dismissed unless, in the unanimous opinion of the other members, he has ceased to fulfill the required conditions.

2. Formal notification thereof shall be made to the Secretary-General by the Registrar.

3. This notification makes the place vacant.

## Article 19

The members of the Court, when engaged on the business of the Court, shall enjoy diplomatic privileges and immunities.

## Article 20

Every member of the Court shall, before taking up his duties, make a solemn declaration in open court that he will exercise his powers impartially and conscientiously.

## Article 21

1. The Court shall elect its President and Vice-President for three years; they may be re-elected.

2. The Court shall appoint its Registrar and may provide for the appointment of such other officers as may be necessary.

## Article 22

1. The seat of the Court shall be established at The Hague. This, however, shall not prevent the Court from sitting and exercising its function elsewhere whenever the Court considers it desirable.

2. The President and the Registrar shall reside at the seat of the Court.

## Article 23

1. The Court shall remain permanently in session, except during the judicial vacations, the dates and duration of which shall be fixed by the Court.

2. Members of the Court are entitled to periodic leave, the dates and duration of which shall be fixed by the Court, having in mind the distance between The Hague and the home of each judge.

3. Members of the Court shall be bound, unless they are on leave or prevented from attending by illness or other serious reasons duly explained to the President, to hold themselves permanently at the disposal of the Court.

## Article 24

1. If, for some special reason, a member of the Court considers that he should not take part in the decision of a particular case, he shall so inform the President.

2. If the President considers that for some special reason one of the members of the Court should not sit in a particular case, he shall give him notice accordingly.

3. If in any such case the member of the Court and the President disagree, the matter shall be settled by the decision of the Court.

## Article 25

1. The full Court shall sit except when it is expressly provided otherwise in the present Statute.
2. Subject to the condition that the number of judges available to constitute the Court is not thereby reduced below eleven, the Rules of the Court may provide for allowing one or more judges, according to circumstances and in rotation, to be dispensed from sitting.
3. A quorum of nine judges shall suffice to constitute the Court.

## Article 26

1. The Court may from time to time form one or more chambers, composed of three or more judges as the Court may determine, for dealing with particular categories of cases; for example, labour cases and cases relating to transit and communications.
2. The Court may at any time form a chamber for dealing with a particular case. The number of judges to constitute such a chamber shall be determined by the Court with the approval of the parties.
3. Cases shall be heard and determined by the chambers provided for in this article if the parties so request.

## Article 27

A judgement given by any of the chambers provided for in Articles 26 and 29 shall be considered as rendered by the Court.

## Article 28

The chambers provided for in Articles 26 and 29 may, with the consent of the parties, sit and exercise their functions elsewhere than at The hague.

## Article 29

With a view to the speedy dispatch of business, the Court shall form annually a chamber composed of five judges which, at the request of the parties, may hear and determine cases by summary procedure. In addition, two judges shall be selected for the purpose of replacing judges who find it impossible to sit.

## Article 30

1. The Court shall frame rules for carrying out its functions. In particular, it shall lay down rules of procedure.

2. The Rules of the Court may provide for assessors to sit with the Court or with any of its chambers, without the right to vote.

## Article 31

1. Judges of the nationality of each of the parties shall retain their right to sit in the case before the Court.

2. If the Court includes upon the Bench a judge of the nationality of one of the parties, any other party may choose a person to sit as judge. Such person shall be chosen preferably from among those persons who have been nominated as candidates as provided in Articles 4 and 5.

3. If the Court includes upon the Bench no judge of the nationality of the parties, each of these parties may proceed to choose a judge as provided in paragraph 2 of this Article.

4. The provisions of this Article shall apply to the case of Articles 26 and 29. In such cases, the President shall request one or, if necessary, two of the members of the Court forming the chamber to give place to the members of the Court of the nationality of the parties concerned, and, failing such, or if they are unable to be present, to the judges specially chosen by the parties.

5. Should there be several parties in the same interest, they shall, for the purpose of the preceding provisions, be reckoned as one party only. Any doubt upon this point shall be settled by the decision of the Court.

6. Judges chosen as laid down in paragraphs 2, 3, and 4 of this Article shall fulfil the conditions required by Articles 2, 17 (paragraph 2), 20, and 24 of the present Statute. They shall take part in the decision on terms of complete equality with their colleagues.

## Article 32

1. Each member of the Court shall receive an annual salary.

2. The President shall receive a special annual allowance.

3. The Vice-President shall receive a special allowance for every day on which he acts as.President.

4. The judges chosen under Article 31, other than members of the Court, shall receive compensation for each day on which they exercise their functions.

5. These salaries, allowances, and compensation shall be fixed by the

General Assembly. They may not be decreased during the term of office.

6. The salary of the Registrar shall be fixed by the General Assembly on the proposal of the Court.

Regulations made by the General Assembly shall fix the conditions under which retirement pensions may be given to members of the Court and to the Registrar, and the conditions under which members of the Court and the Registrar shall have their travelling expenses refunded.

8. The above salaries, allowances, and compensation shall be free of all taxation.

## Article 33

The expenses of the Court shall be borne by the United Nations in such a manner as shall be decided by the General Assembly.

## CHAPTER II
### Competence of the Court

### Article 34

1. Only states may be parties in cases before the Court.

2. The Court, subject to and in conformity with its Rules, may request of public international organizations information relevant to cases before it, and shall receive such information presented by such organizations on their own initiative.

3. Whenever the construction of the constituent instrument of a public international organization or of an international convention adopted thereunder is in question in a case before the Court, the Registrar shall so notify the public international organization concerned and shall communicate to it copies of all the written proceedings.

### Article 35

1. The Court shall be open to the states parties to the present Statute.

2. The conditions under which the Court shall be open to other states shall, subject to the special provisions contained in treaties in force, be laid down by the Security Council, but in no case shall such conditions place the parties in a position of inequality before the Court.

3. When a state which is not a Member of the United Nations is a party to a case, the Court shall fix the amount which that party is to contribute

towards the expenses of the Court. This provision shall not apply if such state is bearing a share of the expenses of the Court.

## *Article 36*

1. The jurisdiction of the Court comprises all cases which the parties refer to it and all matters specially provided for in the Charter of the United Nations or in treaties and conventions in force.

2. The states parties to the present Statute may at any time declare that they recognize as compulsory *ipso facto* and without special agreement, in relation to any other state accepting the same obligation, the jurisdiction of the Court in all legal disputes concerning:

a. the interpretation of a treaty;

b. any question of international law;

c. the existence of any fact which, if established, would constitute a breach of an international obligation;

d. the nature or extent of the reparation to be made for the breach of an international obligation.

3. The declarations referred to above may be made unconditionally or on condition of reciprocity on the part of several or certain states, or for a certain time.

4. Such declarations shall be deposited with the Secretary-General of the United Nations, who shall transmit copies thereof to the parties to the Statute and to the Registrar of the Court.

5. Declarations made under Article 36 of the Statute of the Permanent Court of International Justice and which are still in force shall be deemed, as between the parties to the present Statute, to be acceptances of the compulsory jurisdiction of the International Court of Justice for the period which they still have to run and in accordance with their terms.

6. In the event of a dispute as to whether the Court has jurisdiction, the matter shall be settled by the decision of the Court.

## *Article 37*

Whenever a treaty or convention in force provides for reference of a matter to a tribunal to have been instituted by the League of Nations, or to the Permanent Court of International Justice, the matter shall, as between the parties to the present Statute, be referred to the International Court of Justice.

*Article 38*

1. The Court, whose function is to decide in accordance with international law such disputes as are submitted to it, shall apply:
   1. international conventions, whether general or particular, establishing rules expressly recognized by the contesting states;
   2. international custom, as evidence of a general practice accepted as law;
   3. the general principles of law recognized by civilized nations;
   4. subject to the provisions of Article 59, judicial decisions and the teachings of the most highly qualified publicists of the various nations, as subsidiary means for the determination of rules of law.

2. This provision shall not prejudice the power of the Court to decide a case *ex aequo et bono*, if the parties agree thereto.

CHAPTER III
Procedure

*Article 39*

1. The official languages of the Court shall be French and English. If the parties agree that the case shall be conducted in French, the judgment shall be delivered in French. If the parties agree that the case shall be conducted in English, the judgment shall be delivered in English.

2. In the absence of an agreement as to which language shall be employed, each party may, in the pleadings, use the language which it prefers; the decision of the Court shall be given in French and English. In this case the Court shall at the same time determine which of the two texts shall be considered as authoritative.

3. The Court shall, at the request of any party, authorize a language other than French or English to be used by that party.

*Article 40*

1. Cases are brought before the Court, as the case may be, either by the notification of the special agreement or by a written application addressed to the Registrar. In either case the subject of the dispute and the parties shall be indicated.

2. The Registrar shall forthwith communicate the application to all concerned.

3. He shall also notify the Members of the United Nations through the

Secretary-General, and also any others states entitled to appear before the Court.

## *Article 41*

1. The Court shall have the power to indicate, if it considers that circumstances so require, any provisional measures which ought to be taken to preserve the respective rights of either party.

Pending the final decision, notice of the measures suggested shall forthwith be given to the parties and to the Security Council

## *Article 42*

1. The parties shall be represented by agents.

2. They may have the assistance of counsel or advocates before the court.

3. The agents, counsel, and advocates of parties before the Court shall enjoy the privileges and immunities necessary to the independent exercise of their duties.

## *Article 43*

1. The procedure shall consist of two parts: written and oral.

2. The written proceedings shall consist of the communication to the Court and to the parties of memorials, counter-memorials and, if necessary, replies; also all papers and documents in support.

3. These communications shall be made through the Registrar, in the order and within the time fixed by the Court.

4. A certified copy of every document produced by one party shall be communicated to the other party.

5. The oral proceedings shall consist of the hearing by the Court of witnesses, experts, agents, counsel, and advocates.

## *Article 44*

1. For the service of all notices upon persons other than the agents, counsel, and advocates, the Court shall apply direct to the government of the state upon whose territory the notice has to be served.

2. The same provision shall apply whenever steps are to be taken to procure evidence on the spot.

## Article 45

The hearing shall be under the control of the President or, if he is unable to preside, of the Vice-President; if neither is able to preside, the senior judge present shall preside.

## Article 46

The hearing in Court shall be public, unless the Court shall decide otherwise, or unless the parties demand that the public be not admitted.

## Article 47

1. Minutes shall be made at each hearing and signed by the Registrar and the President.

2. These minutes alone shall be authentic.

## Article 48

The Court shall make orders for the conduct of the case, shall decide the form and time in which each party must conclude its arguments, and make all arrangements connected with the taking of evidence.

## Article 49

The Court may, even before the hearing begins, call upon the agents to produce any document or to supply any explanations. Formal note shall be taken of any refusal.

## Article 50

The Court may, at any time, entrust any individual, body, commission, or other organization that it may select, with the task of carrying out an enquiry or giving an expert opinion.

## Article 51

During the hearing any relevant questions are to be put to the witnesses and experts under the conditions laid down by the Court in the rules of procedure referred to in Article 30.

### Article 52

After the Court has received the proofs and evidence within the time specified for the purpose, it may refuse to accept any further oral or written evidence that one party may desire to present unless the other side consents.

### Article 53

1. Whenever one of the parties does not appear before the Court, or fails to defend its case, the other party may call upon the Court to decide in favour of its claim

2. The Court must, before doing so, satisfy itself, not only that is has jurisdiction in accordance with Articles 36 and 37, but also that the claim is well founded in fact and law.

### Article 54

1. When, subject to the control of the Court, the agents, counsel, and advocates have completed their presentation of the case, the President shall declare the hearing closed.

2. The Court shall withdraw to consider the judgment.

3. The deliberations of the Court shall take place in private and remain secret.

### Article 55

1. All questions shall be decided by a majority of the judges present.

2. In the event of an equality of votes, the President or the judge who acts in his place shall have a casting vote.

### Article 56

1. The judgement shall state the reasons on which it is based.

2. It shall contain the names of the judges who have taken part in the decision.

### Article 57

If the judgement does not represent in whole or in part the unanimous opinion of the judges, any judge shall be entitled to deliver a separate opinion.

*Article 58*

The judgement shall be signed by the President and by the Registrar. It shall be read in open court, due notice having been given to the agents.

*Article 59*

The decision of the Court has no binding force except between the parties and in respect of that particular case.

*Article 60*

The judgement is final and without appeal. In the event of dispute as to the meaning or scope of the judgement, the Court shall construe it upon the request of any party.

*Article 61*

1. An application for revision of a judgement may be made only when it is based upon the discovery of some fact of such a nature as to be a decisive factor, which fact was, when the judgement was given, unknown to the Court and also to the party claiming revision, always provided that such ignorance was not due to negligence.

2. The proceedings for revision shall be opened by a judgement of the Court expressly recording the existence of the new fact, recognizing that it has such a character as to lay the case open to revision, and declaring the application admissible on this ground.

3. The Court may require previous compliance with the terms of the judgment before it admits proceedings in revision.

4. The application for revision must be made at latest within six months of the discovery of the new fact.

5. No application for revision may be made after the lapse of ten years from the date of the judgment.

*Article 62*

1. Should a state consider that it has an interest of a legal nature which may be affected by the decision in the case, it may submit a request to the Court to be permitted to intervene.

2. It shall be for the Court to decide upon this request.

## *Article 63*

1. Whenever the construction of a convention to which states other than those concerned in the case are parties is in question, the Registrar shall notify all such states forthwith.

2. Every state so notified has the right to intervene in the proceedings; but if it uses this right, the construction given by the judgment will be equally binding upon it.

## *Article 64*

Unless otherwise decided by the Court, each party shall bear its own costs.

## CHAPTER IV
## Advisory opinions

## *Article 65*

1. The Court may give an advisory opinion on any legal question at the request of whatever body may be authorized by or in accordance with the Charter of the United Nations to make such a request.

2. Questions upon which the advisory opinion of the Court is asked shall be laid before the Court by means of a written request containing an exact statement of the question upon which an opinion is required, and accompanied by all documents likely to throw light upon the question.

## *Article 66*

1. The Registar shall forthwith give notice of the request for an advisory opinion to all states entitled to appear before the Court.

2. The Registrar shall also, by means of a special and direct communication, notify any state entitled to appear before the Court or international organization considered by the Court, or, should it not be sitting, by the President, as likely to be able to furnish information on the question, that the Court will be prepared to receive, within a time limit to be fixed by the President, written statements, or to hear, at a public sitting to be held for the purpose, oral statements relating to the question.

3. Should any such state entitled to appear before the Court have failed to receive the special communiation referred to in paragraph 2 of this Article, such state may express a desire to submit a written statement or to be heard;

and the Court will decide.

4. States and organizations having presented written or oral statements or both shall be permitted to comment on the statements made by other states or organizations in the form, to the extent, and within the time limits which the Court, or, should it not be sitting, the President, shall decide in each particular case. Accordingly, the Registrar shall in due time communicate any such written statements to states and organizations having submitted similar statements.

## Article 67

The Court shall deliver its advisory opinions in open court, notice having been given to the Secretary-General and to the representatives of Members of the United Nations, of other states and of international organizations immediately concerned.

## Article 68

In the exercise of its advisory functions the Court shall further be guided by the provisions of the present Statute which apply in contentious cases to the extent to which it recognizes them to be applicable.

## CHAPTER V
## Amendment

## Article 69

Amendments to the present Statute shall be effected by the same procedure as is provided by the Charter of the United Nations for amendments to that Charter, subject however to any provisions which the General Assembly upon recommendation of the Security Council may adopt concerning the participation of states which are parties to the present Statute but are not Members of the United Nations.

## Article 70

The Court shall have power to propose such amendments to the present Statute as it may deem necessary, though written communications to the Secretary-General, for consideration in conformity with the provisions of Article 69.

# D. U.N. General Assembly Resolution 44/23, 9 January 1990. ("United Nations Decade of International Law").

RESOLUTION ADOPTED BY THE GENERAL ASSEMBLY
[without reference to a Main Committee (A/44/L.41 and Add.1)]
44/23. United Nations Decade of International Law

*The General Assembly*

*Recognizing* that one of the purposes of the United Nations is to maintain international peace and security, and to that end to bring about by peaceful means, and in conformity with the principles of justice and international law, adjustment or settlement of international disputes or situations which might lead to a breach of the peace,

*Recalling* the Declaration on Principles of International Law concerning Friendly Relations and Co-operation among States in accordance with the Charter of the United Nations[1] and the Manila Declaration on the Peaceful Settlement of International Disputes,[2]

*Recognizing* the role of the United Nations in promoting greater acceptance of and respect for the principles of international law and in encouraging the progessive development of international law and its codification,

*Convinced* of the need to strenghten the rule of law in international relations,

*Stressing* the need to promote the teaching, study, dissemination and wider appreciation of international law,

*Noting* that, in the remaining decade of the twentieth century, important anniversaries will be celebrated that are related to the adoption of international legal documents, such as the centenary of the first International Peace Conference, held at The Hague in 1899, which adopted the Convention for the Pacific Settlement of International Disputes[3] and created the Permanent Court of Arbitration, the fiftieth anniversary of the signing of the Charter of the United Nations and the twenty-fifth anniversary of the adoption of the Declaration on Principles of International Law concerning Friendly Relations and Co-operation among States in accordance with the Charter of the United Nations,

1. *Declares* the period 1990–1999 as the United Nations Decade of International Law;

2. *Considers* that the main purposes of the Decade should be, *inter alia*:

(a) To promote acceptance of and respect for the principles of international law;

(b) To promote means and methods for the peaceful settlement of disputes between States, including resort to and full respect for the International Court of Justice;

(c) To encourage the progressive development of international law and its codification;

(d) To encourage the teaching, study, dissemination and wider appreciation of international law;

3. *Requests* the Secretary-General to seek the views of Member States and appropriate international bodies, as well as of non-governmental organizations working in the field, on the programme for the Decade and on appropriate action to be taken during the Decade, *including the possibility of holding a third international peace conference or ohter suitable international conference at the end of the Decade, and* to submit a report thereon to the Assembly at its forty-fifth session;

4. *Decides* to consider this question at its forty-fifth session in a working group of the Sixth Committee with a view to preparing generally acceptable recommendations for the Decade;

5. *Also decides* to include in the provisional agenda of its forty-fifth session the item entitled "United Nations Decade of International Law".

*60th plenary meeting 17 November 1989*

---

[1] Resolution 2625 (XXV), annex.
[2] Resolution 37/10, annex.
[3] See *Carnegie Endowment for International Peace, The Hague Conventions and Declarations of 1899 and 1907 (New York, Oxford University Press, 1915).*

# Index